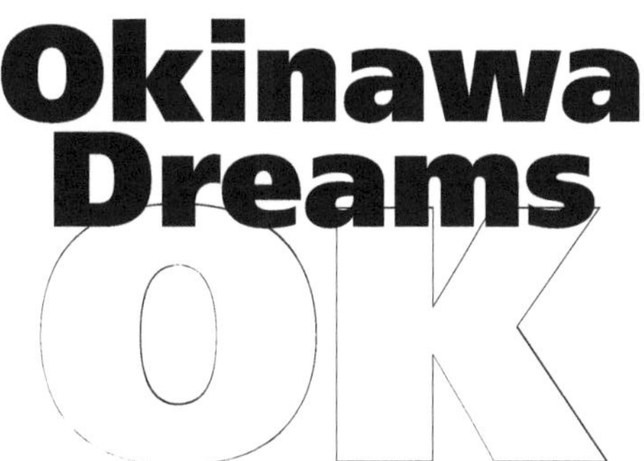

Okinawa Dreams OK

Tony Barrell
Rick Tanaka

Produced by Private Guy International

16 Fourteenth Street, Hepburn, VIC 3416, Australia

Email privateguy@zoho.com

Originally published in 1996 by Die Gestalten Verlag, Germany

Reprinted 2014

Copyediting/index: **Doug Cooper**/Syllepsis Editorial

Design/Production: **Eddy Jokovich**/ARMEDIA

Cover design: **ANTART**

Die Deutsche Bibliothek -
CIP-Einheitsaufnahme
Barrell, Tony:
Okinawa dreams ok / [Tony Barrell ; Rick Tanaka]. -
Berlin : Die-Gestalten-Verl., 1996
ISBN 3-931126-11-0
NE: Tanaka, Rick:; HST

978-0-9808242-8-5

CONTENTS

Introduction		4
The world can learn from our history	Itokazu Keiko	10
The whole Pacific Ocean	Col Stuart W. Wagner	18
The first time Okinawan people have said no	Chibana Shoichi	26
Empty hand, full noodle		34
We are the go-between, between civilisation and nature	Kina Shokichi	44
I'll probably never know why I make films	Takamine Go	54
Talking Taketomi	Uesedo Yoshinori	66
I'm an amateur politician	Ota Masahide	76
The best of both worlds	Maj. Memi and First Lieut Dutko	90
Okinawa is where I want to be	Paul Newman	102
Let nature take its course	Teruya Rinken	112
The persuasive voice of development	Inamine Keiichi	120
Inject the fun factor	Tamaki Mitsuru	130
What this place needs is a fun park	Shimoji Mikio	142
Taketomi Special	Kohama Haeko	150
First-generation Okinawan	Byron D. Jones	158
Spirit from the land of peace	Higa Masakuni	170
Semper Fi	US Marine Corps	182
Go home and be happy	Ahagon Shoko	198
Thanks		210
Resources		211
Index		214

OKINAWA DREAMING

Okinawa means different things to different people. To martial arts enthusiasts worldwide it's the home of karate. During the 1960s, it was the buzz word for politically active Japanese students and workers protesting against US imperialism. Many Americans know Okinawa because of two atrocities fifty years apart: the Battle of Okinawa in 1945 during which many thousands of US marines and GIs died and the rape of a twelve-year-old girl in September 1995. The rape also involved marines—three of whom were found guilty of the crime and gaoled. Until that tragedy many Americans would have thought of Okinawa only in terms of its continuing strategic significance and the heroics of the Second World War.

Few of the hundreds of thousands of Americans who came and went in their tours of duty on Okinawa would have questioned the reason for their being there. It was an accepted part of the geopolitical logic for five decades that the USA needed forty separate military bases in Okinawa. It would be fair to say that for the years between 1945 and 1995 most of the rest of the world would have been in a state of either indifference to, or ignorance of, the conditions of life in Okinawa.

Our work took us there twice during the 1980s—before the end of the cold war—to experience the unique reality of Okinawa's militarisation first-hand. In 1983 we were there to make a radio documentary for a series called 'Japan's other Voices' for the Australian Broadcasting Corporation. Our series offered a critique of the dominant view being promoted in the West at that time that Japan was the source of a flawless system of industrial harmony and consensus politics based on social and cultural homogeneity—some kind of model that could and maybe should be emulated. That model has since been subjected to a decade of Japan-bashing, but Okinawa has until now remained obscure.

It was through Okinawa that we were able to see the fallacy of the homogeneity model. Okinawa was clearly 'Japan' but it was—and is—imbued with all kinds of 'difference', with its own rich history and complex living culture, because, as the Ryukyu Kingdom, it had for centuries developed that culture independent of control by Japan.

We also realised how tightly the island prefecture was locked into the cold war framework, and how little notice was taken of any criticism of that policy outside Okinawa. The time of that first visit was soon after the wild promise made by Prime Minister Nakasone Yasuhiro that Japan would keep its part of its security arrangement with the USA by acting as an 'unsinkable aircraft carrier' in the Asian region. It was bizarre: in 1945 Okinawa had lost more than a third of its population in the crossfire of that kind of thinking.

We also discovered how people who had hoped the Reversion of Okinawa to Japan—over ten years before—would usher the military out and an era of enhanced economic activity in, had those hopes dashed. The USA and Japan seemed incapable of giving up their conviction that Okinawa must be the 'keystone' of the Pacific and the eighties did not bring Okinawa a share of the Japanese economic 'miracle'.

When we visited Okinawa again in 1989, on the eve of the end of the cold war, nothing much seemed to have changed on the anti-base front. If anything there was more disillusionment. But there was obvious evidence that the construction industry had moved in and that Okinawa was beginning to 'enjoy' the fruits of resort tourism. In 1983 people had been wary of this. They had talked about Okinawa's potential for small-scale 'cultural' tourism based on Okinawa's 'exotic' attractions—music, dance, cuisine, subtropical climate, coral reefs and the rest. Popular though they were and are, they couldn't compete with international capital's fondness for developing concrete holiday destinations for that 'international' experience. The modest ideal of low-impact tourism was almost swamped.

In a sense 1995 has changed everything, but not in the way many outsiders we've spoken to seem to expect. Even the hardest core Okinawan anti-base campaigner is not anti-American per se. Though local outrage was immediately directed against the rapists, it was the lack of action by the Japanese government and the ignorance on the part of the mainland public that aroused the most intense rage. The three suspects were not handed over to the Japanese police but detained inside a US base. When the central government turned a blind eye to this the island erupted. Initially, the mainland media continued to display its endemic lack of interest and public demonstrations in Okinawa were not reported on NHK, the national broadcaster, until September 18, ten days after the case became publicly known in Okinawa.

Since then things have changed. The Japanese and world media has swooped in and the consensus is that as far as the military presence is concerned—either US or Japanese—Okinawans have decided 'enough is enough'. If anything, the atmosphere we felt in Okinawa in 1996 was similar to that of the Baltic states in the late eighties when people there were fighting for independence from the Soviet Union.

This is where Gov. Ota Masahide has played such an interesting role, not unlike some of the 'non-politicians' who have been attempting to rescue parts of Eastern Europe from centralism's leaden hand. When we first met him in 1983 he was a university academic, quite gloomy about the struggle to have the American presence removed or even reduced, but for a decade and more he had been thinking the issues through, devising plans for action and gathering supporters.

It took the fall of the Berlin Wall to provide him with an opportunity and a platform for a dynamic political strategy on which he was subsequently elected: remove the bases, increase economic activity—especially planned tourism—boost Okinawa's chances for more autonomy within Japan and develop stronger diplomatic contacts with the region, as in the days when, centuries ago, the Ryukyu Kingdom had been a potent little trading power in East Asia.

His strategy tapped a new sense of destiny that has long been growing within Okinawa, a deep sea change which now resonates around the region—certainly in Japan. It remains to be seen whether he and his supporters can persuade the USA and Japan to shake their cold war belief that their alliance is the only sure protection against all the threats that lurk in the Asia–Pacific region, but Ota is definitely now a national figure.

The effect that the Okinawa 'crisis' has on politics and society in the rest of Japan may develop for practical as well as political reasons. Philosophically, Ota's challenge to the centre has significance in many parts in Japan where people are fed up with the centralised control of decision-making in Tokyo. Many of those decisions served to keep the remoter parts of Japan poor. Practically, a Tokyo-centred Japan has meant people in the regions have had to live with an ongoing rash of environmental disasters and authoritarian dictates. Its ugliest and most dangerous manifestation has been the location of all kinds of poisonous but necessary 'facilities', such as nuclear power stations, toxic waste and leaky fuel depots, as far away from Tokyo as possible. The justification has been easy for the bureaucrats. They are part of the need to pursue overriding 'national' goals.

Forcing Okinawa to host US bases has been no less noxious, but the way the policy came unstuck there has been noticed by people in other parts of Japan who want to get rid of their own unwanted facilities—and the iron hand of control by Tokyo. The prefecture's plan to rehabilitate its post-base economy, by demanding special conditions such as visa-free visits and an expanded tax-free zone, makes a direct challenge to the very mechanisms of centralisation. Its implementation would mean real decentralisation of bureaucratic control.

The dramatic events of 1995 gave people an opportunity to show the world just how determined they are to reclaim their identity. The governments of Japan and the USA had to respond. They set up a Special Action Committee on Okinawa (SACO) to devise a plan for the bases that might suit all parties.

The fact that Okinawa is furthest away from the centre, is the poorest of all the prefectures and maybe the most desperate would, in the past, have made protest irrelevant and resistance impossible, but now a new landscape seems to be emerging, an ideological archipelago growing throughout Japan. There is potency and potential in Okinawa now and it's fitting that Okinawa should lead the challenge against Tokyo. The 'national goals' model on which Tokyo runs Japan dates back more than a hundred years to the nation-building schemes of the Meiji government. In one of its first acts to extend power over the regions, it seized the Ryukyu Kingdom and incorporated it into Japan as the prefecture of Okinawa. The Meiji model might end where it started.

If SACO fails to convince people in Okinawa that the bases will eventually all be removed, we feel sure people will intensify their campaign, that it will gain more and more support from the rest of Japan and that other regional campaigns will also intensify their activities. We can only make this assertion on the evidence and testimony of the people we've talked to in Okinawa.

As the independence movements inside the old Soviet Union and its Eastern European bloc helped dismantle one superpower, the other player in the cold war may need to beat its own retreat from its remaining zone of influence—the Asia–Pacific—where its major military footholds are now confined to Korea and Japan. If Pax Americana was and is powered by military might, Okinawans' challenge to that presence may give what is left of the pillar of US hegemony a really good shake.

The bulk of this book is made up of interviews we conducted in Okinawa in the first part of 1996 for a radio series. Most of our funding came from prize money awarded to the ABC for our program 'Tokyo's Burning', which won the Special RAI prize at the Prix Italia at Bologna in 1995.

The idea to turn the radio series into a book came after a night out with people who helped us in our researches. While it first occurred to us to write such a book ourselves, it soon seemed a better idea to publish a more direct presentation of what people are saying, feeling and planning at greater length than could be done in radio—which is why the interviews we did appear here in full. Some were done in English while others are translated from the original interviews done in Japanese.

Subjects include the major political and strategic story, of course, and the economy, but there's also music, dance, food and drink, future plans and the historical past—the life and experience that gives substance to the politics. We have included some background facts, our own impressions and opinions and the occasional tiny wedge of trivia.

This is not the definitive book on Okinawa. The situation is so fast-moving that some stories may become out of date but the trends are irreversible. This is a record of voices we have heard there since 1983. They have a universal quality, a local variant of a world mood that continues to disturb the global geopolitical 'order'.

Tony Barrell, Rick Tanaka
October 1996

A note on words

Throughout *Okinawa Dreams OK* we have used the conventional Japanese way of naming—family names followed by given names—except when people are well known by the Western order. For example, we note that while the pronunciation is the same, singer Kina Shokichi is now also being promoted as Shoukichi Kina.

Most Japanese words appear in italics, such as *awamori,* Okinawa's distilled alcoholic drink, and *sanshin,* the three-stringed musical instrument. Others like sake, karate and miso that have entered the English language in their own right or that are proper names are not italicised. To provide clarity for readers not familiar with Japanese or Okinawan, placenames like Kokusaidori are rendered Kokusaidori street, even though *dori* means street.

There have been conflicting conventions with regard to the phonetic rendering of Japanese words in English, especially in words involving long vowel sounds or those with consonants such as *l* and *r.* Words like Ryukyu, one of the essential words in this book, have both. Over the years Ryukyu has been spelt all kinds of ways, including Loo Choo and Roo Choo or Lew Chew and Liu Chiu or even Lequese and Lieuchieux. The same is true of another key local concept word, *champru,* which can also be spelt champloo or champroo.

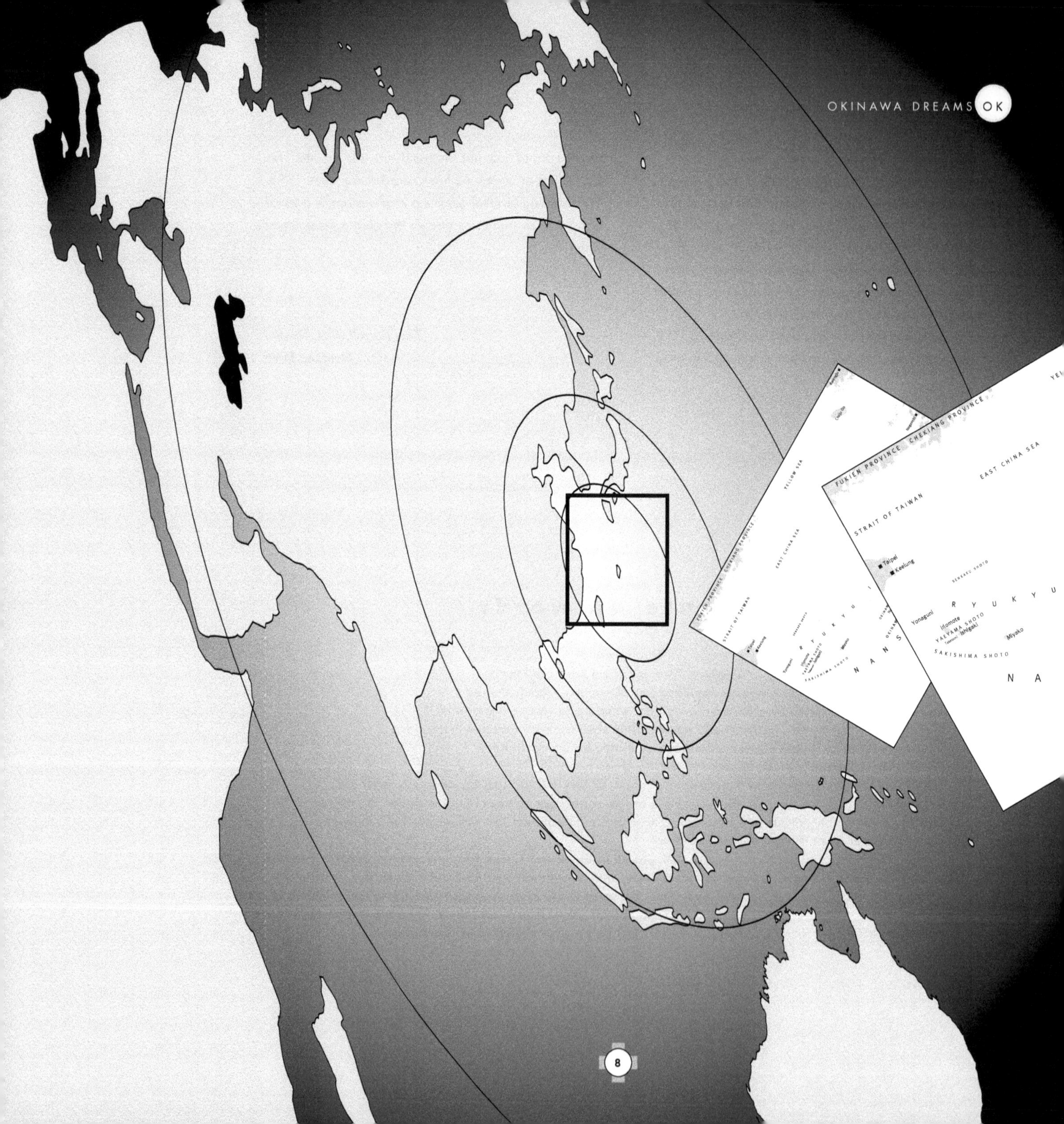
FUKIEN PROVINCE
CHEKIANG PROVINCE
EAST CHINA SEA
STRAIT OF TAIWAN
Taipei
Keelung
R Y U K Y U
Yonaguni
Iriomote
YAEYAMA SHOTO
Ishigaki
Miyako
SAKISHIMA SHOTO

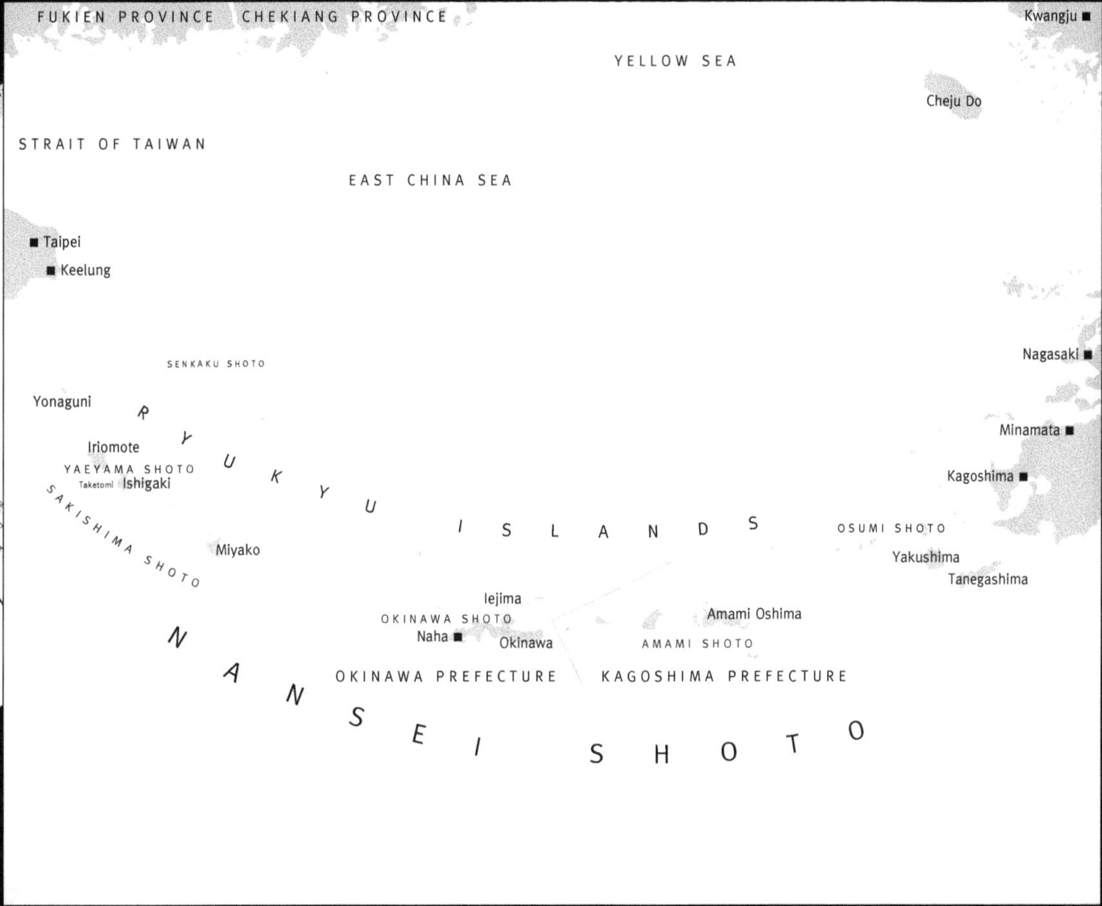

FUKIEN PROVINCE
CHEKIANG PROVINCE
Kwangju
YELLOW SEA
Cheju Do
STRAIT OF TAIWAN
EAST CHINA SEA
Taipei
Keelung
SENKAKU SHOTO
Nagasaki
Yonaguni
RYUKYU ISLANDS
Minamata
Iriomote
YAEYAMA SHOTO
Taketomi
Ishigaki
Kagoshima
SAKISHIMA SHOTO
OSUMI SHOTO
Miyako
Yakushima
Tanegashima
Iejima
OKINAWA SHOTO
Amami Oshima
Naha
Okinawa
AMAMI SHOTO
OKINAWA PREFECTURE
KAGOSHIMA PREFECTURE
NANSEI SHOTO

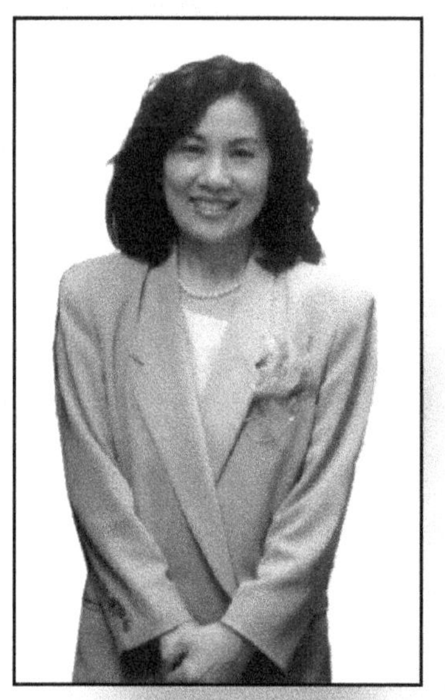

The world can learn from our history

Itokazu Keiko
Prefectual Assembly Member

At the time of our interview, Itokazu Keiko was the only female member in the Okinawa Prefectural Assembly, which has forty-eight members who serve four-year terms. She has been a leading light in the coalition against bases, Okinawan Women Act against Military Violence, and went to the USA as part of the Okinawan Women's Peace Caravan tour to bring attention to the bases issue. She also went to the UN women's conference in Beijing in 1995. She thought she may have neglected her normal constituency work because of these campaigns and she was a little bit nervous about the upcoming election—held June 9, 1996—in which she felt she was in danger of being defeated. As it happens she wasn't and has been joined by two other female representatives.

We began by asking her to give us her analysis of how Okinawa's women are affected by the bases issue and how feminists are involved in the campaign against them.

The issue of the US military bases isn't just a question of talking about the current situation. We have to wind the clock back to the wartime period when the Japanese military behaved just as badly. Our campaign is not anti-US, but against military forces. The Japanese forcibly involved women in Okinawa in that wheel of destruction. During the war, not just women from Okinawa and the mainland but all over the region, Taiwan and Korea, were all called in to serve the requirements of the military. The military always force women into this unproductive process of destruction, that is what their existence and logic is all about.

Only with that sort of logic, war logic, could the destruction of our natural environment and the denial of women's human rights be possible. Women's position has changed little since Reversion. Women are still captives of 'base culture'.

There's no war on now, but it feels like we are still at war. We've been living in a war society for the last five decades. No matter where you are and whose forces they are, the characteristics are all the same. It's a global concern.

When we went to the UN-sponsored women's meeting in Beijing in 1995, we were reassured of that. It's in the very nature of military forces to disrespect women's human rights. That has more to do with this universal, military culture, and little to do with where the soldiers come from, we felt.

We met a few women in the US forces stationed on Okinawa; what's your view of women in the military?

In one sense you have to see it positively, as women getting promoted in 'a man's world'. But we don't believe more women in the forces would change its characteristics. Armed forces are essentially aggressors, their actions driven by the motive to destroy and kill. We think nobody should be involved in the armed forces—men or women. Really, we would like to see more women moving up the ladder in more areas, but military forces are inherently against women.

Do you have a local strategy here to get rid of the bases and a wider global strategy for disarmament?

The decision to hand back the Futenma helicopter base within five to seven years comes as a result of our resolve. It is, in one sense, the result of our collective support as we rallied behind Governor Ota. There has been huge support for the actions he took since that dreadful rape on September 4, 1995. His refusal to override the wishes of landowners and sign the renewal of leases to the military would not have been possible without this popular support.

We said 'enough is enough' loud and clear, and the governor acted upon that widespread sentiment.

I'm pleased that Futenma is to be returned and it will be good to see the plans getting implemented. There are already plans devised by Ginowan city and the prefecture. On the other hand, you have to note that the return of Futenma is not really a removal of its functions, but a relocation and rationalisation, which really strengthens and redefines the military alliance between the US and Japan.

Futenma's 'return' is conditional on the function being moved elsewhere, either to another base in Okinawa, most likely to Kadena Air Base, or to a US base on the Japanese mainland, such as Iwakuni in Yamaguchi prefecture. Already there's a big public outcry from residents around those bases. They're making it loud and clear that it is not welcome.

NO SHOWA

Lots of great and famous people have made fleeting and significant visits to Okinawa. Few of them stayed long. Emperor Hirohito never made it after he ascended to the Chrysanthemum Throne but he did drop in at Yonabaru on March 6, 1921, when he was still only the crown prince. He was on his way by boat for a grand tour of Europe. He caught a tram to Naha and then went by rickshaw to Shuri. He must have enjoyed the ride because it was a special model imported for the occasion equipped with inflated rubber tires.

It just shows how long we have lived with and tolerated so many 'unwanted' facilities in Okinawa. We should now aim to get rid of these operations altogether, not just move them around. With the 'return' of Futenma and the Northern Training Area, in the north of Okinawa island, the land area used for the military will decrease significantly. Yet we cannot be overjoyed if the military's posture and strength remain the same, just because the function is moved or added to existing bases elsewhere.

Many landowners do willingly rent their plots to the military. How can wives and daughter play a part in changing the attitude of those who do take the rent?

It's essential to convert the landowners who rent out their land to the bases for money. They should and they will understand that allowing the bases here encourages the conditions where rapes could take place anytime. The rape of a twelve-year-old girl took place not inside the base, but outside the base, on the street. By hosting them, it could happen anywhere in Okinawa and it's been ongoing for more than fifty years.

Women are at risk wherever the bases are, so I'm asking those landowners who take the rent to recognise the risk and also look hard at their future. They have to realise that living on rent from a military base will not be possible in the twenty-first century; sooner or later, the day will come when the bases go. The landowners should be thinking about alternatives now—using their land for something more productive, especially for future generations—rather than taking rent so their land can be put to military use. No matter how stable it looks, a life that relies on rent from such a destructive industry is not good for our children. I am sure the landowners will eventually understand.

What are the alternatives?

Governor Ota is very keen on tourism.

Before I was elected to the assembly, I was in tourism as a tour guide for twenty years. I agree with Governor Ota that tourism is the key to rehabilitating our economy. It's already a ¥3.5 billion industry, bigger than the income from the military presence, and when the bases are returned it will expand even more.

It's based on three features. Our subtropical climate; nowhere in Japan has a climate like here and it's an attractive environment. Secondly, Okinawa is a perfect place to learn the meaning of peace. Our recent history is violent but we can make a positive message out of our sad history. Visitors can learn about the reality of war—like how armies aren't really there to protect civilians and that women, children and old people are the first to suffer when war breaks out. We also know how the war spread to affect other people, like in Korea and Taiwan.

Some 130 000 students have visited here in organised school expeditions to learn just that. We are becoming a part of a triangle of peace studies, along with Hiroshima and Nagasaki. I think it's important for young people to learn how to construct peace, and Okinawa is a great place for that.

The third feature we have is our reputation for longevity. So people can come here to learn about what contributes to a long life, especially the role of our diet.

So there are lots of positives on which we base our attraction as a tourist destination. It is the industry we believe our future hinges on, and certainly weighs a lot when deciding what to do with the returned bases.

We discovered a disused coal mine along a river on the island of Iriomote but the local people either didn't know about it or didn't want to talk about it. The boat company manager told us we shouldn't go and look.

As I have been in the field of tourism, I understand the reluctance on the part of local residents to tell of the ruin of the dark past and promote the 'bright' side of tropical paradise. I am sure there are plenty of people who would be happy to tell you about the story of coal mining in Iriomote island but you do make a good point.

There are things in our past apart from war that need to be discussed, to be told and shown to visitors, and the coal mining experience in Iriomote is one such example. The quality of tourism, what attracts people here, is something I've been interested in for a long time and since becoming an assembly member, I've managed to persuade the government to set aside a budget to train tour guides with sufficient knowledge in local history so that they can tell people these stories.

Governor Ota—himself a war survivor and historian—is keen to support this scheme and the program is just about to start producing guides. It connects with his initiatives to construct peace. We had to devise a training program from scratch, from writing texts to selecting teachers. Trainees go through both lectures and field training. The scheme is up and running, and just as we speak, 100 people are getting trained, 50 to become peace studies specialist guides and, together with 50 general guides with historical knowledge, they will hit the streets in three months.

This is real progress towards setting Okinawa at the centre of a campaign not just opposing military bases but as a focus for creating peace.

On the future of the bases, Kadena is a huge airfield, what else could it be used for?

There is already a plan in existence for Kadena. The town developed a detailed plan about four years ago. Its main use will be as an international hub airport for freight as well as passengers. And the huge

VOTE NO

Community-initiated referenda took place in Japan for the first time in 1996—a significant addition to the country's democratic processes. These referenda aren't legally binding but a big vote is a powerful political tool. In Japan's prefectural areas, where Tokyo has long planted many of its undesirable, dangerous yet necessary 'facilities', these referenda are likely to be used more and more to express displeasure at centralised authority.

Several local communities have voted on such issues, and the first ever in July saw 60 per cent of the people of Maki in Niigata prefecture vote against proposals to build a nuclear power station there.

The referendum in Okinawa was the first to be held throughout an entire prefecture. It was initiated by Rengo Okinawa, the peak union body, and ratified by the prefectural assembly. Two per cent of eligible voters' signatures are required to submit a petition to hold a referendum and Rengo gathered more than 34 000—nearly double the required number.

Votes were cast September 8, 1996. Nearly 60 per cent of those eligible to vote did so and 90 per cent of them said no to military bases. That's nearly half a million 'nos' compared to only 46 232 'yeses'. The 'nos' represented more than half the people eligible to vote—enough according to the organisers to indicate that the majority of the population is against the bases.

nearby Chibana ammunition depot—between Kadena and the beach—could be converted to a retirement home complex and the beach nearby could easily be developed as a seaside resort. These plans already exist. What we need now is a timeframe so that we can get them up and running.

We saw a private resort at Okuma which was partly used as a beach for military personnel and partly as an exclusive resort for paying customers only. It seemed strange to us to find such a combination of restricted access in Okinawa.

Yes, I agree. Why should local people have to pay to get access to one of their own beaches—or be barred from another. The government has prepared a new law to prevent the private appropriation of beaches. But I have to say that private beach owners do say that one of the advantages is that they do spend time and money on the upkeep of beaches. We have to make it clear that if we do de-privatise these resorts, people will have to take on the responsibility of keeping them clean.

Your opinion of the April 1996 visit of President Clinton to Japan?

The problem with these leaders is they don't talk or listen to people who know about the subject best. If President Clinton really seeks a solution to the Okinawan issue, he should talk to Governor Ota, who represents us. He has been to the USA many times trying to talk to the US administration to discuss the matter over. They should listen to us. Direct talks would be best.

Japanese bureaucracy is slow to respond. It was the US government who responded quickly. And the US action then triggered action from Japan. So there is still some hope left in the democratic process.

While we were touring the US with the Okinawan Women's Peace Caravan we were often asked why we were not campaigning against the Japanese government. I told them, to get the Japanese government to act, the quickest way is to make the argument to the US government. This is the crux of the issue—getting our voice heard.

THE FATAL ATTRACTOR

During the Occupation access to Okinawa was strictly supervised. Between 1945 and 1972 all visitors needed permits or visas to travel there, and Okinawans had to carry a form of passport to go to Japan—a bureaucratic regulation which, because they were the only Japanese to carry such ID, institutionalised discrimination against Okinawans throughout Japan.

The tourism thing in Okinawa is quite recent. In 1966 there were a mere 100 000 visitors. The revenue generated from tourism raised only ¥18.5 billion. At the time of Reversion in 1972, the number of visitors was just over 450 000 and total income from tourism was only half the amount brought in by the US bases.

It was only after 1972 that Okinawa was heavily promoted as a tourist destination both for affluent Japanese, whose income had more than doubled during the previous decade, and those who wanted to access a cheaper version of the wider blue Pacific lifestyle—but couldn't quite afford Hawaii or Micronesia.

Its first real big boost came when a massive Marine Expo was staged mostly with government aid money at the northern town of Motobu in 1975. That year over 1.5 million visitors came with ¥125 billion, an amount which was, for the first time, more than the amount generated by the US bases. By 1991 it was double the income from the bases, and with 3 million visitors per year, tourism earns nearly 20 per cent of the prefecture's income. It is a ¥300-billion-a-year industry.

The bulk of tourists—95 per cent—come from the Japanese main islands.

Since Okinawa is made up of islands, access from the mainland is important. Japan's two major airlines, Japan Airlines and All Nippon Airways, dominate the tourist supply route, as well as traffic among the Okinawan islands.

As more and more individuals and couples are going it alone or in pairs to discover their own wild selves, the package-tour holiday may be in relative decline, but it's still the bread, butter, cream, jam and cherry-on-top of tourist-industry profitability in Japan, where people still prefer travelling by all-inclusive, pre-paid, guided group tours, even on their honeymoon.

The simple economic fact is that very little of the money actually spent ends up in the pockets of people who live at the destination. It's most likely that the airline conglomerates, who own the hotels and maybe even the companies that built them, take the biggest bite. So a lot of that tourist yennage doesn't ever get to, let alone end up in, Okinawa, any more than it does in Hawaii, Queensland's Gold Coast or Thailand's Phuket.

As well as money, tourism also brings crowds and development—and many people are unhappy with its impact. Since the mid-eighties the Japanese government has poured in more and more aid for infrastructural projects linked to tourism to help Okinawa 'catch up' with booming Japan. It hasn't, but it's been a profitable enterprise for banks, airlines and construction companies.

The speed of this spending over the past fifteen years has seen a rash of resort developments which have sprouted throughout the islands like a rash of concrete boils. Whole hillsides of limestone have been quarried, crushed and converted into cement for roads, seawalls and huge hotels, and there is serious concern that the influx of twice the local population every year will mean Okinawa won't have enough water. Already most small islands, like Taketomi, have to ship it in from bigger islands nearby.

For more than two decades a row has continued on how to expand Ishigaki's airport to accommodate this traffic. One plan would have meant building a runway out to sea across a coral reef, which would have been destroyed—thus removing one of the island's main attractions! The scheme was finally vetoed by Governor Ota, but an alternative site which pleases everybody on Ishigaki has yet to be found.

Many people who live in Okinawa still yearn for a less intrusive and more culturally appropriate, eco-friendly or low-impact kind of tourism. It does exist on small islands such as Yonaguni and Taketomi—which has its own 'preservation order' to prevent overdevelopment—but the big profits can only be made from lots of people coming in on quick-turnaround short-stay visits in semi-luxury resorts.

Tourism can also be physically exclusive. As well as being kept out of the profit zone, some beaches are off limits to Okinawans too. The US military have their own beach at Okuma, which no-one but service personnel and their families can use. Amazingly, locals are also not allowed in the privately owned resort right next door.

However the idea of 'history tourism' looks like it has some kind of future in Okinawa. With the prompting of Itokazu Keiko, the government has funded a program to train tour guides to tell stories from Okinawa's tragic history as well as reciting its scenic attractions. Itokazu was herself a tour guide for twenty years and learned that people got more out of their visit if they were told the truth about what happened during Japan's military period rather than having to guess or ignore it. The first hundred-strong brigade of fully trained guides started their duties on June 23, 1996, the fifty-first anniversary of the end of the Battle of Okinawa. It seems appropriate to have launched the program then because the day's significance is observed as a public holiday only in Okinawa and not by the rest of Japan. It's just another way the Okinawans remind mainlanders they have their own history and their own reasons for remembering; and they now have the guides too.

Dark areas indicate US-occupied areas.

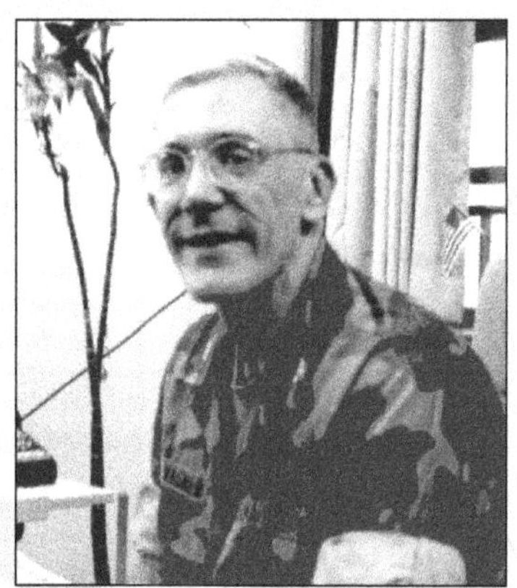

The whole Pacific Ocean

Col Stuart W. Wagner
Director, Public Affairs, III Marine Expeditionary Force and Marine Corps Base Camp Smedley D. Butler

Like other Marine public affairs spokespersons we've met, Colonel Wagner was polite and forthcoming. He's slightly built, softly spoken, cooperative and interested. We had approached him to line up some young marines to talk to us. He chose those we spoke to, and because in our letter we had said, 'young men and women marines', one of the group was indeed a young woman. We were surprised that there were no African-Americans in the selection, and when we pointed this out, Colonel Wagner said we didn't ask for them. We had, he said, more or less asked for a female, so he assumed if we'd wanted Blacks, we'd have asked for them too. We had no answer for that.

Have you had a long tour of duty here?

No, as a matter of fact I got here July 27, 1995, and took the office over about a week before the rape, but this was my second time here. I was here twenty years ago as a lieutenant.

So you knew the set-up here?

I spent a year here but there were some differences. They switched the side of the road they drive on and the yen rate was a bit different: 89 as opposed to 320 to the US dollar!

You inherited a tricky and fast-moving situation last year that caught the world's attention. Was it something that had been waiting to happen?

That's difficult for me to gauge but there had been concerns by the Okinawan people for some time and probably a combination of events led to what happened. First being the horrific nature of this crime; second, the readiness of the Japanese government to listen to the Okinawan people—and coinciding with the fiftieth anniversary of the end of the war, there being a lot of publicity about that.

People are excited here and are on a persistent campaign to try and get the governments to remove the bases. It puts the 'men on the spot' on the spot really—you're doing your duty according to the agreements, so how do you cope with it all?

It does put us on the spot. The important thing to remember is that we recognise the concerns of the Okinawan people—first. Second, we believe that there should be a remedy to our amount of intrusiveness. The problem is there is no easy fix and it has to be balanced out with security needs and there's some hope that it will be done through the Special Action Committee on Okinawa (SACO) at the bilateral level. But most importantly, we recognise that this is a process and that this is going to take some time, even if all the demands of the Okinawan prefectural government are met.

It's incumbent upon us to emphasise the fact that there's an absolute requirement to be good neighbours. So it's a continual education process. We've redoubled our education programs to talk about 'host-nation sensitivities', the requirement for people to have proper conduct and also learn about another culture, so there's a lot of work that needs to be done on a continuing basis.

One of the problems is that for years it's been a fact of life that wherever there is a military base there will be some problems interfacing with the local population—whether it be minor crime or people not getting on with each other, or prostitution. Is Okinawa special in some way?

We do have problems here like everywhere else, but Okinawa is special in one way, in that it is located in a very strategic location and the USA has made a commitment to put forces here, to put forces forward—as a forward presence—and so it becomes special in that it is a linchpin to our strategy and so it increases the requirement to be good neighbours and have a good relationship.

Is the USA dependent on its presence here after the loss of its bases in the Philippines?

I don't think so. What we lost in the Philippines were two main things: our ability to have large naval shipyards and we have been able to go to other places in the world to do that, although it's been more expensive. The second thing we lost in the Philippines was to have aircraft training and we have looked for other ways to do that—that's been the biggest loss.

There's no doubt that this part of the world is very important. Come the twenty-first century, seven of the ten leading countries of the world will come from this area. Given the fact that if something breaks out it will happen very fast, it will be too late to get ready once the bell rings. You have to have commitment and our forward presence is that commitment.

What is the technical structure of your command here?

There are three things about the Marines. First they are maritime. They are part of the Navy, inextricably linked to the Navy. That's important because, with our ability to get aboard ships, we can travel the world. And when you consider that 80 per cent of the world's population lives within 300 miles of an ocean, that's a pretty important thing to be able to do, to travel the oceans without any interference.

The second thing is that the Marines are an expeditionary force, a force that can move very quickly to a contingency or a crisis. And the third thing to remember is that it's not a stand-alone force. Marines work in combination; they have an air, a ground and a logistics portion to them and whenever they deploy, they work in that combination. It gives them their strength.

The headquarters of the Marines in this part of the world is in Hawaii, called US Marine Forces Pacific. We are part of that as a Marine Expeditionary Force. There are three MEFs, we are one of them. Another is located at Camp Pendleton in California, and the other at Camp Lejeune in North Carolina. We're the only one overseas and the largest force overseas of Marines. There are 16 000 on Okinawa, 3000 on mainland Japan.

What's the average age of marines here?

NOTHING SACRED

The Special Action Committee on Okinawa (SACO) was established in November 1995 by the Japanese and US governments to counter Okinawans' outrage. SACO was given one year to come up with a plan, ostensibly to reduce the burden on Okinawa without reducing the current strength of the US–Japan security alliance.

The committee's interim report was released in April 1996. It proposed the transfer of some military facilities, thus giving land back to the community. But since these facilities are to be moved to other areas, there would be no real reduction in the overall military presence. The Okinawan government's reaction was mixed: pleasure and appreciation that changes were being made, but disappointment that the changes were not significant and recognition that they would not satisfy Okinawans.

It's under twenty-two. The Marine Corps is a young force. The things that marines have to do require a young force. There's about 40 000 that come into the service and out of the service every year—that's a requirement to recruit to.

That's one of your problems. You have a lot of teenagers together here in Okinawa.

It is something we have to consider. When we have marines that come here, they spend a pretty good amount of time at what we call the Joint Reception Center learning the culture and the customs of Okinawa—Status of Forces Agreement (SOFA) issues. What it's like to live in a different country, and we also emphasise the things to do in Okinawa: there are some of the best diving areas in the world off Okinawa; not only the ability to take in another culture but there are educational opportunities. We want to get them out of the barracks and experience being in a different culture.

You mentioned being ready for a crisis situation. What kind of crisis are you expecting the Marines to be ready for?

I can't really speculate about what kind of crisis we might have, but if you look around the Pacific rim it doesn't take a genius to figure out what are some places that marines could go to. When you look at North Korea, that's one area that concerns us. Last spring it was the alliance here that was effective in freezing the North Korean nuclear program.

And we are also able to train bilaterally with a lot of countries. Well, we really have to be ready to go anywhere. Our concern is that if the United States leaves this area it leaves a vacuum, the barriers come down, and then countries that tend to be mischievous can do a lot of things.

You have to be *capable of going anywhere in this region.*

We don't *have* to be capable—we *are* capable.

You would have gone to the Persian Gulf from here?

HOW CUSHY IS THE SOFA?

Host-nation sensitivity is a buzz phrase around US bases these days. The US Marine Corps in Okinawa has a web site, for example, to tell new recruits the curious dos and don'ts on the island.

Under the SOFA (Status of Forces Agreement), US service personnel have various rights, privileges and special protections, not just in Okinawa but throughout Japan.

Perhaps most cushy is the controversial protection the SOFA provides in Article 17, Section 5(c):

'The custody of an accused member of the United States armed forces or the civilian component over whom Japan is to exercise jurisdiction shall, if he [sic] is in the hands of the United States, remain with the United States until he is charged by Japan.'

So, US military personnel suspected of crimes in Japan are not handed over to the local police before a formal indictment.

The original SOFA, signed in 1960, still stands, but following the September 1995 rape outrage the US government changed the practice; since October 1995 it hands over a crime suspect to local police if requested. A twenty-year-old sailor from the guided-missile frigate USS *McClusky* became the first to lose the protection of SOFA's Article 17 and was handed over for an alleged break-in and attempted murder to investigators in Sasebo, Nagasaki, in July 1996.

There are some units that went to the Gulf, but this region is the Pacific and that's our main area of focus.

What's the range of the Pacific?

Good question. I've got a map up there of Pacific Command, it goes all the way from one coast of the USA—the waters of it—throughout the Pacific Ocean. So basically we are talking about the Pacific Ocean.

The Marine forces in the Pacific that are stationed in Hawaii come under the Commander-in-Chief of the Pacific (CINCPAC), so wherever he would tell us to go we would go—and he of course will be told by someone in Washington.

To maintain the Marines' presence on Okinawa, is it absolutely necessary to have the Futenma Air Base?

The importance of Futenma is that it's a helicopter base for us—and as the Marines are not a stand-alone force and wherever they go they work in combination, when we have infantry marines that move somewhere, we take helicopters with them. They train together, they transport marines that way, we can transport supplies, so we want to have a helicopter base close to where we have our infantry and that's the importance of Futenma. If you strip the air assets at Futenma, then you weaken the ground forces here—they can't train together, do their things together on a regular basis.

Are there are any facilities that aren't really all that essential, or have they all been stripped back already?

The SACO is looking at a lot of issues and I don't want to speculate on what's going to come out, but there will be a report that will identify areas that will be able to be given back to Okinawans over a period of time.

★★★★★

Two days after this interview, the Japanese government announced that it had reached an 'interim agreement' with the USA to remove the helicopter base at Futenma and return the land to its owners within five to seven years. The helicopter facilities would be relocated—probably to another base in Okinawa.

Floating Futenma

With its 2800-metre runway, Marine Corps Air Station Futenma occupies 483 hectares of land—just about a quarter of the entire city of Ginowan in the centre of the island. Since a plan was announced by both the US and Japanese governments in April 1996 to relocate the station, landowners have been approached by real estate brokers and businesses to sell their plots. The price offered for a square metre is said to be around ¥150 000 and is set to rise as the promised return gets closer. Due to its close proximity to Naha and flat topography, the returned land is said to be ideal for housing development. In September, on his first visit to Okinawa as prime minister, Hashimoto Ryutaro revealed an alternative site for Futenma. The Americans, he claimed, had floated an idea to float the facility—literally, somewhere at sea. Meanwhile, both the Japanese and the Americans have requested a ten-year extension from the landowners whose leases expire on May 14, 1997! Just in case.

BASE ECONOMICS

Since it reverted to Japan in 1972, Okinawa has become less dependent on the income derived from rent paid for the use of land for military bases. It used to be 15.4 per cent of the total economy, now it's 4.9 per cent. That's perhaps why it is now easier to discuss their removal than it was in the fifties when Uncle Sam's contribution amounted to nearly half the entire income of the prefecture. The bases still bring in more than ¥150 billion annually—now paid by the Japanese government—and provide almost 8000 jobs, or just over 1 per cent of the local working population.

The bases have significant spin-offs that bring in income less directly than rent. Military personnel are paid in US dollars and spend a proportion of that income off base—but their purchasing power had much more impact two or three decades ago when the dollar was worth more. In recent years it has hovered around ¥100 and has been known to dive down to the mid-seventies. So US service pay in Japan would barely allow military personnel and their families to eat regular meals off base, let alone go nightclubbing and souvenir-hunting.

The downside of the 'base economy' is obvious. First there's land loss. Military facilities are concentrated on two islands—the main island of Okinawa and nearby on the small island of Iejima. Together bases and facilities take up 20 per cent of the land area. Such an intrusion prevents any systematic and coherent land use by local authorities who are restricted by what they can do and have no capacity to embark on much needed long-term community projects. In some areas bases intrude on as much as half the town area (but in the case of the town of Kadena, 80 per cent!) and their councils cannot come up with the most basic of planning schemes. The scarcity of nonmilitary land in Okinawa is another problem because it has inflated the price to rank amongst the highest in Japan.

Hosting an 'industry' that is made up of 30 000-plus soldiers from a foreign culture must incur all kinds of social and environmental costs not always measurable in cash terms. There are always interactions between the armed services and the local population; nearly 4800 criminal cases involving US servicemen have been reported since Reversion, nearly 200 a year.

More than 500 involve violent crimes: murders, break-ins, arson and rapes, and it's fair to say that any organisation the size of the US military presence in Okinawa must by definition contain 'bad' or antisocial elements.

To add insult to injury the Okinawans have also

Marine chopper over Futenma.

had to endure semi-institutional injustice. Because they were protected by the SOFA (Status of Forces Agreement), US servicemen could for years quite literally get away with, or at least from, crimes they committed in Okinawa.

In 1995, for example, three US servicemen who were wanted by the Japanese police for murder, rape and theft were able to avoid being charged. In the cases of eleven civilians murdered since Reversion, only one arrest was allowed to take place inside a base and two off base. The other eight suspects were able to stay protected on base until they were eventually charged. The change of practice to the SOFA in late 1995 now allows for the transfer of suspects to the Japanese authorities.

Because all the bases and facilities are primarily for military use they have a negative impact on the local environment. Noise pollution from heavy military machines is impossible to contain when the bases are encircled by civilian housing. Bushfires started by live ammunition are common occurrences that enrage the local people as do the discharge of polluting agents and the degradation of the natural vegetation and topography.

The most dramatic impact comes from the large number of accidents that have occurred involving military hardware, a hundred involving planes, since Reversion. Some have killed and injured locals.

The cultural impact is hard to measure. Some people have welcomed American influence but the tendency of service personnel to behave badly on foreign assignment can't be overlooked. No matter how often they are told to be 'good neighbours' they are the professional military who have been taught to destroy and kill and their morale on overseas postings is never as high as it is when they are defending the home turf. Poor morale is often at the heart of antisocial activity.

Historically, US military behaviour in Okinawa would seem to compare favourably with that of the appalling conduct of the Imperial Japanese Army in its foreign occupations, especially in China and especially when it came to the ill-treatment of civilian women. However it seems that despite the advantage of a higher standard of living, the benefits of postwar progress and better education, US military personnel are on the same slippery slide to the same berth in hell.

It's not so much to do with their character, or social and cultural background. Regardless of the rhetoric of 'preparedness' and 'deterrence', the simple, plain and unavoidable fact is they are trained in the trade of violence.

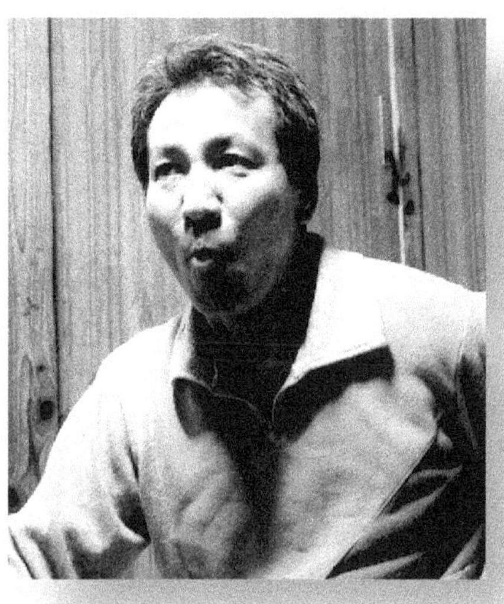

The first time Okinawan people have said no

Chibana Shoichi

Chibana Shoichi runs a small grocery store in Yomitan village and lives nearby with his family, which includes his parents as well as his wife and three children. The day we went to visit him was a day when citizens of neighbouring Kin city were to hold a protest rally against the testing of live ammunition in their neighbourhood by the US military. We thought he might be there to give them support. We tried to get hold of him last time we were in Okinawa some nine years ago without success. In the end, we decided to go to see him.

It's an extraordinary situation for people living around Kin. Fifty years after the end of the war, they still have to bear the outrage of regular rounds of artillery bombardment, as live shells are fired by US guns across a road closed off to local traffic. The artillery is on one side and the target is up in some hills on the other and the citizens of Kin are supposed to carry on their normal business while all that US ordnance flies over their heads. They are persistently assured by the Americans that no harm will come to them, but on several occasions it has. People have been killed by 'stray' US shells fired in these fatuous but dangerous tests, which are pompously deemed by base officials to be a 'necessary' part of maintaining their 'preparedness'.

Kin city isn't far from Yomitan village. They are on either side of the narrowest part of Okinawa's main island—it's 'waist' as it were—the easiest spot for the US landings of 1945. Yomitan has the heavier history because it's where a large number of people died in the first days of the battle, eighty-three of whom killed themselves and their children in the Chibichiri cave mass suicide. Chibana often escorts students on school tours and tells them what happened in that cave.

Chibana was not at the Kin rally. It was a cold and windy day at which only the hardy faithful turned up—plus 300-odd junior high school kids who'd been dragooned into attending to 'learn' about the bases issue. We left them in the capable hands of their teachers, a platform full of local councillors and city elders and at least seven TV crews and sped across the island to Chibana's little family store in Yomitan where we met his wife Yoko. She explained that he'd only just come out of hospital after an operation and if we came back later he'd probably be happy to see us, which we did and he was.

The land that Chibana wants back is located inside the Sobe Communications Site run by the US Navy. It's a listening device designed to eavesdrop on communications traffic. This kind of clandestine activity is often known as ELINT, but nobody will say exactly what that traffic is or why the US Navy wants to hear it. Because of its huge array of antennae, surrounded by a giant fence-like circle, it has earned the nickname 'Elephant Cage'. It also looks like an electronic Stonehenge.

Chibana tells his story in his recent book *Moeru Okinawa, Yuragu AMPO* (Okinawa's rage undermines AMPO), which is available only in Japanese. His previous book, *Burning the Rising Sun*, has been published in English by South Wind. Norma Field wrote a large section about him in her 1990 book *In the Realm of the Dying Emperor.*

We started our interview in relative silence, with his old parents happy to turn off the TV while we talked. Later Chibana's kids came home from an expedition and proceedings were cut short, but in the interval we got a good idea of what he and his anti-base landowning supporters are all about.

Chibana has for a long time been telling people that it's not just a question of farmland being usurped by the military. His analysis goes to the pivotal role of the Mutual Security Treaty between the USA and Japan—AMPO as it is generally known in Japan—and he claims that this strategic defence agreement should be resisted with just as much vigour as the bases, because it's the most likely cause of another military catastrophe that would bring suffering and death to the people of Okinawa.

However, we started by talking about the plot of land that Chibana owns inside the communications facility.

I have about 236 square metres of land inside the Sobe Communications Site used by the US Navy. We call it the 'Elephant Cage'. It is believed to be engaged in ELINT, electronic intelligence-gathering activity. The rental contract with the Japanese government, who in turn let to the US military, expired at the end of March 1996. The government now has no legal grounds to keep occupying my land.

You don't take rent?

Since it expired, the Japanese government tries to pay me rent—they send people every day with the money but I always refuse it. I'm not letting my land, so there is no reason to receive rent.

There are about 3000 landowners like myself who refuse to sign the leases—antiwar landowners—and 30 000 landowners who agree to let their land for military use. I'm one of 450 whose land is inside the 'Elephant Cage'. It's a tiny plot of land really, which originally belonged to my grandfather, who had his house on it. If returned, it could quite easily be turned back into a housing plot and I'd like to get it back, but the Japanese government insists on occupying it—illegally.

Okinawa has always been used for war—in Korea, Vietnam, the Gulf. When the US starts a war, Okinawa is the launching pad for its operations. People talk about AMPO—the security treaty with the USA—as if it's there to protect Okinawa. I don't think that's the case. The bases put Okinawa on the front line. The security treaty is merely there to allow the USA to wage its wars and that's why I'm against the existence of their bases here.

Do you just want to walk across your land?

Legally speaking, I have the upper hand and the court will doubtless give me the right to go in and walk over my land. At first, the government just said no to my request but it has to agree on conditions, like who can accompany me and how many. I am sure we will be able to set foot on our family plot of land for the first time in fifty years.

BAREFOOT ENTRY

On May 14, 1996, Chibana was allowed to walk inside the 'Elephant Cage' and have a look at his plot of land. According to reports, he entered the site with family members and fellow antiwar landowners, as well as musician Kina Shokichi. Chibana went barefoot so that he could 'feel the spirit of his ancestors'. On the family plot no family member had reached for fifty years, they all celebrated the occasion over *awamori,* and sang and danced to the *sanshin.*

That won't be enough will it?

No. Up to now I've been asking to walk in and have a look, but I am also fighting in the courts to get it back and that's what I want—to get back my grandfather's land—that's the point of my court battle. It may not be easy. My chance of getting it back is small, because they cannot physically return just my land as a parcel on its own, since it's part of a whole block leased to the US military, but I've heard they may be returning the entire site to us. If that is true, I would be really ecstatic.

CAGEY ON THE CAGE

It's called the 'Elephant Cage' because it's so big: 200 metres in diameter, 37 metres tall. There's another one at Misawa in northern Honshu and at least two similar installations run by the Japanese Self-Defense Forces in Hokkaido and on the Sea of Japan. No-one will say what any of them do.

In August 1996, the USA and Japan floated the idea of moving the Yomitan cage to Camp Hansen in nearby Kin. The villagers of Kin immediately issued their own statement—no thanks—despite the promise that live artillery sessions out of Camp Hansen might be transferred to other sites in the rest of the country.

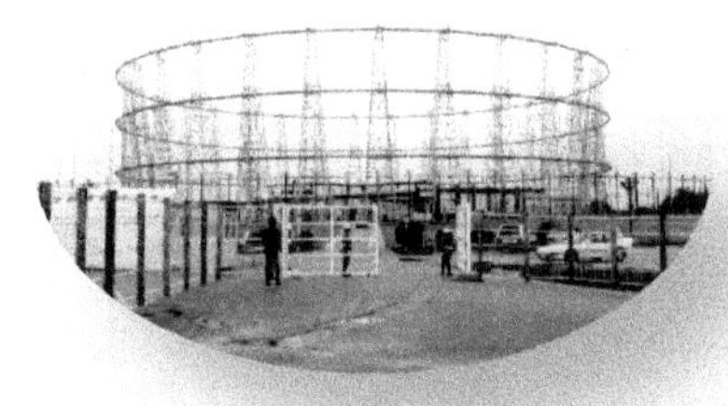

Okinawa is always discussed in the context of the security treaty between Japan and the USA. Our existence and future is always affected by that. So much so that, until now, both governments have not taken notice of Okinawa. This is the first time people in Okinawa have said no since we were taken over by Japan some 120 years ago. This marks the beginning of our taking control of our future, towards self-determination.

Is Governor Ota right to refuse to sign the leases that landowners have refused to sign?

Yes. We agree with the direction he is taking now.

Do you know what the 'Elephant Cage' does?

We landowners are told hardly anything about the function of these US facilities. Anything military is simply top secret. There are lots of huge antennae there, so it's obviously some kind of powerful listening device 'eardropping' on information transmissions—an intelligence-gathering device. Certainly it has nothing at all to do with the defence of Okinawa.

Unless the whole framework and thinking patterns change, what will happen next is the US and Japanese governments will try shifting some of these facilities from Okinawa to other parts of Japan. So getting rid of them from Okinawa will be only a partial solution. The real solution is absolute closure of the bases and reduction of forces. Relocation of an unwanted facility from here to somewhere else is not a real solution. So we will have to keep tabs on what is actually in the 'removal' package and that means we need to keep in contact with people in the mainland, where it's been suggested those facilities may well be relocated.

It's been suggested by some that maybe other countries would take them. There are people in Australia who would like to see them relocated in the Northern Territory, around Darwin. What do you think of that idea?

Squeezing the US forces out of Japan won't be the solution if they are moved somewhere else. If your suggestion is based on fact and they do shift some of Okinawa's facilities to Darwin, we should be in touch with people over there and tell them not to accept. Believe me, it's not worth it.

What happened to your grandfather?

My plot of land inside the 'Elephant Cage' is where my grandfather lived in his house. He was killed on April 1, 1945, the first day of the Battle of Okinawa, so I never knew him at all. My father remembers very little of him as well. He was one of the first casualties, because the American soldiers landed right here in Yomitan.

Why did you burn the Japanese flag in 1987?

To me the hinomaru has always been a symbol of the tragedy of the Battle of Okinawa, as is the kimigayo, the imperial song. They represent imperial militarist Japan. When I was researching the deaths of the people who killed themselves in the Chibichiri cave at Yomitan, I could see a direct connection between their decision to take their own lives—and those of their tiny infants—and the rhetoric with which they had been indoctrinated during the war.

The flag and the song are symbols of that very rhetoric. They caused the loss of so many lives. I cannot see them any other way. The Japanese were responsible for those people losing their lives, not the Americans. The Americans were attempting to rescue those villagers hiding in the cave. It was the militaristic indoctrination put out everywhere by the Japanese government that was responsible for their deaths. This may be forgotten in Japan and elsewhere, but not here. So, when the crown prince was visiting Okinawa to open the annual national athletics meet, I had to make this point clear for everyone in Japan to see and let them know we have not forgotten.

THE ABSOLUTE END

When the three-month-long bloody Battle of Okinawa finally came to a close, a quarter of a million people were dead, the majority Okinawan civilians. When the message finally got through that resistance was futile, the military surrendered. The day after it was all over a magazine published a photograph of a tiny, ragged girl bearing a stick with a white cloth attached to it—a rudimentary white flag. More than forty years later movie footage of the same scene was rediscovered and widely shown and the girl carrying the white flag was identified as Higa Tomiko. She was born and brought up in the old capital of Shuri but during the last days of the war had to flee to the southern end of the island, where the scene was shot on June 25, 1945.

The picture showed her staggering along a road followed by a group of despondent Japanese soldiers. She later claimed it was always her idea and she hadn't pushed in front of them. The images were shot by US Army photographers. John Hendrickson took the still and Richard Bagley, the movie. Tomiko later grew up to work for the American Express company and in 1990 told her story in *The Girl with the White Flag*, published in English by Kodansha International.

Final solutions, easy explanations

It's a phrase that easily springs to the lips but is a 'mass suicide' really possible? After all, if many of those who died in the cave at Chibichiri near Yomitan were children, how come they killed themselves? Doubtless they were killed by their parents; or perhaps the father alone killed his family before killing himself.

Proper excavation and fact-finding studies of the 'mass suicide' did not begin until 1986, but by the forty-second anniversary, April 2, 1987, the cave was ready for public viewing. A plaque carrying the names of victims was unveiled, and villagers erected a Statue of Peace at the entrance of the cave to remind the public of the horror of war and the indoctrination that went with it. Acts of mass self- or group destruction in modern times have been hard to explain and tend to acquire instant mythological status. The mass poisoning of people at Jonestown, Guyana—supposedly at the behest of their spiritual leader, Jim Jones—helped 'explain' mass suicide in terms of mass hysteria. Whether Jonestown or Chibichiri were voluntary suicides or organised mass murders we may never know—but it seems clear that what we usually call 'mass suicide' is not what it seems. The final acts of desperate civilians in caves during the war should not be explained too glibly in terms of their cultural predilection.

In any of these events that have involved families and extended social groups, it's obvious that many of those who die are too young to know why and too young to do it themselves. So it has to be concluded that they, at least, were murdered.

According to Chibana in his book Burning the Rising Sun, the 'suicide' was a result not only of fear and indoctrination but also active encouragement by members of the group supportive of the self-sacrifice rhetoric of the imperialists—tennoists, supporters of the Emperor system.

He explains that a whole group of other people—as many as a thousand who had been hiding in a different cave, called Shimuku—had surrendered to the Americans the day before the Chibichiri tragedy. The reason why they gave themselves up? According to Chibana, they were persuaded to leave the cave by an Okinawan expatriate who had lived for years in Hawaii and, presumably, convinced people the Americans would not kill them. He and others like him were later described by the tennoists as 'unpatriotic'.

The Statue of Peace was destroyed early on the morning of November 8, 1987. A Japanese flag and a note were left at the scene. It read, 'It is too early for peace for the village that burns the national flag. Here is a punishment from Heaven.'

It was obvious that a group of tennoist foot soldiers had done the deed as a protest and condemnation of Chibana's earlier flag-burning. The statue was restored only just in time for the fiftieth anniversary in 1995.

THE IRISH OF THE EAST SAY NO

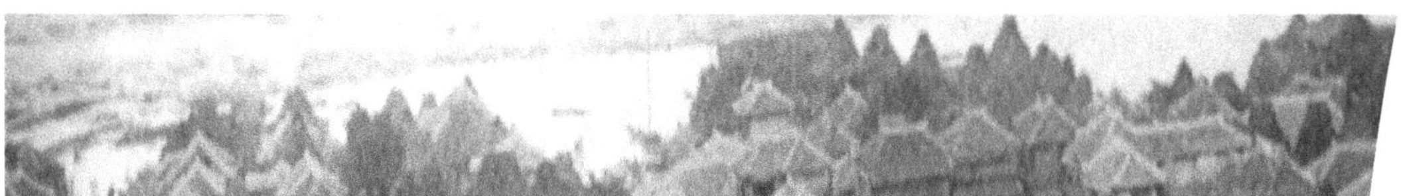

When we were in Okinawa in 1983 we spoke to Lt-Col Jerry Shelton, who was the Marine Corps public relations officer at the time. One of the more interesting things he raised was that the Okinawans are the 'Irish of the East', saying that both people had similar temperaments as well as similar historical predicaments. Whether or not either people have such a thing as an identifiable national 'temperament' as such we wouldn't know, but there is definitely a tendency to see people who have been colonised or marginalised as adopting similar postures when it comes to dealing with the dominant culture.

Nearly sixty years before Jerry thought of it, a novel was written about Okinawa in 1926 that got its author into trouble for characterising the people of Okinawa in a charitable but patronising manner. It was called *Samayoeru Ryukyu-jin* (Wandering Ryukyuans) and you won't find copies of it now because, after a protest from the Okinawan Youth League, the author, Hirotsu Kazuo, asked his publisher to delete it from its catalogue and it went out of print.

The reason the protest occurred was because of Hirotsu's misguided philanthropy. The main character, a Japanese mainlander, sympathises with the predicament of the impoverished islanders he encounters, but the writer expresses his feelings with the kind of patronising pity usually reserved for lesser species. According to a reference in their 1963 book *Okinawa,* Hika Shuncho, Shimota Shoji and Arasato Keiji say Okinawans were portrayed by Hirotsu as antisocial, slack and objects of pity with all their negative characteristics well to the fore.

The Okinawans did not like themselves being stereotyped as undesirables and also complained that the way the term 'Ryukyu' was used in the book was quite derogatory. The authors of *Okinawa* agree, suggesting it was similar to the term 'Chinks' for Chinese.

This protest happened long before the days when 'postcolonial' theory provided the context for the struggle of subject classes and certainly decades before people ever used terms such as 'stereotyping' to identify race- or class-based slurs in contemporary literature. In that regard the Youth League's successful challenge shows just how potent and pro-active Okinawan attitudes to identity have been for a long time, especially given

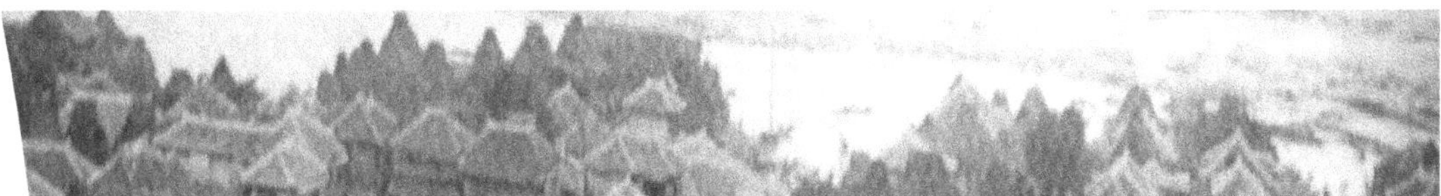

the extraordinary lengths to which the mainland culture of the colonising power went to try and eradicate the Okinawan difference.

Since Okinawa's incorporation into Japan from the 1880s on, education of the young to be 'Japanese' was so intense and comprehensive that anything indigenous to Okinawa was officially characterised as inferior and undesirable, so that all local tradition, including dialects and cultural activities were seen as the expression of a lower form of life.

The author of *Samayoeru Ryukyu-jin* may have had positive intentions in trying to find sympathy for the plight of the poverty-stricken islanders, but as is often the case with such works the result was insulting to the people he was trying to help. The author's decision to apologise and not reprint was praised by the locals. In Japanese literature of the 1930s other writers often characterised Okinawans in terms of them dying out as a race, in much the same way that Aboriginal people in Australia were treated and characterised at the same time—and long afterwards.

All through the Showa era, in the most basic form of communication—language—mainland Japanese expressed their attitude to Okinawa by blatant ignorance, overt simplification and discrimination against anyone who ever used anything other than 'standard' usage. Anyone pursuing local arts, crafts and performance was not recognised as legitimate, let alone equal to their traditional Japanese counterparts. Okinawa's deeply sophisticated forms and practices were simply not seen and their use of language was deemed unacceptably undeveloped.

Ironically, it was the US rulers who encouraged local culture in Okinawa during the Occupation, but it was done more to defuse desires to revert to Japan rather than to elevate Ryukyuan traditions. They wanted to occupy Okinawa as long as possible without interference from anyone—including newly democratised Japan. Were it to be reverted to Japan, Okinawa would have come under the same democratic and civil rights protections and guarantees that were included in Japan's Constitution—which the USA had helped draw up! The Americans weren't keen on that and that's why they put a lot of effort into persuading Okinawans to believe they were 'different'.

Empty hand,
full noodle

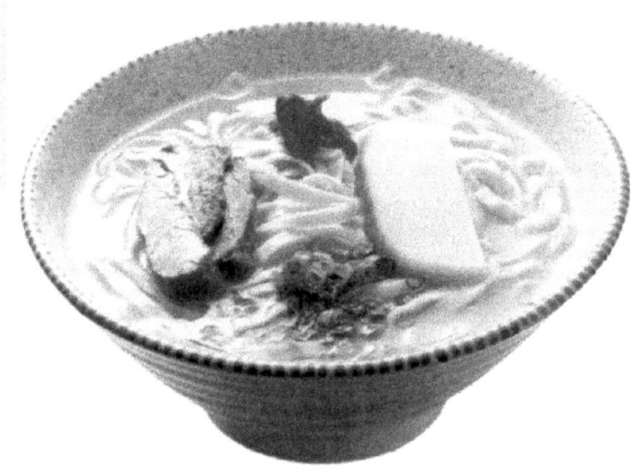

We had heard that Okinawans 'invented' karate, or that it was so different from the version promoted throughout the rest of Japan, it was another indicator of Okinawan cultural survival. Its exact heritage in Okinawa needs a book of its own, but it seems clear that the reason it was developed the way it was can be traced back to the time when the population was disarmed. The 'empty hand' became the only means for mortal combat even for warriors.

There are some who claim that this lack of weaponry indicates a spontaneous expression of pacifist values, that Okinawans are by nature peace-loving people with no history of warfare—which isn't exactly true. The unification of the main island from three small fiefdoms into one and the emergence of the Sho dynasty with its Ryukyu Kingdom based at Shuri castle could only have been achieved by force of arms.

Nevertheless the skill and intensity of karate as a self-defence discipline in Okinawa is awesome. We saw it for ourselves when we attended a one-day karate friendship festival organised to demonstrate the skills of Okinawan karate side by side with the techniques of a kung-fu troupe from neighbouring Taiwan. The demonstration event was held on the stage in a huge community hall near Itoman in the southern part of the main island. The leaflet explained that the occasion was to promote understanding and exchange between the people of Ryukyu and Taiwan. At the back of the wide stage were draped the flags of Japan and Taiwan.

When it comes to dealings with China—and that includes Taiwan—some old traditions never die. While we noticed organisations such as the Okinawa–Peru Association and the Okinawa–Korea Association, for connections with China, such groups use names that designate them as being Ryukyu, as in the Sino–Ryukyu Association.

The karate performers we saw showed their skill with great concentration, gusto and discipline and wore the traditional white linen garb of the martial arts fighter. The kung-fu troupe wore fancy silks, displayed the occasional bare chest and performed throughout to a backing tape of Chinese opera-style music. They were highly theatrical and also poked real swords and spears at each other to show off their capacity to withstand pain.

It was very convincing but one young Taiwan trouper later told us he thought it was a bit of a circus compared to what the Okinawans had done, and that he admired the power and passion that seemed to be at the heart of their craft. Despite such differences, we detected real mutual admiration between the practitioners of these two martial arts cousins, and the party they had afterwards was a warm and jovial affair despite the language difficulties. Everyone seemed to be chatting away, but we could detect no lingua franca. It certainly wasn't

Karate exhibition at Tomigusuku.

English. There were many thank-you speeches and exchanges of gifts, club T-shirts and souvenirs, and the karate masters moved enthusiastically through the throng making sure people ate all the delicacies and had enough awamori or Orion beer.

The show itself convincingly displayed the power of Okinawan karate to intimidate, as old men, young women and tiny kids demonstrated a terrifying exchange of fierce grimaces and furious fists.

We plucked one of the organisers of the event from a seemingly endless exchange of toasts to tell us what it is all about. Senaha Shigetoshi is a senior karate master, so mild-mannered that we would never have guessed the power he held in his empty hand if we hadn't seen it for ourselves only minutes before in the auditorium.

★★★★★

Why is karate so important in Okinawa?

When the Shimazu clan from the Satsuma region of Japan took control of Okinawa they banned weapons, so people developed karate to defend themselves. It combines the local tradition of te, or hand-to-hand fighting, with the martial arts from Fukien in China. It was designed to counter a whole range of attacks, as a means of self-defence.

Karate literally means empty hand, but it also means Chinese hand. You know, kara is Japanese for T'ang. T'ang was for a long time the generic term for China. So karate is both Chinese hand and empty hand.

The hand movements reminded us of the way people in Okinawa use their hands while they dance—the gestures seem to be related.

I'm not sure about that. Chinese kung-fu uses movements that imitate the actions of certain animals. Some schools of Okinawan karate use the fist for the Tiger stance, and there's also the Crane movement, but neither of these are anything like their Chinese origins now.

There were a lot of young kids on show today. Is it important for them to learn karate?

Yes, because it teaches them how to withstand pain and that's important because those who know what it feels like to be hurt, as well as to strike out, are much less likely to resort to violence and become school bullies. It teaches them good behaviour, how to be good citizens.

Is it very different from Japanese karate?

Karate in Okinawa is never done as a competitive sport. It's often described as 'one strike means certain death' and that's what it really is about, so we don't see how that can be treated as a competitive sport as is done in Japan where they have to pull back from the fatal blow all the time. The deep essence of karate is perhaps lost there completely. They probably never realise what Okinawan karate really still is—a genuine method of self-defence, not a sport.

Mainland karate tends to mould everyone into the use of a similar style, it's showpiece karate really and we don't go in for that in Okinawa. Some Americans, servicemen usually, come to learn Okinawan karate so it has spread throughout the world. But we do try hard to keep the essence of Okinawan karate the same, without falling into the temptation of joining the international competitive arena.

It's different from Taiwanese karate, which, aside from those 'animal' movements, allows for the use of weapons and is therefore much more effective than karate at close range. The other difference is that we have techniques for using the closed fist. And the way we take a stand with the closed fist may look more menacing, but once a battle gets into close-range contact, I'm not too sure about karate's effectiveness against kung-fu.

In Okinawa we've had a history of different rulers—China, Japan, the USA. But actually the Chinese were never really in power here—they took tribute. The Satsuma and the Japanese interfered more and then, of course, the Occupation was very direct, but all those phases prove that we have a capacity to keep our own culture alive.

Karate is one way we can show that we can make our own way, that we are peace-loving people and that we don't want anything to happen here again like the Second World War, which took nearly a quarter of a million lives.

How do you think the bases should be used once they are evacuated by the Americans?

I'm just a karate master, I don't really know about that. The best I can say is that we should use them as bases to enhance our culture, especially that part which loves peace. That's all I can say.

★★★★★

Okinawa is the only Japanese prefecture which has absolutely no rail transport. Since the war hardly any money has been spent on public transport so, aside from the private bus services, there's little option but to drive. The buses are okay, but take their time, so we hired a small Nissan in Naha and immediately discovered that traffic congestion has increased exponentially over the years since we last visited. There are more highways and motorways that bypass the jams, but as they take up more of that rarest commodity on the main island—open space and valuable land—they hardly seem to be a positive addition to the overall environment.

After talking to the karate master, we decided to head north, to get out of the din and density of overdeveloped Naha, so we went up the artery of the island's National Highway 58. The main island of Okinawa is small—only 100 kilometres or so from the southern tip to the north at Cape Hedo.

On our way we stopped off to look for something to eat at Hentona. It was a Sunday in April during Shimeisai—the time for grave-viewing—but it was overcast, raining on and off, and aside from a few stalwarts sheltering under tarps, very few families had ventured out to

their ancestors to pay tribute and party in the usual way.

Hentona is just a tiny dot on the map off No. 58. The one-lane village seemed all locked up until we spotted a tiny noodle bar in a side street, just wide enough for our small Nissan to pass. We were immediately welcomed by a group of elderly women who were drinking tea and eating cakes. They seemed to have been sitting there all day long, just chatting. They got curious straightaway, wanted to know who we were, what we were doing there and then immediately volunteered all kinds of information and insights into things major and minor, which they thought we ought to know about.

One was a survivor from Saipan as a young girl after the end of the Second World War and was shocked to see how terrible conditions were in Okinawa. As she put it, 'There weren't even any snakes to eat'. We were regaled with detailed reminiscences, such as the time one thought they were being rescued by a Japanese battleship but it turned out to be the American invasion.

As to the bases, they were extremely eloquent and forceful in their opinion that although there were no significant military areas around Hentona it was a matter for solidarity on all parts. Everyone should agree to getting rid of the bases so that events like the Battle of Okinawa couldn't ever happen again. Nobody wants any bases on Okinawa, thank you!

While we slurped noodles they chatted to each other, including us in the conversation, about Shimeisai, how things had changed, how the old 'turtle-shaped' graves, which could contain the remains of several generations of an entire family, were out of fashion now in favour of smaller square-shaped graves for individuals.

'The old graves are natural, like a woman's body, don't you think?'

The conversation rambled on to the quality of Okinawan soba—and how to suck it up with gusto—sweet potatoes, which they gave us to eat after we'd finished the noodles, families, children, Australia and the weather. We were in their eternal tea drinking'n'chatting session. Time

HABU AND HABU NOT

Habu is a venomous Okinawan snake. They become more active during the summer and when sighted the police are called in to catch them. According to statistics for the 1995 season, 223 were captured and 178 bites were treated. No deaths by *habu* bite have occurred since 1993.

seemed to bother no-one. They may do this every day.

A younger woman sitting at another table said over her bowl of soba that although she'd been living in Hentona for fifteen years she was still regarded as a mainlander. There was no rancour and everyone laughed. When we left, we were asked not *if* we were coming back, but when.

We got back into our cramped little Nissan with its sewing-machine acceleration and headed north through the rain, wondering when and where was the last time we got such instant and warm acceptance.

No rail to monorail

Okinawa is an automobile country. Highways, motorways and tollways crisscross or snake around the US facilities on the main island. For a population of 1.2 million there are more than 700 000 cars. Okinawan roads seem no more crowded than those of Tokyo or Osaka, but there's no alternative—no subways, no suburban trains, no trams, no fixed-rail traffic at all. What light rail there was—and there's a crumbling reminder of a tram car on display at the entrance to Ginowan city hall—disappeared under the rubble of the Battle of Okinawa in 1945 and no-one ever thought to replace it.

In fact the US military ruled without any consideration for an alternative. The hegemony of the petrol head dominated the landscape ever since.

Parts of Okinawa directly reflect US suburban values, with six-lane highways, drive-in shopping centres, supermarkets, and fast-food outlets—all your favourites—generously equipped with capacious car parks to make the anxious motorist feel at home.

Traffic congestion may not seem above 'normal' but the road-toll statistics tell the true story. Okinawa has one of the highest rate of deaths per 1000 kilometres in Japan.

Since nearly 90 per cent of the prefecture's population is concentrated in the southern half of the main island, traffic there is often chaotic.

Diesel buses are the only alternative but they have a dismal efficiency and break-down record. As their trip time progressively lengthens, so their patronage declines—buses now carry only slightly over 10 per cent of travellers.

A plan to build a 13-kilometre monorail line connecting the airport and the centre of the town has been approved. Since the building of a similar service in the sixties to link Tokyo with Haneda airport, most monorail systems seem to have been built more for fun than efficiency and tend to service amusement parks or tourist traps, so it's strange to see such an ugly intrusion replicated in Okinawa—although any public transport system with a fixed infrastructure must be a welcome measure if it mitigates the ever-exploding auto population.

In other islands, transport is much the same—mainly cars but sometimes animals. In the days following Reversion, islands with any substantial population, such as Ishigaki or Iriomote, were provided with one major road system, usually a 'ring' road around the coast with a few inland spurs to service beauty spots.

CHOP PHOOEY

According to *The Cambridge Encyclopaedia of Japan,* karate wasn't introduced into mainland Japan until the 1920s. Even then it never caught on until the late 1950s when university students discovered it.

There have been various names for the different martial arts practiced in Japan, Korea and China and sometimes they change with the times. Up until the fifties what we now call judo was widely known as ju-jitsu, although the actual Japanese word was *ju jutsu.* The change to ju*do* indicates that it had become less of a martial art pursued by warriors—*jutsu* means something like skill—to a leisure activity or sport pursued by enthusiasts. Nevertheless, judo was banned by the US Occupation authorities in mainland Japan because they feared it was too militaristic. It returned soon after they left in 1952 and was accepted as an Olympic sport for the Tokyo Olympiad in 1964. Karate was never outlawed by the Occupation in Okinawa but only became popular in mainland Japan around the time judo was rehabilitated.

Chinese fighting techniques were all once known as *wu shu,* literally meaning martial arts. When China became a republic in 1912 they were all renamed *kuo shu,* or national arts, but since the Communist victory in mainland China they have reverted to using *wu shu.*

Kung fu is a very loose term which can mean any kind of exercise or disciplined movements. One Western way to write the Chinese name of Confucius, the great philosopher-teacher of the sixth century BC, was K'ung Fu-tzu. Kung fu tends to be used in the West in the same way as *wu shu.* Its actual origin is probably *ch'uan fa,* which means rule of the fist.

One legend says all these skills were invented in India by a great prince 5000 years ago and then brought to China—together with Zen Buddhism—in the sixth century AD by a monk called Bodhidharma. Another legend claims there was already a form of wrestling in China and something called *go-ti,* a way of fighting against monsters, and that these techniques came from ancient skills invented in China thousands of years ago. Much of the spiritual elements found in the various kung fu disciplines can be traced back to the Taoist teachings of Lao Tzu, who lived at the same time as Confucius. The appeal of kung fu and the rest may come from their reputation as being 'secret' arts, with the implication that they may involve magic.

The form now called karate took a long time to get to Okinawa—but it undoubtedly came directly from China sometime in the fourteenth century when it was known as *to-te,* or Chinese hand. Some people now call it *Okinawa-te.*

It was banned in China during the seventeenth century, which is when it really took off in Okinawa. Three schools developed—at Shuri, Naha and Tomari—which vary in how 'hard' the attack is. Hard-school devotees are supposed to be able to kill a bull with one blow using a technique called *shuto,* or sword hand.

Kung fu was hugely popularised in the West by the Hong Kong films of Bruce Lee and 'Kung Fu', the American TV series that starred David Carradine as a wandering martial arts monk—both made in the seventies. Lee movies, such as *Fists of Fury* (1971) and

Enter the Dragon (1973), were more physical than mystical. They introduced Western audiences not only to martial arts moves and Bruce Lee's miraculous upper-body muscle tone but also to the styles and techniques of traditional Chinese theatre adopted for and by the Hong Kong film industry to feature characters who perform semisupernatural feats such as flying, disappearing and reappearing —as in 'Ninja', the Japanese TV series of the sixties.

Lee himself died suddenly of a mysterious brain disorder in 1973 and became an instant legend who, like Elvis and James Dean, is believed by many to live on and is often spotted in all kinds of unlikely or ordinary situations such as football stadiums or the local mall.

The Bruce Lee myth was made even more mysterious because, before he died, he fathered a son who grew up to be movie actor Brandon Lee, who himself died tragically when a gun, which was supposed to be loaded with blanks, went off while he was filming *The Crow* in 1993, itself a movie with a magical martial arts undertow.

A new generation of young Westerners know karate from a series of American films that began in the mid-eighties. *The Karate Kid* (1984) and *Karate Kid 2* (1986) were directed by John Avildsen, who also launched Sly Stallone with the original *Rocky.* Compared to the Bruce Lee series they feature a more kindergarten karate. Then there's Jean-Claude Van Damme, Chuck Norris and all the other heroes who save the West from various kinds of fundamentalist devils.

The 'karate kid' is a tiny Californian who learns to beat back the school bullies thanks to martial arts and intellectual discipline taught to him by Mr Miyagi, the kindly Japanese handyman—played by Morita Noriyuki, usually known as Pat—who helps out at home. Miyagi is the real name of a great Okinawan karate teacher who invented his own style: *goju ryu* karate. The *Kid* opus also owes something to the Carradine TV series, which also features a wise old master who mutters ambiguous mottos which help the hero—whose own origins are also ambiguous—to make his way in the wicked world of the West.

In *Kid 2* the kid and Mr Miyagi actually go to Okinawa for a chop out with the handyman's arch enemy and dysfunctional family. *Karate Kid 3* (1989) and *The Next Karate Kid* (1994), released to coincide with the fiftieth anniversary of the Second World War, includes a lot of rough stuff with war veterans and both have the same smooth moves, fractured Zen and sensible role modelling as the original but not the zip and charm. Pat Morita has had many minor roles in all kinds of movies in need of a wise old man of the East. His huge list of credits include *Even Cowgirls Sing the Blues, American Ninja* and *The Battle of Midway.*

If you must, there's a Karate Kid home page at http://tribea.ios.com/~wooster, and many more serious karate and martial arts sites for fans of the real thing that can be accessed simply by loading a search engine with 'karate'. Many of them have Okinawan connections.

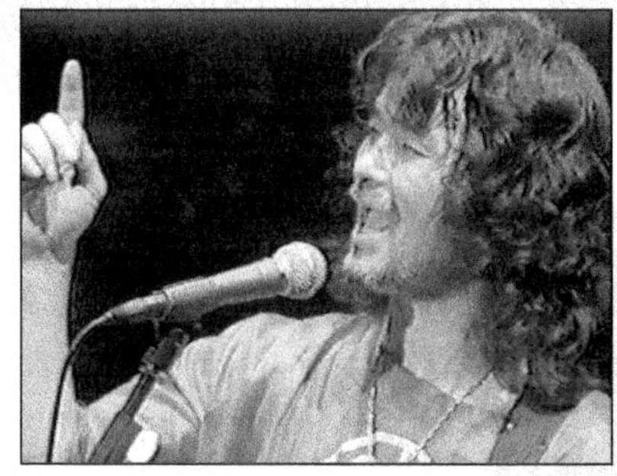

We are the go-between, between civilisation and nature

Kina Shokichi

The first time we really heard Kina Shokichi's music was in the early 1980s when we were hosting a monthly radio show on Sydney's JJJ-FM. His music soon became a staple of our program, as Okinawan elements became more and more influential on the work of the more interesting musicians among the Japanese mainlanders. No doubt they had the same response to the intoxicating feel of Okinawan music.

At that time Kina had become the international face of the Okinawan scene. He may not be a household name yet in the West as such, but his music is widely known throughout Asia and is appreciated by a significant and growing number of fans worldwide. He has many admirers and collaborators, including Ry Cooder, David Byrne and a score of Japanese musicians and may be remembered as one of the performers at the Atlanta 1996 Olympic Arts Festival.

We met him in his theatre club, Chakura, in Kokusaidori street, downtown Naha, where he tends to hold court for visiting journalists and people who want his ideas and opinions on all manner of things. Later in the evening he played a live gig at the club to a small but respectful and enthusiastic audience that included his mother and father. When he is not touring elsewhere, he plays there every night. A number of hard-core fans came down from the mainland to see the show. His big hits are 'Hana' and 'Hai Sai Ojisan', both of which have been recorded by other artists

From the Kina Shoukichi and Champloose Live *video.*

in Japan, and in the case of 'Hana', much further afield.

Tell us about your family background and traditions regarding music.

My father Shoei was a talented master musician and my mother is a very good communicator. My grandfather was a 'medicine man', using herbs and natural stuff to heal people. That seems to be my family's traditional business, on father's side. My mother's line is that of determined warriors. Her father used to hide in the mountains after the official abdication of the Ryukyu Kingdom during the Meiji period. One of the things Japanese mainlanders did was to ban the traditional Okinawan hairdo. So he went into hiding in the bush to avoid cutting his hair off. I think I have inherited qualities from both family lines.

I was surrounded by my father's music students when young. Strangely, though, I never learned music. My sisters were practicing every day. I did not touch an instrument until I was sixteen. I just picked up the sanshin one day and immediately the song 'Hai Sai Ojisan' was born. It just happened all at once, I picked up the instrument and the song came out. It was just like that. Even though I'd never touched an instrument, I grew up looking at people practicing. Later, I learnt that my ancestors on father's side indeed had many excellent music masters, so I must have been born with that musical talent in my blood.

When did you start doing 'new' versions of traditional music?

I was never consciously trying to create anything 'new'. When I did it, first people thought it something totally opposite to tradition, but if you listen to "Hai Sai Ojisan' now, it sounds very traditional and sits well in the traditional repertoire. It must have sounded very new at the time, because I used guitars and other instruments. But as proven over time, I was not doing anything new. I was just carrying on the tradition.

Are you a bridge between traditional Okinawan music and new styles?

I'm not sure if 'bridge' is apt because most of the time tradition is maintained and handed down by those who only practice the old pieces, while what I do is creation. I have always believed that Okinawan music is active, it is as vibrant as other living music such as rock, jazz and even classical music. Just like any living music style, Okinawan music can incorporate all sorts of influences from outside, yet still sound distinctively Okinawan.

My creative life began around the time of Reversion, when Okinawa became a part of Japan again. In the early seventies I think it is correct to say I was the musical representative of the mood at the time. We are heading to an equally turbulent time now and I am needed again. Every time the society goes through a turbulent time, I seem to be required.

I am a successor of that Okinawan tradition which fosters creativity during turbulent times—as during such times when we were an independent country. All those turbulent times in our history are in my soul.

From my viewpoint, the current struggle against the US bases has much the same quality as the Reversion movement. Not many people here have realised but I may be the answer to these turbulent times of Okinawa. It is my pleasure to make some contributions.

I don't belong to Japan, I don't belong to the USA, I don't belong to China. I am talking about my spirit. But because it does not belong to any one of them, I can communicate with them all. That's why I can receive messages from Australian Aborigines and the indigenous peoples of the Americas, like Hopi people. I can communicate with them all because my spirit does not have any national allegiance.

You could say my spirit exists in the terrain that lies beyond national borders. My music comes from there. That is why Okinawans can absorb all sorts of musical influences, classical music, rock music, yet still make it our own. If you don't have your own identity, those influences would absorb you, instead of you absorbing them.

The folk music scene and its links with the protest movement of the sixties had a significant impact in many places including Japan. How do you relate to international music movements around now?

World music is perhaps what you mean. It should be used to describe exactly the sort of music we—Champruse—have been playing for a long time, I suppose. David Byrne tried to create a version of it by fusing black and white music but he failed to come up with something successful because he forgot to include any Asian musical ingredient; he realised that when he heard my music. But I've been doing that kind of thing for years!

I'd love to get more people interested in our music. If mainstream music learns from my music, copies it or whatever, it would be better, but, in reality, it is afraid to incorporate my music.

The folk music boom of the sixties didn't last long in Japan because it hadn't got deep enough roots. It was a very superficial and imported phenomenon. The recent boom of world music has firmer roots but no vision. When I make music, my concern is to combine these two together successfully.

The sixties and seventies was a very political time in Japan. Every time the security treaty needed to be revised—in 1960 and 1970—there were nationwide mass protests. Some said to me that the reason there was no popular anti-AMPO movement around 1980 in Japan was because, after Reversion in 1972, the Okinawa factor was no longer there to ignite the flames.

It was a time when the USA and the Soviets were offering different models of utopia for the rest of the world to follow. The USA was offering their promise of liberal democracy, while the Soviets were talking about workers' heaven. It was a period of confrontation, but we saw a light in the darkness. John F. Kennedy seemed to offer something new at the beginning of the sixties when he declared that the torch is handed down to the young people. He was talking about what the ideal shape of the society should be.

It was refreshing and encouraging—but he was killed and the light was gone—but the seeds of idealism were blown all over the world and some did take root. After the assassination of JFK, many young people started to pursue other ideas—personal ideas from the inside. Some Westerners went to Asia for answers, many to India, some to Japan. I feel like I am very much a part of this spiritual give-and-take cycle and I don't think it's just a coincidence that I was invited to Atlanta for the Olympic Games.

I inherited the spirit from the US in the sixties and I feel my spirit is being called back to the USA as part of a global exchange of creative spirits.

How is Okinawan music different?

Because it feels different. Of course the scale and rhythm are different, but more than anything else, what makes Okinawan music so distinctive is that it reflects the way of life here. Its appeal comes from the Okinawan way of life and attitude that remains here, but that have been lost elsewhere. We are a nonmaterialist culture, we have long contact with the dead, our forefathers, and that puts power into what we do. And that's why so many outsiders get attracted to our music.

RY RECALLS

In the sleeve notes to a 'best of' album—*Peppermint Tea House*—put out by Warner Brothers in 1994, Ry Cooder describes what happened in the studio when he recorded with Kina for the *Blood Line* album sessions in Honolulu in 1980. After the voice track for 'Hana' had been laid down by Tomoko (she was Kina's wife in those days), Kina insisted on having it played back over and over again 'until he had wrung himself out'. Cooder says he later missed Tomoko's mournful voice and the 'chunk-band groove' of those sessions.

We were lucky enough to hear Tomoko's amazing emotional range close up and personal at her *minyo* karaoke bar in Naha in April 1996 when she agreed to sing a half hour of hits, including 'Hana', just for us and a couple of devotees from Tokyo. Of all the versions of 'Hana'—including Kina's own—her vocals are the only ones which give the song its full power without turning sickly sweet.

I think Okinawan music has the vigour, the essence of life, which people of modern civilisation have all lost. See, many people are feeling they've come to a deadend chasing the dream of consumption. Okinawan music comes from a totally different philosophy.

What will happen in Okinawa in the near future?

To put it simply, I believe we can achieve something the rest of the human race has failed to achieve. After all, we have the longest life expectancy in the world here and there must be something cultural in that. Our indigenous culture has real value and we could play a world role in offering that to everyone. Someone has to play that role, otherwise there will be no circulation of energy and the balance in nature will be completely disrupted.

I guess the role we could play is the go-between, between civilisation and nature. See, there are people who know what's wrong with this world and what to do, like all those indigenous people, but they have not really convinced the world, the world of modern civilisation. In turn, civilised people have failed to reach the same depth in understanding of the Earth that many indigenous people have.

You could say we are in that rare position to bridge the two. In a few years time I think Okinawa will become the meeting point between 'native' culture and modern civilisation.

What should happen to the US bases?

Looking at it over a long period it wasn't so bad they were here because they've been a reminder of what twentieth-century civilisation is all about—peace maintained by nuclear deterrence, the means of mass destruction, the very existence of nuclear weapons maintains peace. Is it the sort of peace we are after?

That's not a mature way to keep peace and it is about time we grew up. We should look for some more mature alternative form of security such as love or truth, or celebration, instead of bombs.

The twenty-first century could turn out to be our golden era, only if we can establish a world order based on such mature forms of trust and confidence. There, I believe Okinawans can play a role. We in Okinawa

NOT SO FAST

The Okinawan prefectural government has a Base Return Action Program to develop the land now occupied by the military when it is returned. However, Okinawan greens criticise the plan because it has been drawn up by a mainland Japanese consultancy and is insensitive to the fact that although a lot of land has been destroyed or polluted by military use, a lot more of it is pristine and wild—in fact, the only 'natural' vegetation left on the main island. The construction industry might be keen to get in there and 'use' it, but large parts—especially the Yanbaru forest in the north now used as a training area—should be kept as nature reserves.

have some credentials, because we renounced weapons hundreds of years ago. No other country has done that. Local history shows we never had slaves. So we could be of use.

Personally I have been organising festivals inviting indigenous people from all over the world for the last ten years. This is all preparation for the future. My personal network will become valuable to the people of Okinawa.

Maybe we should move the United Nations here and start moves towards disarmament at once. Maybe Okinawa could stage a new form of the Olympic Games with a spiritual basis instead of being devoted to competitive games which come from military origins anyway. You know, all those races were designed to train spies to run fast! The javelin event was based on throwing spears; the discus was for throwing bombs as far away as possible. We deserve better than this. We can have an Olympics based on spiritual celebrations, music and meditation.

This is what Okinawa should be doing anyway, and the bases should be turned into something useful towards that direction.

One of your albums is called Nirai Kanai. What does that mean?

To put it simply, you can say 'paradise'. Literally *nirai* means where the sun rises and *kanai* where the sun sets, together, it represents the circulation of life around the universe. It is where the sun resides. Our legends handed down from our ancestors say we came from there to Okinawa. And we will go back there. *Nirai kanai* is the gate where we come from and go back. The cycle of life is an essential part of our tradition.

You know, many gods reside here. They seem to like this place. I'd like to introduce them all to the rest of the world. [Laughs heartily] That's my message.

You have a song called 'Sabani'. What is sabani?

Sabani is a curved log boat. I have not yet completely understood its significance but you know, before Okinawa became widely known as such, it was also called Ryukyu. Now, before that, it was called Uruma, it meant the island of the *uru*. *Uru* now is understood to mean coral, so Uruma literally means the coral island. But I think there is something deeper

HEAVEN OUT THERE

One of the most potent of ancient Okinawan notions is nirai kanai—'heaven off the coast' or 'the home of the gods across the sea'—an 'out there' sort of concept many Pacific Islanders share. Rice is believed to have arrived from there.

It's the subject of many Okinawan songs, including one which Kina recorded for his 1980 Blood Line album. More recently when the Nenes, a female group of singers who perform regularly far away from their home base of Ginowan, did a cover version of the 'Banana Boat Song' with new lyrics in the Okinawan language, they transformed it into a song about nirai kanai.

than that. If you look around, there is a place in Iraq called Ur, now an old ruin on the Euphrates river near Basra. The word means the son of god as well as the universe. Ur's the place which appears in the Bible as Ur of the Chaldees. Sumerian civilisation was established there.

There is a hypothesis that our ancestors came from there on *sabani* and called this place Ur's land. I like the idea but I'm afraid I haven't found any evidence to prove this yet.

Champru rules

Champru is one of those words that's been spelt by outsiders so many different ways. It's pronounced 'champ-roo'.

Kina Shokichi's band is variously known as Champrus, Champroos, Champruse and more recently Champloose. But in their own language, it has always been spelt and sounded the same. His *champru* music is often said to have come from the *champru* town of Koza. What is this thing called *champru?* It means a mixing together, or mixture, and may have its origins in Bahasa Indonesia. The word is certainly used in Indonesia as *campur* and appears in Nagasaki as *champon.*

Indonesia's *nasi campur* (also pronounced 'champ-roo') is a plate of cooked rice and an assorted mixture of side dishes, pieces of meat or fish, rather like Japanese *bento* lunch boxes. Nagasaki's *champon* is a Chinese derivative noodle dish, rather like fried noodles with mixed gravy on top. *Champru* in Okinawa is a stir-fried mixed dish. Most popular is *goya champru* with tofu. *Goya* is a summer vegetable, known as bitter melon in English. Other *champru* dishes include *mamina* (bean sprouts), *chiribira* (garlic shoots), *somin* (fine rice noodles and tinned tuna), *tamana* (cabbage) and *fu* (gluten).

Recipe for *goya champru* (to be cooked with light oil in a wok): Lightly fry bite-size tofu first, then set aside. Cut *goya* in half and get rid of seeds, slice thin in crescent shapes, salt and let sweat for half an hour to reduce bitterness (optional as you become addicted to the taste). Rinse off salt and dry. Stir-fry thin pieces of pork (optional) and *goya* slices, then toss in cooked tofu and bonito flakes (optional) and stir in lightly beaten egg just before turning the heat off. Salt to taste. Locals often add a dash of *awamori* with chilli.

HAI SAI SET

Kina's single 'Hai Sai Ojisan' did for Okinawan music in Japan what Bob Marley's 'I Shot the Sheriff' did for reggae in the UK and farther afield. Literally, the title means 'G'day, Buddy'. It opened the door to the mainland for Kina and his *champru* Okinawan music. The single was so popular that the huge Nakano Sun Plaza hall in Tokyo was sold out on his first Japan tour in 1977.

Before Kina, the only music that made it out of Okinawa was heavy metal by bands like Murasaki—purple in Japanese, and deeply committed to the plush power of the Hammond organ—and Condition Green—named after the military term which means you are absolutely ready to go over the top, and they did.

Heavy metal was the favoured genre for US servicemen at the time, and they more or less dictated the kind of music played in the live venues around the bases on Okinawa and, of course, on FEN—the local US service radio station—the Far East Network. Mainland record company executives picked up the same taste, so Okinawa's early music exports were mostly big guitar bands.

Kina made it outside because of the talent-scouting prowess of Kubota Makoto, who, because of his activities as a prolific record producer around the region, ought to be nicknamed 'the Phil Spector of Asia'.

In the early seventies Kubota played and recorded with a band called the Sunset Gang which favoured the sounds of Deep South blues. On a visit to Okinawa he took back a bagful of traditional-style singles put out by local record companies—Okinawa is perhaps the only part of Japan outside the urban centres which has a number of independent music labels—one of which was Kina's 'Hai Sai' single.

So the legend goes, Kubota passed on a copy to Hosono Haruomi who was later to form the Yellow Magic Orchestra. Hosono included a variety of Okinawan tinged tracks on his pre-YMO solo work, including the *Tropical Dandy* (1975), *Bon Voyage Co.* (1976) and *Paraiso* (1977) albums; a track called 'Roo Choo Gumbo' was included on the *Bon Voyage Co.* album.

Kubota's Sunset Gang (subsequently transmuted to Sandii and the Sunsetz) made an album called *Hawaiian Champroo* (1975) which included a few Okinawan-style compositions, so it's fair to say that in the mid-seventies Kubota and Hosono introduced rather than 'discovered' the modern Okinawan *champru* music style to Japan.

Kubota with Sandii and the Sunsetz persisted with a recognisable blend of 'chunky *champru*' and while YMO was hardly Okinawan in its style you can hear the occasional notation floating through.

YMO's most internationally successful member Sakamoto Ryuichi has *champrued* the occasional track on his solo albums and for his early nineties world tour enlisted the support of the Nenes. His 1996 world tour included his version of 'Asatoya Yunta', an ancient love ballad from Taketomi. We were lucky enough to hear a traditional rendering of this song for ourselves, sung by one of

Taketomi's oxcart drivers, outside the house he claimed was the heroine's home.

Okinawan music in the nineties is seen as Japan's contribution to 'world music', and as such pops up on the mainstream charts. Ry Cooder preceded that with 'Going Back to Okinawa' on his *Get Rhythm* album (1987). One recent example came from a popular mainland group called The Boom, with a nationwide hit single with obvious Okinawan influence.

Today, the most accessible way to enjoy folk-style music in Okinawa is at a *minyo sakaba,* a traditional music bar, where singers and *sanshin* players perform often late into the night. Some include karaoke facilities so that customers can fill in between sets; this has a mixed appeal depending on the ability of the singer to hold a tune. Strict traditionalists tend to frown on the concept of mixing *minyo* and *awamori* drinking in bars, and if you're not a karaoke fan you'd have to agree with them.

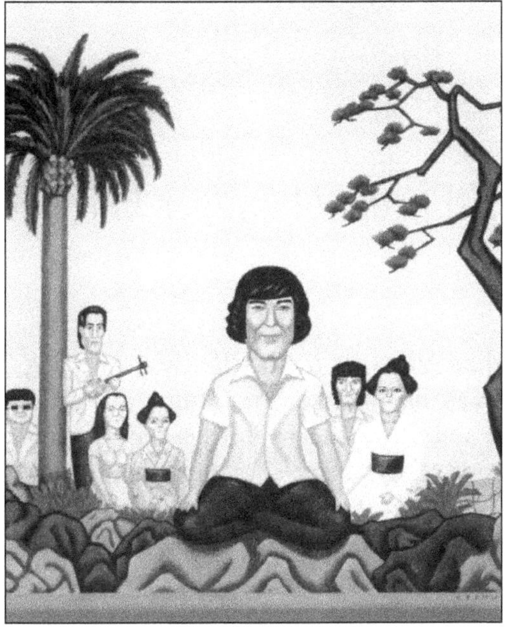

Minyo bars in Okinawa are a comparatively recent tradition that started in the seventies. The first was called the Mikado, set up in Koza and run by none other than Kina Shokichi. In the Mikado's early days, Kina performed with the Champroos as did his father, Kina Shoei. Other regulars included the Sanshin Trio, which featured Teruya Rinken and China Sadao, who is credited with putting together the female chorus group called the Nenes and writing most of the music for them, as well as being a singer-songwriter-producer in his own right.

Kina may have come a long way since then, but he still performs to small audiences at his new club in Naha.

It's not only Kina's words, music and peace ventures which inspire homage from admirers and imitators. The cover for his self-titled debut album *Champrus* was designed by Kawamura Yosuke, whose graphic work is well known and emulated by Western artists, especially the hipper T-shirt designers. Kawamura had already designed covers for Kubota's and Hosono's albums.

Cover art from Kina's first album.

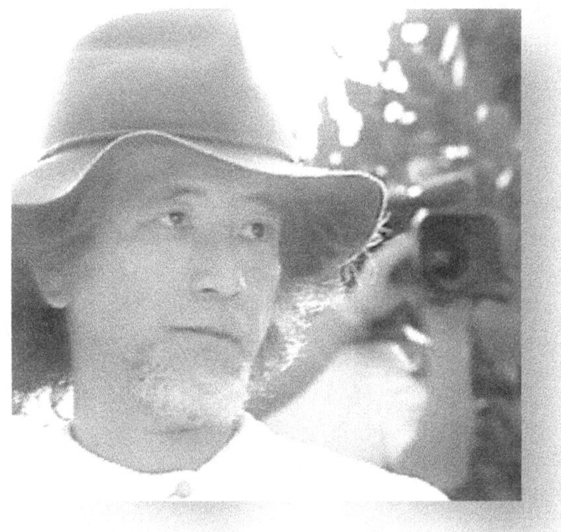

I'll probably never know why I make films

Takamine Go

Ever since we saw Paradise View in a film festival in 1985, we wanted to talk to its creator. Its attraction was an intense and grainy surrealism. Filmed in the jungle, beach and village, the story and the characters lurch seamlessly between dreams, madness and mundanity. Takamine lives part of his life in Kyoto, which has a version of Japanese reality far removed from the sensibility of his home islands. Since *Paradise View*, he made a second Okinawan feature in 1989 called Untama Giru, and his most recent work is a documentary about his beloved traditional singer Kadekaru Rinsho—a video-only release.

We heard he was 'on tour', filming with legendary underground Lithuanian director, Jonas Mekas. It seemed a suitably surreal situation, and we put out a message for him to find us. Eventually he tracked us down at Kai's Bar, a location too noisy to record a lengthy interview.

We met again—with a crowd of friends and onlookers—in the lobby of a major hotel decked out in the current international style of brass rails and potted palms. Takamine was dressed in an unseasonably long overcoat, an extremely battered pork-pie hat, a beautiful green and purple shirt and a hand-held digicam, which he was using to record his 'on the road' experiences with the visiting Mekas. Before we opened proceedings, we were able to try traditional *bukubuku* cha tea, Orion beer and a special dark

Takamine from his Kadekaru Rinsho *video.*

bitter drink served in a china cup—which the hotel staff claimed was 'coffee'.

We decided to move beyond the Muzak zone and settled for the plastic chairs around the hotel's empty swimming pool. It was warm, but still too early for summer life so no-one else was there. There may have been no water in the pool, but in the background there was the constant trickle of a fountain and birds that seemed to be piped through the hotel's PA system.

Takamine was in filming mode and mood and taped us recording our interview with him. He identified himself as 'Go', even though his given name is Tsuyoshi. He started off by explaining how he chose it. Ready, steady, go, Go.

That's really a different pronunciation of the same Chinese character. Nothing special. It's just much easier to say.

I was born in Kabira village on Ishigaki island, miles away from Okinawa island. When I was five we moved to Naha. I grew up there until I was nineteen. My mother still lives in Naha. After finishing school, I went to Kyoto to study painting at university and that's where I live part of the time now. Sometimes I'm there, sometimes I'm here with my mother.

I don't know where I will be living in the future, but I have my family in Kyoto. My wife teaches music at high school and basically she supports our family of five. We have two daughters and her mother lives with us too. I'm a good filmmaker but not so good at money-making. So it's really up to her where we will be living, because she supports us all.

Tell us about the problems you face making films on the island where you were born. How strong is the pull from your roots?

When making films I make them from a very subjective point of view. My films aren't objects or objective, they are more like self-portraits. If Tokyo or Kyoto people want to make films there in their own way that's fine, but I make films in Okinawa because it's the best place I can express myself. I'm not interested in making films of the place as such. I don't overrate the place, you know, I like some aspects of life here in Okinawa, but there are many that I hate here as well.

How difficult is it working in Okinawa, especially if your films are so personal?

It's as difficult here as it is anywhere else to raise money to make feature films. The added degree of difficulty of making films set in the place of your own origin depends on how well you can merge with the environment—with the air. Even though my films are 'personal', they aren't private or introverted. I always want to make films from my own personal perspective but for everyone to enjoy.

I make lots of films in Okinawa but none of them portrays Okinawa from an 'objective' perspective.

What's so special about Okinawa?

It's the air, or the atmosphere. Everywhere it's different. My films deal with politics, culture, history, but to me, the local air is something I really like to portray. You can make a film with lots of messages, but the unique characteristics of the film as a medium aren't exploited to the full that way. A good film can

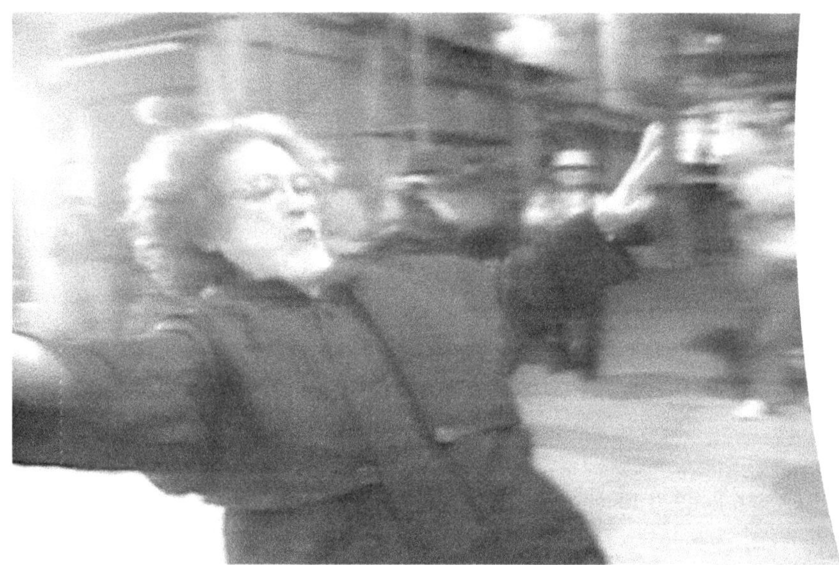

create atmosphere.

I want to share the unique air of Okinawa with other people through the medium of film. We have an Okinawan word here, *mabui*, which roughly

Still from Kadekaru Rinsho.

RUDE NAMES

Okinawa has a lot of nicknames, some nice, some nasty. Its ancient name is Uchina and people still use that term. Some say the name Okinawa itself is derived from Uchina. A book of contemporary culture put out in mainland Japan in 1996 is called *Uchina Pop.*

Fodor's Guide to Japan and East Asia of 1964 described the Ryukyu Islands as 'presently administered by the American army' and a source of 'irritation to Far Eastern stability for centuries'. Writer Stuart Griffin subtitled his chapter 'Okinawa: Orphan of the Pacific'.

A 1982 special edition of *AMPO* magazine, the English-language Japanese quarterly, described Okinawa as the 'concealed colony'. Anti-base campaigner and women's protest movement organiser Takasato Suzuyo used the phrase 'prostitute daughter'. Both Japan and the USA have long referred to Okinawa or the Ryukyus as 'stepping stones to Asia'. *Fodor* '64 also uses the old nineteenth-century term 'Keystone of the Pacific'. *AMPO* '82 said such strategic stupidity would likely render Okinawa the 'nuclear bullseye'.

As to the topographical attractions of Okinawa, in *Fodor* '64, 'Ireland is no greener' and the deep waters of California 'no more sparkling' and, weirdly, 'the beaches of Burma no more inviting'. Griffin tells us that *awamori* can be distilled from sweet potatoes as well as rice, that Okinawans play their own football—*kemari*—do bullfighting, karate, and bare-knuckle boxing—*jodam omote*—which, he says, means smiling face.

One interesting suggestion from Griffin in '64: once the Americans leave, Koza city, which he says is 'a fascinating and frightening garish boom town' which grew up around Kadena Air Base basically to service the huge number of US personnel stationed there, might become 'the Far East's ghost town'.

The people of Okinawa, said Griffin, did not let 'their status as pawns in the giant East-West conflict disturb their daily lives of hard work and hard play'. They were 'untroubled, amiable, and easygoing', 'warm-hearted', 'most of them are very gentle with hardly any suicides', 'blood pressure at the minimum and insanity almost nonexistent'. Their gentility, said Griffin, earned them the nickname 'ladies of the Pacific' and added that like typhoons, common in the area, and women, Okinawans too could be 'fickle, flighty, and unpredictable' and had a reputation for 'failing to turn up when expected'.

By the way some guidebooks claim that as many as forty-five typhoons can hit 'the region' in the course of a year.

'Here is an archipelago dreaming in the Pacific sun' where the people will 'grope their way from a shackled past into a free future, a people who are, and only ask to be, allowed to live in peace'.

translates as soul, or perhaps a state of ecstasy, and it's that state I want people to experience when they watch one of my films. But to be honest, I really don't know why I make films now and I'll probably never really know. That doesn't matter at all though.

Here I am talking about the 'ecstatic' state that only the best use of the medium can bring about. Many filmmakers around the world have the same attitude and aspire to do as I do. If they didn't, their films wouldn't mean anything no matter how interesting and important the subject matter is.

I use many aspects of our history, culture—music and dance—very distinctively Okinawan things in my film. They are not mere plot or background stuff just to add colour and movement. They are filtered through my own perspective to achieve that sense of ecstasy which only this medium can achieve.

> Your film Paradise View was quite surreal—it took its viewers into another world, as if it were a painting, with no obvious barriers between what is and isn't real.

It's a fairly common theme here in Okinawan culture where reality mixes with nonreality. You'll hear people talking about nirai kanai a lot here. Nirai kanai is where happiness-bringers reside. Nothing religious, nothing unique about it. Many people all over the world have their own version of nirai kanai.

We stress that we live side by side with dead folks here a lot, but everyone does. And my use of these concepts is my interpretation of an Okinawan version of a universal human quality.

My films often traverse between what is and isn't real. I consider it part of entertainment to the audience to have your senses tested, by arguing within yourself: is it real or not? It should be left to the individual viewer to interpret that. It's certainly not the role of the director to reveal it.

To nu yu kara Yamato no yu	From the rule of China to that of Yamato
Yamato nu yu kara America yu	From the rule of Yamato to that of the USA
America yu kara Yamato nu yu	From the rule of the USA to that of Yamato
Yamato no yu kara Uchina yu	From the rule of Yamato to that of Okinawa
Hirumasa kawataru kunu Uchina	Oh, how often changes occur in this Okinawa

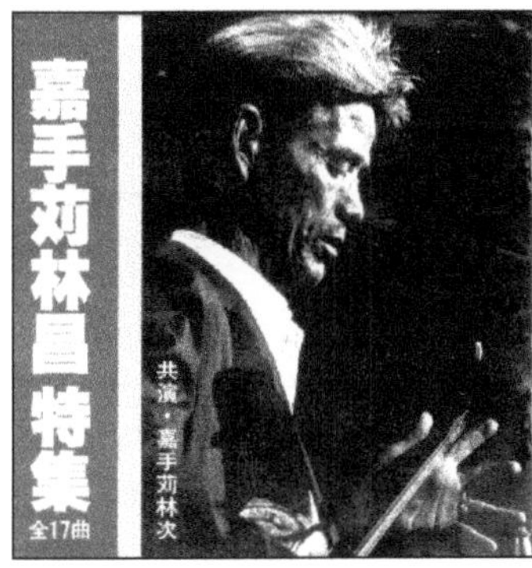

Kaderaku Rinsho's anthology album cover.

Maybe the best way to sum up what I mean is to sing this song written by Kadekaru Rinsho, called 'Jidai no nagare', or 'The flow of time'. It goes like this:

That song was originally written by Kadekaru Rinsho; it's about how China was the great power behind the Ryukyu Kingdom. Then we were taken over by the Japanese and when they got defeated after the war in 1945 we were conquered by the Americans, and then given back to the Japanese in 1972. But now people are talking about independence. I must stress that merely becoming politically independent is not necessarily my idea. I'm wary of nation-states of any kind because any state is authoritarian and I have to include any independent state of Okinawa in that category.

Political independence as a 'nation-state' is not all that an attractive option to me. I don't see why we should have to belong to Naha, or whatever, instead of Tokyo. What's the difference? To me, the only real solution seems to be the creation of a kind of federal state of individual islands in the chain, maybe you could call it the federal republic of the Ryukyu islands—but no, not the Republic of Ryukyu!

By the way, I said Kadekaru wrote the song, but I should say my version has an extra two lines. His version traces the story up to the rule by the USA, the second line, then to the last line. I have inserted the two other lines. This interpretation and adaptation of songs written by others is a pretty typical Okinawan tradition. Maybe we still believe they are public property that we can interpret and add our own thing to them. I think it's a good tradition—adding something new to that which already exists.

Anyway, a federal republic of islands needn't be based on any particular ideology. It should encourage people to express themselves, to pursue cultural activities whether it be song, dance, painting or filmmaking. We should just keep other things to a minimum—just keep high technology where it's absolutely necessary in medicine, but at other levels, we don't need expensive buildings, roads and all that. We should get down to basics. Let people do what they want to do. I'm sure it makes everyone much happier.

THEORETICAL BASE

Yanagida Kunio, the man regarded as the founding father of ethnology of Japan, visited in 1921. He believed both Okinawan and Japanese cultures stemmed from a common source, had developed separately for centuries, and said that without studying Okinawan folklore no-one could understand folklore in Japan. He later wrote a book called *The Ocean Road,* in which he discussed many things, including the possibility that rice passed through the Ryukyus on its way to Japan.

You said that people here have a lot of contact with dead souls. What does that mean?

We have a strong worship of nature but especially our ancestors here. It is not religious, but is expressed in everyday life. The dead aren't literally here, but they are alive in our souls, our memory, our subconscious. Maybe it's more obvious here. In April for example, we have a festival called Shimeisai, when people make visits to their family graves. Our graves are very big and prominent. When we go to them at Shimeisai, we go there not only to be reflective but to dance and sing together with the dead souls. [Here he seemed to be taken by his own thoughts. He clapped his hands briefly and paused, as if waiting for a response. We listened in silence. Then a couple of tears rolled down Takamine's cheeks. We felt a presence. It was as if he was silently demonstrating that we were surrounded by souls.]

That's our way of paying respect. Having a kachashi, a dance party, in front of them, they would be happy to see us having a good time, you know. That's our way. Of course we make solemn prayers before we start partying.

[Having made this point Takamine took brief leave and disappeared into the toilet, perhaps, we thought, more troubled by his thoughts than his bladder. Maybe we should have asked why, but we assumed he would have told us if he'd wanted us to know. The interlude had no effect at all on the rest of our conversation.]

What significance do you put on the word chirudai, which was the basis for your 1979 film?

In *Okinawan Chirudai* there's a conversation between a child and his father in which he explains if ever this thing called chirudai should disappear from Okinawa then we'd really be part of Japan. It's a word that to some degree means laziness and does have negative connotations, but it also means a kind of loose floating feeling that's all through the place. You could say it is in the distinctive atmosphere we have inherited from our ancestors. You must have noticed it, that floating feel, when you first arrived here.

I'd say it belongs to mother nature, which you cannot make value judgments about one way or the other. Chirudai is not something human logic has created, but it is something existing within us before we acquired any logic. I believe Okinawa will remain as Okinawa as long as we have chirudai, but once we lose it, we would become Japanese.

Lots of visitors from outside tend to think that it was the Ryukyu Kingdom that created, defined and shaped our distinctive culture. Sure, there are many interesting things from that time, but I'm more inclined to attribute the basic elements that we have to a time before—things like chirudai seem to have been here forever.

ECSTASY TO GO

***Mabui,* the Okinawan word for a spirit, which Takamine interprets as ecstasy, appears as 'Mabui Dance' in Hosono Haruomi's soundtrack music for *Paradise View* and as 'Mabui Dance #2' on his *Medicine Compilation* (1993) album.**

You mentioned before there are things you don't like about Okinawa. What are they?

What I don't like recently is the way Okinawans behave. It may sound strange, but when I have been following the recent protests against the US bases and against the discriminatory way the Japanese government has been handling the issue, the Okinawan people seem to be acting out their roles. You know, they are playing out what Okinawans are expected to be. They don't seem to be using their own

Okinawan language.

You hear the central government and some governors and commentators talk about the 'age of regions and decentralisation'. You know, the sort of argument that regions will have more say and so on. But what I can see is the exact opposite. The centre sucks out from you what it needs, not the other way around. That's why I cannot trust those Okinawan leaders who only play the role expected of them by the central authorities for the Okinawans. Their picture of us has no *chirudai* in it.

Okinawan Chirudai had a Japanese subtitle which translated *chirudai* as sacred laziness because that's how I wanted Japanese people to understand it. I had to say 'sacred' because 'laziness' has such derogatory connotations.

The idea's not religious or ideological, it's just something here. It's a basic characteristic of Okinawan people. See, if our natural environment is destroyed then Okinawa would not be Okinawa. The same is true of *vv*. It's such a basic characteristic that without it we wouldn't be what we are. If you negate *chirudai* you negate a basic human characteristic—which is not just Okinawan either.

What should happen to the bases?

The existence of the US bases is destructive to nature. Once gone nature can't come back again. You know, it takes ages for a stone to become a stone in nature and impossible for it to turn back to its previous state.

I think we should convert the bases into a state-of-the-art, high-grade, high-tech medical centre, a place where people can come from anywhere in the world to get well. Okinawa could become an international healing centre where people come to be cured.

Sacred sighs

One insight we gained wandering around the back streets of the smaller island villages was the way sacred natural sites are marked by ancient stone monuments. A mangrove swamp near the Urauchi river estuary on Iriomote is a haven for huge 'buttressed' rainforest trees, which live together in an ancient clump at the edge of the tidal line. The entrance to the place is marked by a decaying plaque but was clearly not on any current tourist itinerary—we saw no trace either of bus tires near the entrance nor loafer prints in the mud beyond. What we did discover was a low, coral stone wall with an archway 'entrance', a curved stone lintel topped with a ball of stone. Nearby, fallen to the ground were the relics of another little stone archway and some broken columns. They seemed to us to be religious relics but there were no further clues anywhere.

We found a similar construction near Hoshisuna beach at the northern tip of Iriomote. There behind a massive man-made breakwater at the back of the beach was an area given over to several monumental structures. One, the most recent, was a large concrete rendering of a traditional Okinawan curved-prow fishing boat. Behind this was a wooden building, a shrine of sorts, and beyond that, low stone walls similar to the broken ones in the mangrove swamp—again with a gap for a stone lintel and ball.

We saw yet another example close to the centre of the port of Ishigaki, this time in an area rather like a religious compound, which contained a number of shrines of different sizes and ages. Again it was at the back in relative obscurity, beyond a clump of ancient, lopped coral trees.

These old stone monuments seem to be little protected—nor was there any tourist information—and we were later told that this was probably because they were merely 'markers' and that as far as the locals were concerned, it was the place itself or even more likely the coral or the rainforest trees that were sacred, not the man-made monuments.

OKINAWA FRAMED

Okinawa has provided alluring opportunities for filmmakers seeking both 'exotic' backdrops and hard-edged documentary realism.

Renowned mainland director Sai Yoichi, who has an ethnic Korean background, made a trilogy of films set in Okinawa but only the final one had a genuine local theme. *A-Sign Days* (1989) is a semi bio-pic of an Okinawan rock singer called Kiyan Mary, of Mary and Medusa fame. It's set at the end of the 1960s and depicts life in the time of Occupation as seen by this legendary singer and her friends.

A-Sign Days presents a vivid picture of the popular music scene in Okinawa at that time, and as well as Kiyan Mary's own offerings, it shows how American rock music dominated taste with songs like 'Suzie Q', 'Born to Be Wild' and 'Johnny B. Goode' prominent on the soundtrack.

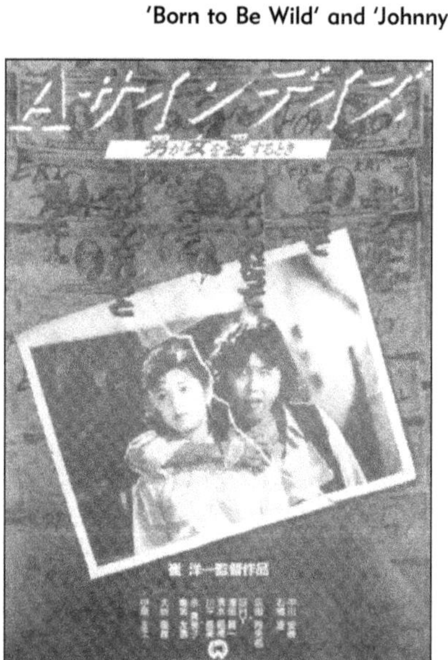

The 'A sign' of the title refers to the US Occupation's seal of approval, introduced in 1952 and issued to about 3000 bars and restaurants around the bases to allow them to trade with US personnel. As the film shows, these A-sign bars were meeting places for US servicemen and the thousands of prostitutes who depended on their patronage for their economic survival.

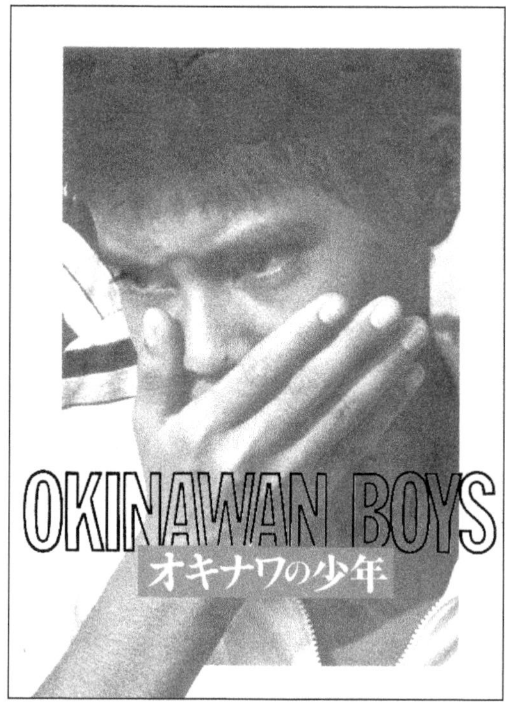

Okinawa's own directors have used film to expose an audience to their unique history and culture.

Okinawan Boys (1983) by Shinjo Taku, is another Occupation melodrama featuring a big name, Japanese mainland star Ogata Ken, known to an international audience for his role in the *Ballad of Narayama,* directed by Imamura Shohei. Shinjo had worked as assistant to Imamura, whose neorealistic style of filmmaking took a surrealist twist when he made *Profound Desire of the Gods* in pre-Reversion Okinawa in 1968. Imamura later said the actors complained so

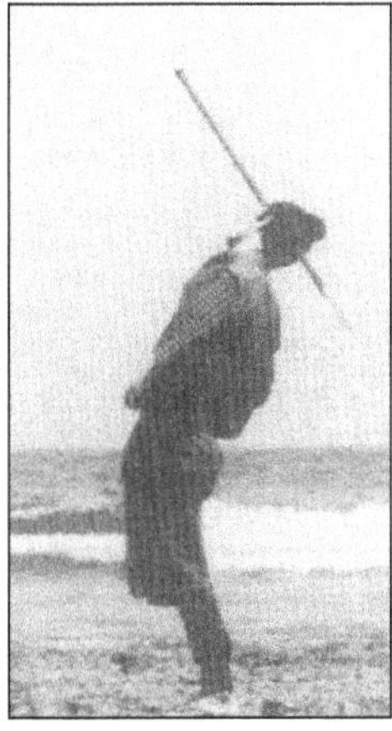

much about being kept on Ishigaki for eighteen months — he himself had no problem with such confinement—he switched to making documentaries for two years.

Takamine Go seems to be the most prolific Okinawan filmmaker. Difficult as it is to raise funds, he's produced an oeuvre of minor classics including *Okinawan Chirudai* (1979), *Paradise View* (1985) and *Untama Giru* (1989). Hosono Haruomi composed a fine Okinawan-tinged soundtrack for *Paradise View* and played a minor role in it together with fellow singer-actor Togawa Jun.

Takamine Go's next project for which he was raising funds when we met him is called *Mugen Ryukyu* (Love's love: An Okinawan dream). The screenplay is set in the historical reality of Reversion but like his other films, reflects on that 'reality' with scenes and themes that draw heavily on ambiguity and fantasy.

There have been many excellent documentaries made in Okinawa, notably *The Old Man and the Sea* (1990), a real-life drama directed by Jan Junkermann. Loosely based on Ernest Hemingway's novel, it's about a fisherman's battle with a marlin off the island of Yonaguni, the furthest west of all Okinawa's islands.

Yuntanza Okinawa (1987) is a documentary shot in Yomitan village in 1986; Yuntanza being the local name for Yomitan, where half of the village land is taken up by US bases and where antiwar sentiment is perhaps the most intense in all Okinawa. The film tracks the tightly knit community of Yomitan uncovering the truth of the wartime mass suicide for the first time. At the same time imperial icons of the past were promoted again at schools in preparation for the annual national athletic meet, the domestic Olympic games.

There's a scene near the end when a couple of high school girls rush up to the stage during their school graduation ceremony and tear down the *hinomaru*—now once again the national flag of Japan. They then stomp on it—presaging the action of Chibana Shoichi five months later when he burned the *hinomaru* at the meet at Yomitan.

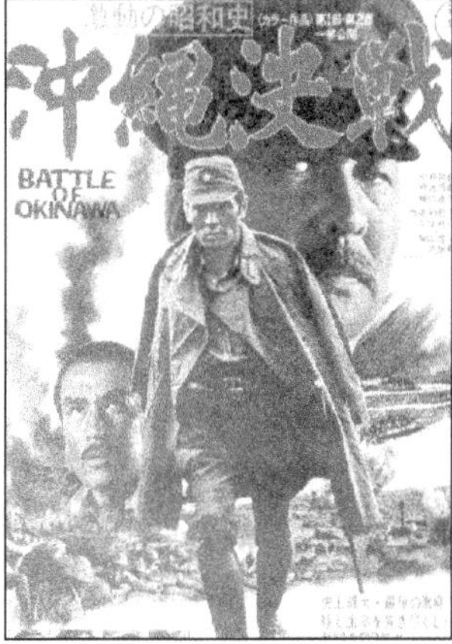

The Toho film company had made a score of successful war films during the sixties, and decided to produce one a year with an annual release date of August 15—the day the war was lost in 1945.

Toho's 1971 feature was the *Battle of Okinawa*. The director, Okamoto Kihachi, concentrated on the fate of three top military leaders and the battle-scene special effects were handled by Nakano Akiyoshi, the man who succeeded Tsuburaya Eiji as FX director of the 1970s Godzilla series—which included the King Shii-saa epic set in Okinawa.

Posters: A-Sign Days, Okinawan Boys, Battle of Okinawa; *still:* Untama Giru.

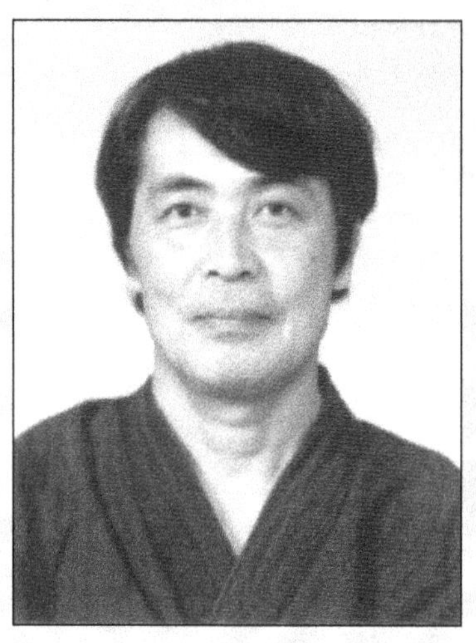

Talking Taketomi

Uesedo Yoshinori

Filmmaker Takamine Go suggested we go to Taketomi if we wanted to get an idea of what the old Yaeyama lifestyle was like. He should know, because he was born in Ishigaki and knew the place. He chose the location for a scene in his documentary film about Kadekaru Rinsho, one of the great older traditional *minyo* singers and *sanshin* players whom Takamine adores. We took his advice and a plane from Naha to Ishigaki—about an hour—then a ten-minute, high-speed and very noisy power ferryboat from Ishigaki harbour out past the massed ranks of concrete-made tetrapods across the coral reef to Taketomi.

It's a bit like a museum piece. The whole streetscape is heritage listed so nobody's allowed to build 'new-looking' buildings—although some were built a decade or so ago. It's small enough to walk around, although some people who live there do use cars to get down to the ferry dock—where you can also hire a bicycle when you arrive. A small fleet of microbuses services the daytrippers who come over for a quick look at the reef and the museum.

Most of the buildings feature coral either in the walls or the compounds that surround them and crushed coral is spread across the road—which, if it's been freshly laid, can make bike riding strenuous. The only other mode of transport is the ox dray, bullock cart or buffalo ride. There are two companies, one

'private', the other 'commercial', which tow a tour of tourists around a three-kilometre wander through village streets for about an hour while the driver alternates between giving out historic anecdotes and singing local songs with *sanshin* accompaniment. The animal that took us around had a hibiscus behind her ear—she was thirty-six years old and her owner said she would live to be fifty. She moved very slowly, which seemed right.

Taketomi is a magical place. We met one woman there—a 'refugee' from Hokkaido who wished to remain anonymous—who claimed on her holidays she can live off what she finds on the beach, especially seaweed and fish. There are about 250 permanent residents, a hundred of whom are over seventy, with the oldest inhabitant being 106 years old. There are two main white sand beaches, but the tide has to be in for the water to cover the coral, otherwise it's a very scratchy swim.

Taketomi's drinking water and electricity come by underwater pipe and line from Ishigaki and aside from the buffalo, there are a few cattle, goats and chickens but no commercial fishing apart from some mangrove-unfriendly prawn ponds which local people think are nonindigenous. We looked in at the only 'industry' on the island, a weaving shed where two women were producing unique Taketomi-designed cotton and silk cloth. We were told that every woman on the island has this skill and that all the carpenters could build one of the wooden looms they use. A touring party from Taiwan dropped by, fingered the wares, were told to move on quickly by a tour leader in a dark blue suit and bought nothing. We caught up with another party from Hokkaido at the local folk crafts museum and watched and listened while its curator, Uesedo Yoshinori, entertained them for about ten minutes. His main concern was to inform them just how different from the rest of Japan these islands were. They seemed convinced and laughed a lot at his jokes. He took a more serious line with us and gave us a potted history of the region which we pass on here.

Uesedo Yoshinori is a keen advocate of the preservation of Taketomi's streetscape, which he believes fitting to the climate as well as the source of local culture. Preserving old stuff properly is a way of tourism development, he claims.

★★★★★

According to archaeological studies, human remains date back at least 1500 to 1600 years on Taketomi. On nearby Ishigaki and Hateruma islands, they found traces of human life dating as far back as 3500 years ago, so it won't be long before we find something similar here. On mainland Okinawa, at Minatogawa, they've found remains of life from 20 000 years back.

There are many theories about where we all came from—whether it was the South Pacific islands or somewhere else. One theory says we are descendants of the residents of a vast ancient Sunda continent in the Pacific. We are talking there about 20 000 to 30 000 years ago. It isn't difficult to imagine people moving from south to north along the edge of the continent and, you know, in those days all these islands were connected to each other.

We know that migration changed its direction around 2000 to 3000 years ago, as people started moving here from the north. Local legends say six different families came to Taketomi about 600 years ago from the north and set up six villages. The area had a loose relationship with the Ryukyu Kingdom until 1500 when Sho Shin, the king of the Ryukyus based on the main island of Okinawa at Shuri, invaded and put it under his direct control.

A revolt against Shuri led by Akahachi on Ishigaki was provoked. People were pushed into a corner and the king took the opportunity to force them into his centralised state. Their defeat marked the end of intra-island warfare and the beginning of their subjugation by Shuri. Once that was done, complete disarmament of the population was implemented. Hence the tradition of the 'unarmed state'. The king ordered all weapons to be collected from everyone, including warriors as well as farmers and put them away in storage. Hideyoshi did much the same in the rest of Japan, except the samurai there were allowed to keep their swords.

About a hundred years later, in 1609, the Ryukyus were invaded by the Shimazu forces and put under Satsuma's control. During that period it was a separate kingdom but literally overseen by Satsuma representatives who made sure nothing happened which might be contrary to their views. That system lasted until 1879 when the new Tokyo government took over direct rule of Okinawa. The kingdom was abolished and a prefecture of Okinawa was created.

From the viewpoint of residents of Taketomi, we've been conquered by successive waves—the Ryukyu Kingdom, the Satsuma, Japan and the USA. You can see from the money on display in the museum that we've got notes from many eras in the currency of the ruling authority.

The B-yen notes were circulated immediately after the war. Then the

ALIENS AT HOME

In the 1983 film *Okinawan Boys,* there's a scene where a traffic cop in Tokyo asks Satoru, a young migrant worker from Okinawa, to show a passport.

When we met director Shinjo, this was his explanation for the scene:

'The passport issue is an essential part of the whole thing. There were lots of ignorant people in mainland Japan. I myself had the same experience—being asked by a stupid cop to present a passport. The passport was a rather strange one, issued by the US military authorities and approved by the Japanese authorities. It stated that the holder is allowed to "return home to Japan". Subconsciously or otherwise the Japanese authorities were accepting the fact Okinawa was a part of Japan, but they failed to explain why only Okinawans had to carry papers while the rest of the population was not required to do so. So while we were considered to be "coming home" when we went to Japan, we were treated like aliens.'

currency switched again when Okinawa was ruled by the USA with the signing of the Peace Treaty. The only legal tender became the US dollar. Then in 1972, with Reversion, the Japanese yen became the currency of Okinawa.

This is the sort of stuff nobody else in Japan has experienced. It's just one example of how Okinawa's history is very different from what is taught as the history of Japan in the classrooms.

As of May 15, 1972, we were handed back to Japan. Some things changed but the military bases set up during the US Occupation still remain. For a quarter of a century, the issue was left untouched. That is one reason for the recent prefecture-wide outrage against the bases.

During the US Occupation, Okinawans living here needed special documents to travel to the rest of Japan. They were like passports, but issued by the US military and authorised by the Military High Commissioner here. For those living in the rest of Japan, they needed to obtain a special certificate issued by the Japanese authorities. You can see passports and certificates in our museum too.

Cop: **Your driver's licence.**

[Satoru hands over his licence.
The cop looks at it.]

Cop: **Okinawa? You from Okinawa?**

Satoru: **Yeah.**

Cop: **Show me your passport.**

Satoru: **What?**

Cop: **I said passport. All aliens are obliged by law to carry their papers around all the time.**

Satoru: **Aliens?**

Cop: **Things may have been different before, but isn't Okinawa governed by the US now?**

The B-yen was issued by the US military here from 1948 and was the only legal tender for awhile. The Americans had total control over monetary policy. They decided how much to issue, how much to circulate.

Their control extended to all aspects of social and political life here. Even though we had an elected council and a civil executive body, the veto lay with the US military authorities. Left-wingers could be sidelined. A Communist candidate, Senaga Kamejiro, was elected mayor of Naha city but was not acceptable to the US Occupation, so he wasn't allowed to take up his rightful position as an elected official.

We have other things in our display cases, like brands of cigarettes, which were never sold outside Okinawa in the rest of Japan where there was a government monopoly on the tobacco market. There's one Okinawan cigarette called

GOODY TWO SHOS

The Ryukyu Kingdom had two separate dynasties during its existence between 1429 and 1879. Before it was unified, the island of Okinawa was divided into three domains, or three 'mountains' as they were known. Mainly for geographical reasons, separate kingdoms existed in the north, middle and south of the island. They all had tribute/trade relations with Ming dynasty China. After years of bloody battles, the island was finally united by a king from the middle, the second king of the first Sho dynasty, Sho Ha Shi, who then ruled from the castle of Shuri. This Sho dynasty lasted only forty-one years, though it had seven kings. Years of infighting, intrigue and power rivalries weakened the line, which was finally usurped in 1469 by the kingdom's former financial manager, Uchima Kanamaru, who then proclaimed himself Sho En, the first king of the second Sho dynasty. It had nineteen kings and lasted for 409 years. In 1983 we met the latest in line and 'pretender to the throne' Sho Sen, who was president of the Small Business Association of Okinawa.

The star of the Sho was unarguably Sho Shin, the third king of the second Sho dynasty. When Okinawans talk about the 'golden days' of the Ryukyu Kingdom, they usually refer to his time. This was when the Okinawan court and high culture flourished, financed by the wealth generated from trade, but ordinary folk enjoyed little return from this dynastic expansionism.

The accumulated power and wealth was used to strengthen the centralised state and expand beyond the main island. In 1500 Sho Shin conquered the Yaeyama group of islands.

Second Sho family logo.

Violet, which came in two varieties, before and after 1972. One has the tax receipt issued by the government of Ryukyu, while the other is issued by the Japan Tobacco Monopoly. These items may seem trifles but what they signify is, I think, enormous.

We have about 260 postage stamps printed for Okinawa-only circulation. These were not available on the mainland, though the actual printing was done by the Ministry of Finance's printing department. The denominations were of course printed in US currency. We have in our collection a very rare one with 'final issue' printed on it, next to the 5c. Have you seen any other postal stamp that proclaimed the country, region, or whatever, where the issuing authority is no longer going to be in existence? That was the last of the series of Ryukyu stamps that had a US denomination but were printed in Japan and only available in Okinawa.

Maybe our experience after the war is not especially dramatic when you compare it to what was happening over in Europe at the same time. But it's very unusual compared to the rest of Japan.

And we should speak out. When a former prime minister of Japan, Nakasone Yasuhiro, made the claim that the Japanese people are a single, homogeneous ethnic group, he was wrong. It showed how attitudes towards Okinawa have been exclusivist but people here didn't make a big issue out of it at the time. They should have spoken out but they didn't.

Within the region, too, we have differences among

ourselves. Sometimes we don't feel we are part of Okinawa. People here in the Yaeyama islands suffered a double occupation historically, you know, by Japan and Okinawa. We don't share the same anti-US base attitudes predominant on the main island of Okinawa, simply because we don't have any military facilities here. We never really had armed soldiers coming here, even when we were under US military rule. Those who came here were more civil administrators. So it's quite natural that people don't feel the same antagonism towards the American bases.

They are more remembered here as the people who did good things. They helped to get rid of malaria by spraying DDT, which, I suppose would have caused lots of environmental concern now.

They built roads and all the infrastructural things, so we didn't really suffer at the hands of the Americans.

During the war, there were about 160 Japanese soldiers on this island. But maybe because it is such a small island, the US forces never took it seriously. There were a couple of bombs aimed at the school building, which was used as the camp for those Japanese soldiers.

There was an airfield on Ishigaki that attracted US attention, but more lives were lost as a result of the so-called evacuation, forced upon us by the Japanese military, into the malaria-infested jungles. So people here suffered more from malaria than battles with the Americans.

[Uesedo showed us one of the museum's best exhibits, an ancient sailing boat used by people to move around the islands.]

It seems local people had engaged in trade with other countries before we were annexed by the Ryukyu Kingdom. One of the Shuri government's motives was to control our foreign trade. Shuri imposed a hefty tax on us here, then the Satsuma leaders imposed a harsh poll tax after the invasion in 1609. Under this rule, the common people were virtually banned from travelling to other countries. From their point of view, it made more sense to tie people to the ground as farmers and tax them, rather than allow them to risk their lives on the sea.

Sabani, the local name for a one-log canoe, I think, was developed after Meiji. *Uminchu,* which literally means person of the sea, used to refer to those who migrated from the Okinawan mainland to this region in the Meiji era, because, you see, after the Meiji restoration we were given more freedom, freedom of movement and freedom of jobs, which encouraged fishermen from the main island of Okinawa to migrate here and set up their hamlets. Some fisherfolk migrated later to other islands like Kohama.

Fishing people have a tradition of migration; like those from Itoman on the main island and Kudaka island, who migrated south to Miyako island and set up their own hamlet. I think those who came down here are part of that migratory movement.

But all this happened after the Meiji restoration and because of it, commercial fishing and migration were allowed. Before that, of course, we had subsistence fishing—catching fish when the tide was out, stuff like that.

> *Where rice came from and how it arrived in Japan has always been discussed in Japan, perhaps because of its imperial connection. Before the war, it was widely believed rice came with the ruling families from the north. Yet, some researchers claim that a different kind of rice might have arrived from the south. What do you think?*

We really don't know how long we have been cultivating rice here. On this island we still grow *akamai,* or red rice. It is said to belong to the Javanica variety, quite different from the Japonica type favoured in Japan or the long-grain Indica from other parts of Asia. One thing certain is that there was more than one 'Rice Road' and more than one variety brought into Japan. Javanica rice was brought into Japan either from mainland China or the South-east Asian islands, definitely via the Ryukyu Islands, that's for sure.

TOO DEEP TO BURY

The 'preservation order' that allegedly protects Taketomi from developmental vandalism is very nice but doesn't seem to have the garbage disposal problem under control. Just as its water and electricity have to be piped and lined in from neighbouring Ishigaki, much of Taketomi's 'portable' waste has to be moved off the island to garbage dumps elsewhere.

The island has recently had a sewerage system installed that pumps out effluent into the sea—a lost opportunity since Taketomi might have been the right place to try out technologies designed to recycle human waste as fuel or fertilizer, or both.

One of the ugliest problems we noticed on Taketomi is the vending machines, dozens of them placed in pairs at every tourist stop and several places in between, all selling canned or bottled drinks. At quiet times of day they make more noise than the visitors and when the tourists are around they're in constant use, as if everyone who comes there feels a natural obligation to keep the Pepsi pumping and the Fanta flowing. Sure enough, empty glass and aluminium refuse can be found almost everywhere.

What is the state of the tourism industry on this island?

We get about 300 000 tourists a year on Taketomi, which has less than 260 people. Only about 10 per cent of them come into our museum, which was set up by a Buddhist monk in 1947. He died in 1983. Everything in it was collected by him since he was a little boy—for sixty years. Everything exhibited was used here on this island, which I think is important. He did not go around collecting the stuff with money.

You could say the tourism industry on this island started with this museum—people used to come to the island to visit it when there was nothing else to see. We try to keep this cultural link with the tourist industry—and we also try to keep the village looking like it did in the old days. It has a preservation order on it, endorsed by the national government in 1987. That's why people keep coming here and our population has now stopped declining, in fact it's actually rising, ever so slightly.

I think culture has economic growth potential. People will come to see the real thing and if you keep your integrity they will keep coming. We know there is money in culture and tradition. If you have something genuine, you can pull in those people who are willing to pay for the real thing. I think we are having some success here on this island.

Taketomi is not unique. On Iriomote, while searching for a secluded beach we'd been told was a beauty spot at the end of a woody winding road, we found not an unspoiled haven but a huge hunk of dumped junk right on one of the entry points to the beach. Mass consumption means mass disposal of products that simply don't break down. The most extreme case is plutonium and there are those in Japan who have suggested that deep-sea trenches off Okinawa would be a suitable dumping ground for civilisation's most durable poison—another example of the 'remote area dump' syndrome that has dominated environmental policies for decades, but which is now facing serious challenges all over Japan.

WHO ARE YOU AND WHAT DO YOU WANT?

One of the most disturbing and confusing aspects of Okinawan history is the way outsiders have persistently tampered with the islanders' identity. Back in history it was assumed that the king of the Ryukyus was technically a 'vassal' of China and even though there were no Chinese troops or mandarins based in the islands to enforce this status, the king was supposed to, and regularly did, provide tribute to the Chinese emperor. The king of the Ryukyus could only be enthroned once his succession had been approved by His Heavenliness.

During the 'medieval' period when Japanese mainlanders started to seriously interfere with Okinawan affairs, this relationship with China became a matter of dispute and ambiguity which lasted right up until 1879 when the then-king was forced to abdicate by the Meiji government in Tokyo. To prevent him getting support from China, he had to be more or less kidnapped.

Since the invasion of 1609, when Satsuma gained sway over Okinawa, people were told to spend less time amongst foreigners, their trade to the Indies and South-east Asia was controlled and restricted and they were allowed to have close communications only with China. They went so far trying to disguise their own presence in the Ryukyus that the Satsuma obliged Okinawans to behave more like the Chinese—not to sing their own songs or wear Japanese-style clothes. Very confusing.

Governor Ota told us back in 1983 this explains why many Japanese find it easy still to think of Okinawans as 'not Japanese'. During the Tokugawa shogunate in the seventeenth century, the Satsuma were instructed to allow Okinawans to keep in touch with foreigners but under supervision, with spies keeping tabs on these contacts. No foreigners were allowed in, as they were at the Kyushu port of Nagasaki.

At the end of the Tokugawa period, a period of what Ota calls 'forced assimilation' began, with all aspects of life in Okinawa being 'Japanised'. Ota quotes a newspaper editorial from 1893 which claimed that unless they pursued Japanese ways they 'would never be happy'. This was the first time they were offered the opportunity to die for the Meiji emperor—in the war with China

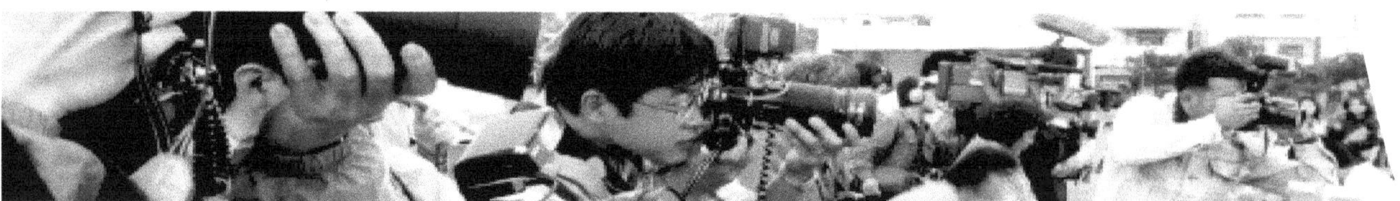

in 1894. Okinawans were told they should be pleased if their sons died in the war because they could then join the Japanese gods at the Yasukuni shrine in Tokyo. At that time they were only allowed to join the infantry (presumably as cannon fodder), and their enthusiasm was reflected adversely in casualty figures. Okinawans who died in that war made up a proportionately higher toll than from any other part of Japan.

During the Showa period, 'Okinawan ways' were again discouraged, not always successfully. One reason so many ordinary people died during the Battle of Okinawa in 1945 was because they were speaking their own language—banned by the military government. Despite the fact that they were obviously local civilians, panicky soldiers from the mainland decided they were foreign spies and shot them. Ota and many other Okinawans believe that the indoctrination of loyalty to the Showa emperor was also the reason as many as 700 Okinawans killed themselves during the battle. They thought that in the face of defeat this was their only alternative.

Many of these unhappy contradictions surfaced again during the US Occupation period when Okinawans were forced to relate to the Americans—who supervised their government—and see Japan as once again a 'foreign' country. During this period, because the American rulers encouraged people to treasure the Okinawan traditional culture, it confused matters once again.

Okinawans rallied around the Revert to Japan movement because they thought it would mean they could achieve political and social equality and get rid of the military bases. In fact, as historian Arasaki Moriteru of Okinawa University says, letting Okinawa go back to Japan was the USA's best option for keeping the bases!

Enthusiasm for Reversion to Japanese rule after 1972 did wane in Okinawa when it became clear that the fruits of 'democracy' as developed in postwar Japan were neither available nor all that desirable. At a prefectural level, Okinawan democracy has been more genuine and effective than regional government throughout the rest of Japan, which is one reason why Governor Ota has achieved such a high profile and suggests that Okinawan confidence in a more autonomous future is based on practical experience as well as ideals or dreams.

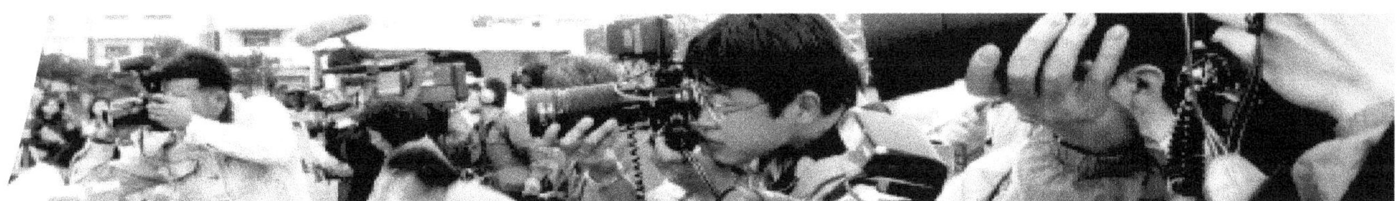

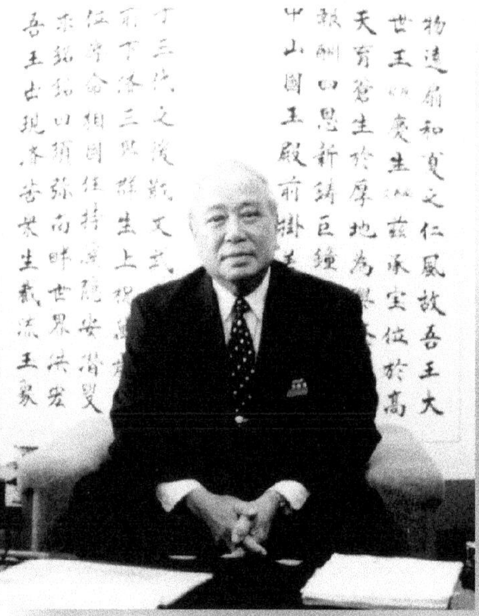

I'm an amateur politician

Ota Masahide

Governor, Okinawa Prefecture

Governor Ota Masahide was a professor of journalism at the University of the Ryukyus when we met him in 1983. We were in Okinawa to record interviews for a radio series for Australia's ABC, which was broadcast as 'Japan's other Voices' in early 1984.

In 1983 there seemed little prospect for success with the anti-base movement and one reason we chose the story was because it was to all intents and purposes a 'forgotten issue'. It was during the prime ministership of Nakasone Yasuhiro, who took a hard line on security matters and had proposed to US President Ronald Reagan that he could rely on Japan to be an 'unsinkable aircraft carrier' in the western Pacific. This is precisely what Okinawa had been for Japan during the Second World War. Such statements only alarmed people with memories of how such nonsensical posturing had ended in 1945.

It might seem now that the fatuous Pacific grandstanding of the 1980s has faded with the cold war, but not so. While we were waiting to talk to Governor Ota, Prime Minister Hashimoto Ryutaro was popping a more subtle version of the Nakasone doctrine into the ear of US President Bill Clinton, this time couched in sensible terms, such as 'widening'—and therefore deepening—Japan's security role in the region, the very kind of 'reason' used to justify keeping US bases in Okinawa for fifty years. Regional 'tension', it seems, is still too significant for there to be any diminution of the Japan–US Mutual Security Treaty's importance in Asia, or for there to be any let-up in the rhetoric devoted to its promotion.

In 1983 Ota had been careful to explain to us the inherent contradictions in Okinawa's history—a peaceful nation of traders, with advanced cultural activities and with no expansionist or aggressive tendencies of their own, living on a group of islands other nations deemed to be strategically significant.

One of the interesting contradictions he had discovered in his surveys of newspaper opinion polls down the years was that in 1962 a total of 88 per cent of the population of Okinawa was in favour of Reversion to Japan, but that ten years after Reversion only 57 per cent was in favour. That dissatisfaction, said Ota, had come because of the failure of the Japanese government to bring either economic prosperity or human rights to the islands—a hangover from a long historical process. Ever since Okinawa had been part of Japan, it had been poor.

One way the Japanese government had curried favour with the population during the 1980s was to increase the amount of rent it paid to landowners to lease their land to the US military bases. At Reversion there were 3000 antiwar landowners who wouldn't take the rent or regarded it merely as 'compensation' for damage done—but in 1983 that figure was down to less than 200. It is now back up near 3000.

Ota is quite well known and respected in wider Japan as an historian of the Battle of Okinawa. He had just turned twenty when he was mobilised into the Tekketsu Kinno Tai (Steel-blooded unit for service to the emperor) and thrown in front of the 'steel typhoon' that was the American invasion. It was an horrendous experience, which shaped his attitudes, especially the anti-military policies he has persistently advocated.

After the war he studied English language and literature at Waseda University in Tokyo on a scholarship sponsored by the US military and then did postgraduate studies in journalism at Syracuse University in New York State.

So, although he's an anti-base campaigner he's hardly an anti-American, and most of his criticisms are aimed at the Japanese government's acquiescence to US military needs. He was once a leading member of the exclusive Kin Mon, or golden gate, Club in Okinawa, whose membership was made up of the Americophile elite of Okinawa and many of his policies are based on his perceptions of US-style democracy. Until the nineties his only claim to fame was as an academic historian and he hardly seemed a likely candidate for political office. However, by 1996 he had become one of the most recognised politicians in the entire country.

The recent outburst of popular protest against the US bases was not simply a grassroots reaction to the rape case. The anti-base position has been gaining strength since the end of the eighties. In 1990 Ota was elected to the governorship on the single issue of the bases and was re-elected in 1994.

There's no doubt that the 1995 rape case made people in government face the issue, but Ota then capitalised on that new receptiveness. He took a provocative step, which also re-established a measure of political autonomy for Okinawa. When leases for land being used by military bases came up for renewal, some landowners refused to sign new ones. The Japanese government ordered Ota to do it on their behalf. He refused. His action made it clear that the Japanese government could not overrule Okinawan resolve and it generated a geopolitical crisis between the US and Japanese governments. It at last focused their attention on the problem Okinawans have faced since 1945.

Ota's political actions made on behalf of a longstanding grassroots movement then set in motion a search by the USA and Japan for a means to 'redeploy' the Okinawan bases, or their functions, perhaps to other parts of Japan, the region, or even Australia. It remains to be seen whether the plan they come up with will satisfy the people.

Moreover, unless a very different kind of Japanese government comes to power, it seems very unlikely that all US facilities will be removed from Okinawa in the near future—so the crisis that started under Ota's governorship will doubtless continue. It may intensify, it may dissipate. We shall see.

Ota or his successors may choose to escalate the issue and put Okinawa's sovereignty at the centre of the debate. While there is no serious talk of political secession yet, tighter ties with the region, as in days of old, are becoming a reality that could yield at least economic autonomy from greater Japan. In this sense history is on Okinawa's side.

As with every politician you line up for an on-the-record interview, we

NUMBER CRUNCH

Okinawa was a terrible battle—110 000 Japanese soldiers died and 150 000 civilians. There were 50 000 US casualties—12 000 dead and missing of which 5000 were sailors. As it loomed, it was dubbed by the Japanese command 'Tennozan', after a decisive battle in Japan's wars of unification at the end of the sixteenth century. Unfortunately, this battle has become the pat answer to why atomic bombs were used on Japan.

In the 600-page study Tennozan: *The Battle of Okinawa* and *the Atomic Bomb,* George Feifer claims the bombs were necessary because the alternative, an invasion of the main islands of Japan planned in two waves for November 1945 and March 1946, would have been even worse than Okinawa. Planners in Washington, he says, estimated US deaths in 'the landings alone' would have been 100 000 and that a million Americans and 20 million Japanese would have died before it was over.

While there's no way anyone can say the Americans wouldn't have suffered such casualties—*if* the war had lasted that long—the figures used by Feifer are not those President Truman and his advisers had before them when they made the decision to use atomic bombs. Their actual estimate of 40 000 dead was bad enough, but it fell well short of Feifer's inflated tally and actually assumed that losses wouldn't have been as heavy as in Okinawa. Feifer's 'million' deaths comes from a figure put around not by planners working on the invasion but by politicians after the war, perhaps to justify the enormity of the atomic holocaust. Ota's version does not stumble into this trap.

were asked by the governor's press office to send a list of questions before an interview would be granted. We thought it best to cover as much ground as possible and composed a list of sixteen questions about historical, contemporary, political, strategic, economic and cultural issues which we duly faxed to Naha. The reply came: cut it to five.

When we met the governor in a spacious conference room full of large, comfy armchairs stacked with staff and friends who wanted to listen in, Ota apologised for not having had time to look at our questions and said we could ask anything we liked. On the wall behind him were poems about old Ryukyu written in large calligraphy telling how the islands prospered by trade and were a peaceful nation.

Governor Ota is used to explaining Okinawa to Japanese mainlanders and foreigners. He's written more than forty books, including one available in English. The Battle of Okinawa, a large-format book full of photographs, was published by Kume in 1984. He has an easy grasp of the main issues, speaks good English and very rarely sounds anything like a politician. If you want to compare him with another political figure of our time, we'd say he's Okinawa's Václav Havel.

You've been campaigning for the removal of bases for a long time, as have many people in Okinawa. The rape case has given you an opportunity to make a higher political profile—has it helped you in your cause?

I didn't particularly want to use this issue to raise local people to oppose the presence of US military bases on Okinawa but it has helped us mobilise people. It is just one of nearly 4000 incidents that the people of Okinawa have put up with involving US military personnel. Often, people did not bring their cases up in public—they always kept all kinds of sorrows and anger to themselves—but with this case the girl was so young.

Back in 1955 a similar case occurred. A six-year-old girl—Yumiko—was raped and killed and it infuriated the local people, it put oil on smouldering

SATO'S PRIZE

While he was prime minister of Japan, Sato Eisaku slated reversion of Okinawa as his top-priority issue in a summit meeting he had with President Lyndon B. Johnson in January 1965 and later that year became the first prime minister to visit Okinawa since the Second World War.

Okinawans had mixed feelings about Sato. Upon arrival at Naha airport in August 1965, he claimed he was aware that 'the postwar reconstruction period for Japan' wouldn't be over be over 'until the day Okinawa reverts to the mother country'. Despite this well-meaning promise, a huge protest gathering of sceptical protesters confronted him later that night. About 50 000 took part in a rally and 20 000 marched along Military Highway 1, as it was then known, towards his hotel to help him firm up his resolve on Reversion.

Sato was out at the time they arrived at one of the military camps—meeting the US High Commissioner. When he learned the marchers were demanding to see him in person, were waiting in front of his hotel, and would not move, he decided to stay overnight on the base. In 1974 he was awarded the Nobel Peace Prize for the peaceful transfer of the islands back to Japan.

flames, because there was also the ongoing land problem at the same time. The USA wanted to build permanent military bases on Okinawa and was expropriating farmers' land. It was during this struggle that the Yumiko case occurred and it made people mad about the presence of the US bases.

And again in 1995, both the US and Japanese governments had been talking about extending the role of the US–Japan Mutual Security Treaty and people here were worried about the strengthening of bases on Okinawa. They want so badly to get their land back.

Twenty per cent of the main island of Okinawa is taken up by US military bases. They are concentrated on the central and southern parts of the island, where more than a million people live. Okinawa is only 0.6 per cent of the land territory of all Japan, whereas 75 per cent of all US bases in Japan are concentrated on this tiny island.

For half a century people have put up with all kinds of incidents and accidents caused by military personnel, but this time they said they had had enough. This is why the case of the 12-year-old girl made people so mad and anti-military sentiment came to a head.

How can you use it to put pressure on the Japanese government? How strong is your hand?

I don't want to utilise the case for political or other purposes. We have been requesting both governments to downsize US military bases here on Okinawa for a long time, and they've been considering it, but no tangible solution had been offered. I paid visits to Washington to meet high-ranking US officials four times in the past five years and requested the Japanese government again and again to address the base-related issues so that the people of Okinawa can cooperate with their local government. Otherwise it will be difficult for the local people to cooperate, particularly as they are so mad. They feel that they are being discriminated against.

Back in 1972, Okinawans were so eager to get back to Japan—Reversion—because they wanted to come under the so-called peace Constitution of Japan. Before that in Okinawa there was no constitution, neither US nor Japanese, and therefore no guarantee of human rights. So they wanted the protection of the Japanese Constitution. After Reversion they were discouraged because they didn't feel they were protected by the Japanese 'peace' Constitution. It specifically guarantees equal opportunity, basic human rights, and the protection of property and so forth, but in reality there were no basic human or property rights or rights to equality, so they were discouraged and at the same time resentful at this situation. So that's why we brought this issue to the court, but the court did not meet our requirements so we had to appeal to the Supreme Court.

There was a period in Okinawan history during the Meiji era known as the 'Do Nothing' era. Was this post-Reversion period another 'Do Nothing' era?

It wasn't exactly the same, but people were saying similar things about it, like they call it the third 'disposal' of the Ryukyus by force. The Battle of Okinawa was the first 'disposal'. Then in 1952 when Japan became independent, Okinawa was separated and placed under US military occupation and people say this was the second 'disposal' of Okinawa by force. And now

THE LAW
THE GOVERNMENT
THE PEOPLE

Japan's Supreme Court made its first pronouncement on the legality of US military bases in Okinawa in August 1996. The delivery took barely ten seconds. It simply stated it had no power to judge the matter.

It was the culmination of a twelve-month legal battle between the prefectural and central governments that began when a number of landowners decided not to renew their leases for use by the military. It escalated in August 1995, when the prefectural governor, who had been obliged three times before to sign on their behalf, also decided to refuse and was taken to court by the national government.

Ota took this stand because he was alarmed by an official US defence report—the Nye Report—released earlier in the year, which declared the USA should maintain the level of its military presence in the Pacific. Despite the Japanese government's pledge to reduce that presence in Okinawa, the US report said the opposite.

In his appeal against the orders Ota argued the concentration of military in Okinawa was historically incompatible with local values and in breach of the Constitution, which afforded people the right to live in peace.

The court wasn't interested. On Friday, September 13, 1996, Ota announced that he would no longer refuse to sign on behalf of the landowners. He was appreciative of the government's offer of cash for the Cosmopolitan City Plan, including an expanded free-trade zone, cheaper air fares between Japan and Okinawa, and no-visa entry for foreign visitors—concessions that could move Okinawa towards greater autonomy but may be difficult to deliver if the central bureaucracy opposes a 'two-systems-in-one-country' solution.

Okinawa Prefecture logo.

because we rely on the legal system of Japan, which doesn't meet the requirements of the local people regarding their property rights and the forced occupation of their private land, this is therefore the third 'disposal' of Okinawa by force.

Okinawa has a long history of independence and self-reliance before US or Japanese domination. How far can you go to create a new, independent Okinawa? How realistic is it to gain autonomy?

It doesn't just apply to Okinawa but also to the rest of Japan as a whole. Centralisation in Japan is very strict and conformity is the sort of culture of Japan. If you differ from the rest of Japan, then usually you will be discriminated against. To that extent Japanese centralisation is strict. But at least the central government is discussing the possibility of autonomy for each prefecture and we sincerely hope that this will materialise.

Back in 1609, Satsuma invaded Okinawa. Before that Okinawa was a tiny independent kingdom, known as the 'land of propriety'. Because they did not carry arms the Okinawans were easily conquered. After the Satsuma invasion there were worries about people rising up in revolt. People were strongly prohibited from carrying weapons, so up until the Meiji era local people never carried any arms, which is why they created karate—Okinawan karate.

Even after annexation by Japan in 1879, when Okinawa became part of Japan, Okinawan people respected independent thinking and valued independence very strongly. The Meiji government didn't force the mainland Japanese system on Okinawa because they didn't want Okinawans to revolt.

So, on one hand, centralisation has been very strict, but on the

ABORTED DELIVERY

The battleship *Yamato* made its large journey to Okinawa towards the end of the Second World War. Named after the old Japanese race, *Yamato's* end was sadly ignominious. It was bigger than anything floating at the time and had nine 18-inch guns, which could fire massive amounts of shells to a distance of nearly forty kilometres.

The truth was it was obsolete, as the days of battleships cannoning at each other had long gone before it was launched. The Japanese should have known that, as they themselves displayed the superiority of air power over great slugs of the sea when they destroyed American battleships at Pearl Harbor and sank the Royal Navy's *Prince of Wales* and *Repulse* off the Malay Peninsula.

The *Yamato* was the only major Japanese vessel still floating when the Battle of Okinawa loomed. *Musashi,* the second Yamato-class hulk had already been sunk near the Philippines and the third, *Shinano,* was hastily converted to a flat-deck aircraft carrier only to be sunk 100 miles south of Tokyo Bay.

It was decided that Yamato should be sent on a sneak-attack mission to Okinawa; if it got through Yamato was to beach itself and blast its guns. In fact it was a kamikaze mission. Yamato left home port for the last time on April 6, 1945, and with virtually no air cover soon became a soft target. The US Navy had fifteen carriers in the vicinity, the Royal Navy had five and the US Air Force was already operating out of airfields taken in the first days after the invasion of Okinawa on April 1.

After receiving twelve bombs and seven torpedoes on April 7, *Yamato* didn't make it.

The name and image of a huge battleship however was salvaged for use in a seventies sci-fi animation movie featuring *Yamato,* the 'space battle cruiser'.

other, in order to keep local people's support, the Meiji government did not change the system or Okinawan customs—things Okinawan.

As the Pacific War neared its end, 'Japanisation' was intensified and people were told to forget about everything Okinawan, like the local language or dialect, and they had to learn the standard Tokyo language. They weren't allowed to carry the sanshin, the three-stringed local instrument, and were prohibited from performing local dances—so that they would conform to the standard Tokyo system. They were educated so that in the event of an emergency, it would be best for all human beings to sacrifice themselves for the emperor. So, in the Battle of Okinawa almost one-third of the population was sacrificed.

With this bitter experience, people abhorred any kind of warfare, and that's why they don't want any kind of military bases here, because they are made for war.

In the Occupation period the Okinawan people were separated from mainland Japan and weren't allowed to go back and forth, confined, in a way, to one concentration camp. In order to live, they had to work in the military bases and so became dependent on the bases.

Now 20 per cent of the main island is militarily occupied and twenty-nine seashores are controlled by the military—like Naha port—and fifteen airspace areas are controlled too. We cannot use our own land, our seashore or our own airspace, so we cannot develop our own industry. Okinawa's income is the lowest in Japan and the unemployment rate is twice as high as the national average. In order to improve such a situation we have to have our own land, our own coast, our own airspace to develop industry to solve these problems.

What industries do you need?

Tourism!

What would you do with all the bases? They can't all be farmland. Kadena is such a huge airfield—would that become an international airport?

Yes, it's already planned to be a civilian freight airport. As you know, the Asia–Pacific region is developing very rapidly. We have very close relationships with South-east Asian countries. We have offices in Korea, mainland China, Taiwan, Hong Kong, and this year we will set up offices in Singapore, Malaysia and the Philippines. Next year we will move to Indonesia, Vietnam and Thailand. So we can be very international in that sense and develop our own industry as they did in the days of the ancient kingdom.

In those days the population was less than 100 000 and they developed trade relationships with neighbouring countries. It was a very prosperous period, lasting almost 400 years. Now we have 1.27 million people and communications have developed so radically we can develop our own business with neighbouring countries.

When we were in Iriomote we realised how close it is to Taiwan. People regard Taiwan as their neighbour. Some people seem like they don't really consider themselves part of Okinawa.

Yes, Yonaguni people listen to Taiwan radio. They have a close sister relationship with part of Taiwan. We want to stick with that kind of relationship with our neighbouring countries. They are very good to us, very friendly to us.

When we talked about tourism in 1983, you were concerned its impact might be destructive as well as bringing wealth. There's been a lot of development here since then—a huge number of resorts have been built. Are you worried they might destroy the natural attractions that bring people here?

We are worried about the destruction of our natural environment, but we are very careful in the way development plans are pushed through. Once we lose the natural environment, Okinawa is not a worthwhile place for tourists. That's why we didn't allow the airport at Ishigaki to be extended across the seashore—we wanted to protect the coral there.

SPECKS ON THE HORIZON

One of Okinawa's tiny neighbours has in the past few years become the focus of a prickly international territorial dispute involving Japan and China that seems to have confused the USA and maybe shaken its monolithic insistence that its presence is the only guarantee of peace and stability in the Asia–Pacific region.

The Senkaku Shoto—the group of islands known in Okinawa as Iigunkuba—are currently administered by Ishigaki city. They were taken by Japan at the time of its victory over China in 1895. Taiwan, the major prize of that war, went back in 1945 but the Senkakus were bagged with the rest of Okinawa by the US then and went to Japan when Okinawa reverted in 1972, despite protests by Chinese students in the USA.

Four of the five islands are privately owned by Japanese. Uotsuri is the biggest of them, but less than 4 km^2. It's known as Yukun by Okinawans and Diaoyu Tai by Chinese. It hosts a helipad built by the Okinawa Development Agency in 1979, as well as the remains of a bonito flake factory. The fifth, Taisho, is owned by the Japanese government and used by US forces as a bombing exercise range like Iejima, the small island off the west coast of Okinawa.

Japan's 'ownership' of the Senkakus has been in dispute ever since their occupation and has proven to be one of the few issues that has united opinion in mainland China, Taiwan and Hong Kong, a phenomenon which has confounded both the Americans and Japanese.

The source of this unity was Japanese citizens. Various ultranationalist groups, with names like the Japan Youth Federation and Death-Defying Unit to Proclaim the Ownership of Senkaku Shoto, have made daring visits to the islands in small boats to erect flags and lighthouses to remind the world that these islands were still Japanese—actions clearly designed to provoke Chinese public opinion.

Seemingly spontaneous demonstrations erupted in Hong Kong and Taipei around the sixty-fifth anniversary of the Japanese invasion of Manchuria in 1996, as many Chinese, it seems, still worry that such death-defying incursions onto the Senkakus indicate that the Japanese as a whole are reviving the nationalism that led them to war in the 1930s.

People in Okinawa know the 'trouble' goes back even further—to the Sino-Japanese War of 1894–95 and twenty years before that. In 1871, when the Ryukyus were still disputed territory, a group of Okinawans were killed in Taiwan. Despite a request from the Meiji government, the Chinese authorities did not take action nor offer compensation. Three years later, Tokyo sent a 3500-plus expeditionary force, most of them dissatisfied ex-samurai, to Taiwan and occupied parts of it until the Chinese recognised that these Okinawans were Japanese citizens, even though they were still technically under the 'protection' of China at that time.

The Japanese authorities used this incident as part of their move to establish total control over Okinawa, which was itself a 'stepping stone' to Taiwan.

The issue will remain confused. Beijing likes the idea of speaking for the Chinese diaspora in Asia and the concept of 'Japan the common enemy' is quite useful in that posture. If all three Chinas can be united against resurgent Japanese nationalism, it's harder for the West simply to isolate mainland China as the belligerent that justifies the continued occupation of Okinawa.

That was a long battle?

Yes. Seventeen years. I had lots of pressure put on me to build that airport, but I said no. We also have the national planting festival, attended by the emperor and empress, and the original site for it was at the northern part of Okinawa. But in order to have the festival, they would have had to cut down almost 10 000 trees, so when I became governor, I changed the site to the southern part, to a site where the battlefield was and we planted trees there which are now growing rapidly, so now we'll have a forest there.

We have passed a regulation—with the cooperation of the prefectural assembly—to protect the natural environment, so that developers have to get approval from the government before they build any resort development.

When we spoke in 1983 you quoted opinion polls, because it was part of your studies to look at opinion polls from the past. What's the situation now, do you have a strong support base for your position?

As far as public opinion is concerned, it's about 70–80 per cent in support of my position.

That's pretty unusual for an incumbent politician.

That's quite true. I don't consider myself to be a politician. I don't want to be a politician. I want to be a researcher like I used to be. I want to be an amateur all the time. I don't want to be a professional politician.

But you will see this one through?

I don't know. [chuckles]

It's fine to strengthen ties with ASEAN and other nations in the region, but the Japanese government still retains the right to make foreign policy. What's your strategy, will the Japanese government allow you to be independent?

Well, maybe the Japanese government doesn't want us to make such diplomatic moves, but it's not 'national' diplomacy, because nowadays it's quite usual for prefectures to make friends with neighbouring countries, as with sister-city relationships. And, as I said before, today in Japan the decentralisation movement is the current trend, so the Japanese government is discussing how to give autonomy to individual prefectures. We feel it's most important to become independent and conduct such diplomacy with neighbouring countries. Even though the central

SWEET AND LOW

Sugarcane is the main cash earner for Okinawan farmers. Its importance is on the wane but it still earned ¥22 700 million or 21 per cent of total agricultural output in 1992.

Production of sugarcane was introduced to Okinawa from Fukien, China, by Gima Shinjo in 1623.

Production and distribution of sugar was monopolised by the kingdom in 1645 by order of the Satsuma, so farmers were no longer allowed to grow sugarcane as they chose. These controls were needed to maintain the sugar price on the Osaka market and the state monopoly and control system were not abolished until 1888.

government does not want us to do this kind of thing, we have to do it to develop a unique local region.

I think this will contribute to the central government of Japan as a whole. It will be good for the central government because our unique regional culture will help strengthen our prosperity and contribute to the national culture and economy as well. So we want to try our best.

Are you talking about a loose federation?

Well, prefectural governors are discussing how to decentralise the Japanese system and some say regional areas can be created—say, the Kyushu area could be one, the northern part of Japan could be another and the central part could be another—but we, as Okinawan people, want to be one part. We want to get as much independence as possible, as much autonomy as we can get, and this current situation is a good trial for us to get autonomy from the central government. Otherwise we cannot develop our own industry.

During the Meiji era, sugar was the only 'processed' export item Okinawa had. But it was really only during the 1960s that Okinawan agriculture became reliant on cash crops like sugarcane and pineapples. Until then, farming was for subsistence. During the 1960s, many lowland rice paddies were converted to sugarcane fields. This pushed many farmers out of labour-intensive farming of peas and rice and into the service sector, including on the US bases. Now the Okinawa Sugar Company is ranked 21st of the biggest 100 firms in Okinawa.

We have been heavily dependent on government funding—almost 60 per cent. This is too much and we cannot go on forever in such a situation. As I said before, the unemployment rate is very high, especially among the twenty-to-thirty age group. We have to solve that problem. It's very serious.

What about industries other than tourism?

For years our main industry was sugarcane, but because of the deregulated market it doesn't do much for the local economy. We are encouraging people to grow orchids, mangoes, things like that.

At the time of Reversion, revenue from the bases amounted to almost 70 per cent of the annual economy, but today it's only 5 per cent. But it still counts a lot. The income from the military bases amounts to $1.6 billion, second to tourism, so we have to do something about it. That's why we have developed the so-called Cosmopolitan City Plan to be fully implemented by the year 2015.

We've told the central government that we want to see the return of the US military bases in three stages. Stage one includes the ten most important military bases, including Naha port and Futenma Air Station, by 2001, and Kadena by 2015.

We hope that both governments will meet our requirements. But we don't know how they will deal with our plan.

SMALL IS COOL, DREAMING OK

Since it was once an independent entity, if not exactly a 'state' as such, what's to prevent Okinawa from attaining that kind of status again? Okinawa is the only region in Japan where secession is seriously on the agenda and people there talk about it all the time as a possibility, even a probability. In the 1950s a Ryukyu flag was designed and in the 1980s a mock constitution was drafted.

Is it feasible? Could a population of 1.2 million support itself and run its own international affairs? Well, Singapore may be the exception rather than the rule, but its population is just a little over twice as big as Okinawa, and in fact, Singapore has made its money in modern times by imitating what you could call the 'Ryukyu model', of old, that is, making profits from buying and selling rather than making and doing. That's how the islanders of the Ryukyus made their wealth hundreds of years ago, roaming the Asian region looking for opportunities. It's how they built their castles, and sustained themselves in much the same way the great city-states of Europe did at around the same time. It was only the intervention and interference of the Japanese in that trade from the beginning of the sixteenth century that virtually ruined Okinawa.

Even before that, before the islands were 'unified' under the Ryukyu Kingdom in the sixteenth century, the smaller regions of the archipelago, such as Miyako and Yaeyama, were their own masters. In the late 1970s people there started **shima okoshi,** or island revival movement, to resist the invasion of resort-style tourism, which helped get a higher profile for the local identity and cultural practice. It successfully encouraged hundreds of young people to return to Iriomote and other islands from Okinawa or Japan.

The fact is that there are nations which do survive now that are smaller than Okinawa. Estonia is a good example of one that has re-emerged from modern serfdom. Tucked into a corner of the Baltic Sea it has about the same population, and from 1940 to 1991 was forcibly absorbed into the former Soviet Union. President Lennart Meri, in a speech to mark the fiftieth anniversary of the United Nations, made the point that there were enough small nations in the world to constitute a 'silent majority'.

Estonia might even provide Okinawa with the vital knowledge, experience and inspiration of how to go it alone. During the Middle Ages, Estonians were part of the Hanseatic League as traders. In modern times, like Okinawa, Estonia was at the periphery of an empire, and, together with the other Baltic states of Latvia and Lithuania and many other former parts of the Soviet empire, was used and abused as a dumping ground for all kinds of military and industrial ugliness.

Estonia removed itself bloodlessly from the Soviet shackles and, admittedly by going gangbusters with free-market privatisation reforms, quickly achieved an economic success none of the other newly democratised countries have been able to match. There are other connections. Estonians drew heavily on their distinct cultural heritage to maintain themselves during the Soviet occupation. Small though it is in the geopolitical scheme of things, the determination by all kinds of Estonians to keep their great choral tradition alive also had a deep influence in keeping the spirit of independence alive too. Huge choral festivals, many of them attracting hundreds of thousands of people from all over the country, were held right under the noses of the KGB and their friends, who didn't realise how potent these events were. They were gathering grounds for the expression of political as well as musical solidarity through the darkest days of the cold war and Soviet intransigence, and the great change in the late 1980s is known as the Singing Revolution. The Soviets didn't know or understand the power of singing and so left them alone.

Okinawa's cultural strength will undoubtedly be its secret weapon in the process of disengagement from Nippon. It may seem both 'remote' and dependent to the Japanese who still think Tokyo is the heart of the galaxy, but it's very well placed for contact with many Asian capitals. Taipei, Taiwan, is a lot nearer to Naha than are Tokyo or Osaka. And would the Japanese really 'need' Okinawa once it has no military bases?

Provided its ties can be extended and strengthened, it's in the region that Okinawa's future must lie. Okinawa is well placed to act as a go-between in regional politics and it has its own experience to offer other countries looking for more autonomy. There's a major diplomatic challenge to be taken up immediately and that's the reluctance by several East Asian countries to realise they need to be weaned off their reliance on the US military presence in Okinawa for regional 'stability'.

The argument against autonomy goes something like this: even though you are the poorest, you are still part of the richest and so you cannot break away. Material wealth is the main reason such action might seem radical.

However, other parts of 'the richest' seem to be developing similar trends. Secession may not be openly touted in Japan's provincial regions, but 'de-centralisation' has become a buzz word and the centre shows definite signs of weakening as the usual tactics for keeping the regions quiet no longer go unquestioned.

The traditional method has been the pork barrel. Compliance and silence have been bought—often at tremendous social and environmental cost. Some remote parts of Japan's main islands have so many nuclear power stations as a result of de facto bribes, such as tax breaks, donations, public works, schools, parks, libraries, anything. Other areas have waste dumps, oil silos—Okinawa has a huge one known as the CTS in Kin bay—airports, military bases, all safely assigned to the periphery, as far away from Tokyo as possible, thank you. However, the accumulated negative effect of this policy is now being vocalised everywhere and bribes to local officials are no longer enough to keep people quiet. Money politics have not been abolished but they no longer rule out opposition.

The 'Okinawa model' was for military bases rather than nuclear power plants close to their backyard, but the effect and the response is the same. Nowadays people in the Fukui region of the main island of Honshu, known as the nuclear 'Ginza' because of its proliferation of nukes, have started saying no in exactly the same way. Fukui won't secede but it can learn from Okinawa. Such re-positioning of public attitudes really questions the solidity of 'Japan' and its capacity to bully its prefectures to stay in line. As we know, a rape can tip the balance quickly and irrevocably away from the conventional wisdom. Think what a nuclear leak, an explosion or meltdown might do.

Design for a Ryukyu flag, 1950.
Blue, white and red from the top.

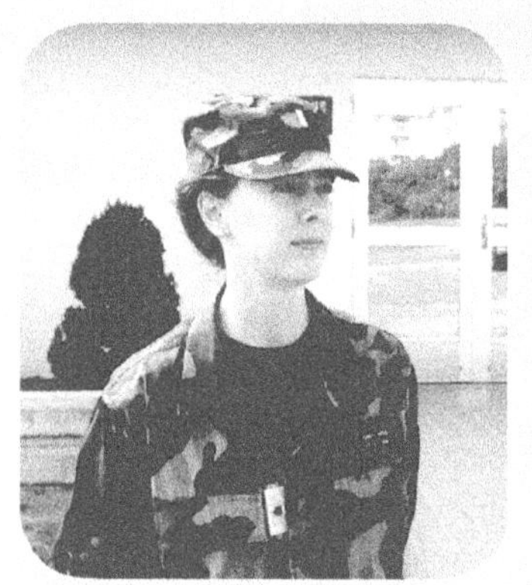

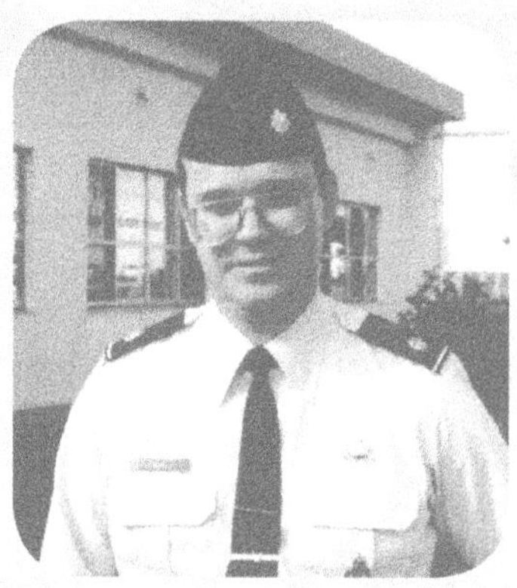

Best of both worlds

Maj. Ed Memi
First Lieut Tania Dutko
Spokespeople for Kadena Air Base

Our trip around Kadena Air Base was noisy and full. We were escorted around the 2000-hectare base by Maj. Ed Memi and his driver-colleague First Lieut Tania Dutko, who gave us nearly two hours of their time to show us how much the Air Force cares about its neighbours.

The team must have done a lot of this guide work around the base for visiting media people, especially in recent times. One side of Major Memi's desk had a collection of *meishi,* business cards, left by visiting journalists from all over the world. We noticed among them some of our acquaintances' names from Australia and Japan. There were fifty or more cards stuck on a noticeboard. He stuck ours up with them in a manner which suggested this was routine.

This was the first time we got inside the base. In 1983 we'd got as close as the nearby observation platform, and we'd been questioned across the fence by a couple of MPs at gunpoint as we were recording our impressions of the location for a radio program. On many occasions we circled around it just to get to the other side of town. But this time, we were inside the fence and seemed welcome.

First impression? It was huge. As our pair of experienced PR hands explained, it's the biggest airfield in the Pacific, and the 18th Air Wing has been

the basis of the Air Force's presence and activities out of Kadena since 1954. There are 30 000 flight hours, or 16 000 missions a year, which was a 'pretty good tempo'.

Before arriving in Okinawa we had written to ask for a background interview and an opportunity to record some sounds of aircraft take-offs and landings for the radio documentary we were making. 'You just want some sound bites', said Major Memi when we phoned him. 'I can do that'. He did that and a lot more. He 'narrated the tour', as he said, showing us many of the facilities inside Kadena. Fans of *Independence Day* stuff would have been ecstatic at the sight of so many sharp-nosed flying machines making so much thunder in our ears.

The major was especially concerned that we understand how much effort and money—mostly Japanese, he never forgot to stress—had gone into the building of 'noise prevention' structures to protect citizens living hard up against the boundary of the base.

His other main thesis, shared by his colleagues, was that there was a big difference between the political agitation against the bases and what people thought 'personally' of the American presence. In fact, any question directed to that issue was deflected along the lines that Okinawans don't actually dislike Americans as such.

A few hard questions about the reality of relations with the community were tried by Beatrice Guelpa, a Swiss freelance journalist based in Hong Kong, but the front was impenetrable: the USA has its commitment and it does its very best to ease the pain for local people; trouble of any kind is exaggerated by the media. Here are some excerpts from the tour featuring mainly Major Memi, with some contributions from Lieutenant Dutko.

★★★★★

Major Ed Memi (EM): Kadena is like a small city with all the facilities that a city would have: fire department, police department, recreational facilities, golf course, gymnasiums, but the primary facility of any air base is the runway—and we have two.

We are a forwardly deployed base and we have F-15s for air superiority to knock out other planes from the sky, the KC-135, which is a flying tanker to refuel aircraft, two E-3 Sentry AWACS—the 'eye in the sky'—and the last type of aircraft we have in the 18th Wing is the HH-60 Black Hawk helicopter. Altogether they form this wing and we are able to deter threats to the region. That's how we support the mutual security treaty.

There's also a naval facility here with P-3 Orion surveillance planes. There's also the AC-130—which belongs to the 353rd Special Operations Group—a cargo plane for dropping things into hostile areas at night. We also have the

Still from Yuntanza Okinawa.

82nd Reconnaissance Squadron, which is an intelligence unit using RC-135s.

Most of the major construction or infrastructure projects on the base are funded by the government of Japan. The current infrastructure spending program is for about $308 million—over several fiscal years—and 75 per cent is funded by Japan.

[Points] There's a 'lemon lot' where people park their cars before they get rid of them when they're going back to the USA.

The munitions area stores 54 000 tons to support the entire Pacific theatre, so if Navy aircraft, or Air Force, or Marines want munitions they come to Kadena and load up. It's bigger than the main base.

There's room on the taxiways for a lot of aircraft because Kadena would be a staging base too—like those used in the Gulf War when we used them to build up forces before going in—they're in Germany too. You need that room to park aircraft. We would double or triple our own aircraft in the event of conflict.

Exercises with other forces are important to promote joint interoperability as they call it, so we can understand how their systems work, allies working together—just like in the Gulf War, which was a 'coalition' effort, not a single action by one military force. You work with your allies in the region and by this mutual training together you understand each other's capabilities and you get this synergistic effect—all forces working together for one purpose, which is to defend both US and allied interests in the region. And as you know more and more of our trade is with Asia—more than over there in Europe—so this region is important.

Most civilian development has been on the north-western perimeter of the base. When the base was first built there wasn't any housing here. But there's been encroachment over the years so that Kadena's farms come right up to the fence and almost 90 per cent of this farming is actually done on base land. There's a tacit agreement that allows them to farm the land and yet they still get rent payments—the best of both worlds.

HOME OF THE SHOGUNS

Kadena is the home of the US Air Force's 18th Air Wing, a unit of the Fifth Air Force headquartered at Yokota Air Base on the mainland. The Fifth Air Force is one of four numbered air forces in the Pacific coming under the command of the Pacific Air Force headquartered at Hickam Air Force Base in Hawaii. Kadena has two parallel 3650-metre-long runways and accommodates more than fifty F-15 Eagles and a dozen KC-135 Stratotankers. Altogether it usurps about 20 million square metres of land and is 'home' to 20 000 people, including 7000 service people as well as their family members. It has just about everything to make the service folks feel at home: dental clinic, barbers and a Burger King, base exchange shops (BX) and post office, supermarkets and cinemas, library, churches, golf course and basketball courts and a ten-pin bowling alley. Three kindergartens, four primary schools, two high schools exist inside the base, and the University of Maryland and Central Texas College both offer courses there. Kadena's annual Open Day lasts for four days and takes place in early July. Kadena has been suggested as a relocation site for the Marine Corps' chopper training facility now at Futenma.

Lieutenant Tania Dutko (TD): You don't hear a lot in the news about the people who support renting their land to the military, you hear about the Sobe Communications Site—and that's only one man making all that.

EM: That matter is for Japan and the government of the USA and individual citizens to resolve. The military is not involved in that. It's an internal government matter.

The reason why you are here has nothing to do with Okinawa really, has it?

EM: We're here because the government of Japan wants us here and if the government of Japan said they didn't want us here we'd be gone. No matter how you look at it, slice it or cut it, that's the truth right there. They want us here and as long as they want us here we'll be here. Both countries feel that the mutual security treaty is very important for the security of Japan and for many allies in the region who want the treaty and support the US presence in the region.

That's tough luck on Okinawa.

I wouldn't say that. As far as the military and the Air Force are concerned, we are taking many actions to be good neighbours, as with the question of noise. We recognise Okinawan concerns and I think the issue is about to be resolved between the government and the Okinawan people.

It's a bit more than noise though, isn't it?

TD: The relationship between the Americans and Okinawan people is very good. Many of our people live off base. Ask the average American person living off base about the Okinawan people and they would say they are the most hospitable people they have ever met.

EM: I'd say 99.99 per cent of American servicemen are law-abiding, contributing citizens and the base hosts a wide variety of community events. We encourage our service members to get out into the community and contribute and be role models. And we do a lot—we sponsor orphanages, friendship lunches between wives' clubs, so there's a

PLANE FACTS 1

The F-15 Eagle is the US Air Force's front-line tactical fighter plane, manufactured by McDonnell Douglas. It was introduced in 1972, modified and upgraded over the years, is still noted for its manoeuvrability and remains on the front line in the European as well as the Pacific theatre. During Desert Storm, F-15s had a 'confirmed' kill ratio of 26:0.

They have been sold to the USA's allies and clients, such as Israel, Saudi Arabia and Japan. Japan's Self-Defense Forces use more than 100.

lot of interaction. I don't think on a personal level any Okinawans are anti-American.

That's a different issue from being anti-base isn't it?

TD: Our leadership does its best to recognise the community. We work with them also and when we are going to fly we let them know and if we have to fly on holidays and certain days.

Your presence is hard to ignore with 72 per cent of the entire US presence in Japan here.

EM: That's more to do with the history of the end of World War II, it's historical.

TD: And it has been reduced greatly.

It's not the Okinawan people's fault for being so strategically important is it? They are poor but they are valuable.

EM: The SACO may come up with alternatives and it will take a year. So who knows.

But if US strategic policy continues, these facilities have to be somewhere.

EM: That's true. The USA is committed to 100 000 in the region with 40 000 in Japan and that has been continuously reiterated by our secretary of defence.

TD: As long as the Japanese government wants it.

EM: That's right.

If Japan said you have to move out, where would you go?

EM: Just like Clark Air Base in the Philippines, they got relocated. It's happened in the past.

Beatrice Guelpa (BG): Are relations that good? I saw signs in Naha saying, 'Army go home' and some bars are closed to US personnel.

EM: Every serviceman I've talked to has never said anything about any anti-American attitude from any Japanese or Okinawan person. There are public statements and protests but on a person-to-person level, relations

PLANE FACTS 2

The C-130 Hercules is one of most popular middle-distance military transport planes in the world. First manufactured by Lockheed in 1954, it's a four-engine cargo plane, which can land and take off in rough and tough conditions. All four US overseas military forces use them, as does the US Coast Guard. They have been deployed in humanitarian aid drops and mercy flights throughout the world, as well as controversial exercises such as Operation Just Cause in which Panama's head of state, Gen. Manuel Noriega, was seized, shackled and taken to the USA from Panama City two weeks after the US invasion in December 1989.

A Hercules can carry more than ninety troops or sixty fully equipped paratroopers, who can jump from two doors on the side of the plane.

Its popularity extends far beyond the US services. Okinawa's immediate neighbour Taiwan purchased a fleet in the mid-1980s and some US allies obtained licences to build their own versions.

The Hercules has also been adapted as a tanker (KC), for anti-guerrilla warfare (AC), electronic warfare (EC), rescue (HC) and other specific tasks.

are not as bad as they are portrayed.

BG: Do you have any Okinawan friends?

EM: Yes, and I actually have Okinawan employees in my office. We have 2800 employees working for the government of Japan working here in the base who wouldn't be employed here if it wasn't for the bases. Even Governor Ota has admitted that a lot of people wouldn't be employed by the bases if the bases weren't here.

Friends are different from employees, aren't they?

TD: I have Okinawan friends. We—my husband and I—live off base and we have Okinawan neighbours. We have them over for dinner and their children are constantly interested in us whenever we go outside.

BG: I was talking to some people yesterday and some of them told me that after last September they lost a lot of friends because of the rape case.

TD: I never heard anyone say that. I have yet to talk to anyone who has Okinawan friends who say that. There are people who have been here for many years—American civilians who are teachers—and they are involved in cross-cultural organisations and they all say their relationships are just as strong as ever.

My husband and I don't go out on base, we go out to eat at least once a week off base. We may only have one opportunity in our lifetimes to live in Japan, especially on this beautiful island of Okinawa which we really enjoy—this is the most popular base to be stationed at in the entire Air Force.

EM: We buy a lot of things off base—I always buy milk off base and then there are all the others things you collect, the items you take home from wherever you go, things that are unique as you move from state to state and country to country. You buy a little bit of each country while you're there; maybe it's little porcelain things, trinkets or in the case of Japan, stereo equipment.

PLANE FACTS 3

First delivered in 1977, the E-3 Sentry is a remodelled Boeing 707 with special AWACS (Airborne Warning and Control Station) capability. Its most noticeable feature is a huge rotating radar dome, which has a range of more than 300 kilometres and is strapped on the top of its fuselage. The Sentry has an airborne data-processing facility, which means as well as collecting data, information and intelligence, it can also manage battle activities.

E-3 Sentries set up a valuable radar defence against the Iraqis at the start of Desert Storm. According to an Air Force 'Fact Sheet' available on the Net: 'For the first time in the history of aerial warfare, an entire air war has been recorded. This was due to the data-collection capability of the E-3 radar and computer sub-systems.'

TD: When I talk to my neighbours they say it's considered a good job to work on base.

EM: It's a big industry. The figure I heard is $187 billion, which is the contribution of the military bases. The entire tourist industry would be half that.

BG: Only 8000 people work here.

EM: You don't think that's a lot of people?

BG: No.

EM: It is—when you realise there's only a million and a quarter here altogether.

Back in the office, no longer deafened by the heterodyne din of F-15s and the rest of the Okinawa aerial armoury, we asked *Major Memi* to give us a bit more detail about why he thought the US needed its 'commitment to forward deployment' on Okinawa.

He said what we expected, despite the end of the cold war, or maybe because of it, with the break-up of the Soviet Union there were strong tensions in the region, even the threat of 'nuclear proliferation'. He fingered North Korea and reminded us that nobody could have predicted the USA would have been in the Gulf War.

EM: If you don't see it coming, you want your forces in the region—you don't want to be sitting here in Japan waiting for help that's ten or twelve hours away in the USA. That's a long time to wait.

The best way to look at the forces at Kadena is to think of us as a spear. The civilian leadership is holding the spear and deciding where we're thrust, into what part of the region, but the fact that we can reach most areas in the region adds to our strategic value and significance in the region. Where we go and where we are involved is a decision made by our civilian government in Washington. They identify the threat and it's hard to say where our next involvement will be.

Paradise blues

Hawaii and Okinawa are like cousins separated by the Pacific Ocean. Their populations are both just over the million mark, both have sub- or semitropical climates and are targeted by the tourist trade as havens for the overstressed in search of paradise. But whatever 'paradise' existed in either has been brutally disrupted since their 'discovery' and exploitation in the past century and a half.

They now share a less dubious attraction, as well as being swamped by golf courses and resort complexes, both have been turned into island fortresses because they happen to occupy strategic junctions on the geopolitical map and are both caught in the crossfire. Okinawa's main island was virtually obliterated in 1945 in a return match for the ruthless surprise attack on Pearl Harbor, Hawaii, in December 1941.

The island kingdom in Hawaii was first discovered by Western interlopers in the person of Capt. James Cook on his famous 1779 trip to, amongst other things, log the transit of Venus and stake a claim to Australia. Hawaii's strategic importance was realised by the USA in the mid-nineteenth century. In 1893 the US government overthrew Queen Lili'uokalani, and soon annexed Hawaii and established it as a forward base for the US Navy. During the 1930s, the Japanese government claimed that the US militarisation of Hawaii and the Philippines was justification for its own aggressive moves throughout the Asia–Pacific region.

After the war, Hawaii's military functions broadened as a 'forward deployment' platform; in 1959 it became the fiftieth state of the Union.

Hawaii was also the destination for the first group of migrants who left Okinawa in 1899 and some 45 000 Okinawan descendants now live there. Both island groups employ about half a million people in the tourist industry and they are basically catering for the same market: middle-class package holiday-makers. Almost all visitors to Okinawa come from Japan, as do about a quarter of the visitors to Hawaii. They spend almost exactly the same amount of time, four days in Okinawa and five in Hawaii, and money, around ¥27 000 or $340.

Tourism accounts for about 20 per cent of Okinawa's total income and more than 30 per cent in Hawaii. Although both tourist industries are now more lucrative, both also make a substantial income from US military bases. Their military infrastructure is of course connected. Both are part of the US Pacific Command (USPACOM) headquartered in Honolulu.

In response to our suggestion that a massive military presence off one's own territory was a thing of the past, he explained that the USA has a strategy for being able to support two simultaneous regional conflicts in the world at once—one in Europe and one in Asia.

When we asked him if there were any nuclear weapons on Okinawa, he said:

We are in compliance with all the treaties with the government of Japan and that will answer your question.

Does that mean they won't be introduced or maintained on Japanese soil without prior consultation? Is that correct?

EM: Again, it's going to be based on those existing treaties and we're in compliance with them.

★★★★★

To give substance to his assertion that he had Okinawan employees in his office, Major Memi introduced us to Higa Masahiro, who was first hired by the US Air Force in 1954. He has been at Kadena as a 'community-relations specialist' since 1973 acting as a go-between to set up meetings for the townspeople of Kadena-cho and Okinawa city to air their complaints about the numerous intrusions on their lives by the bases—usually by aircraft engine noise.

Higa said that he had no complaints about his job—which is why he stayed so long. And that there was no pressure on him from his Okinawan friends to make points to his employers and that the majority of Okinawans felt as he did about the bases—although the bases should go, the strategic issue would be dominant and that Ota's demand for Kadena to be returned by 2015 won't occur in that time. Higa retires in 1997.

Fill 'em up

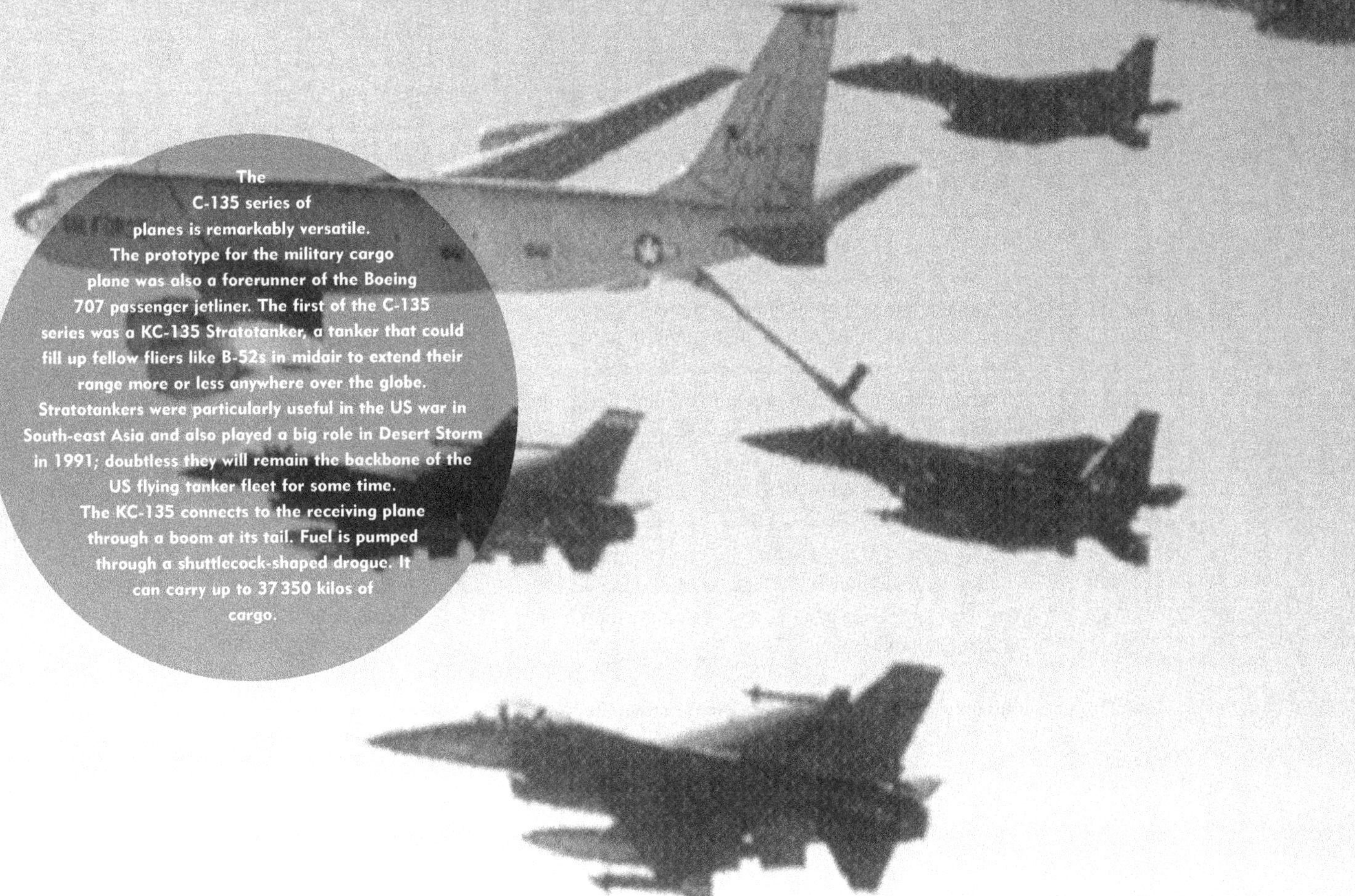

The C-135 series of planes is remarkably versatile. The prototype for the military cargo plane was also a forerunner of the Boeing 707 passenger jetliner. The first of the C-135 series was a KC-135 Stratotanker, a tanker that could fill up fellow fliers like B-52s in midair to extend their range more or less anywhere over the globe. Stratotankers were particularly useful in the US war in South-east Asia and also played a big role in Desert Storm in 1991; doubtless they will remain the backbone of the US flying tanker fleet for some time.

The KC-135 connects to the receiving plane through a boom at its tail. Fuel is pumped through a shuttlecock-shaped drogue. It can carry up to 37 350 kilos of cargo.

MYSTERIOUS 007

The C-135 has spawned a flock of different breeds for specific tasks after its success as the Stratotanker. The EC-135 was developed as an airborne command operations platform for the Strategic Air Command. There's also a weather-watching version of the series, the cutely named WC-135, but the most intriguing version of this model is undoubtedly the RC-135, a reconnaissance, or more truthfully, a spy plane, which can take photos, map landscapes and eavesdrop on both analogue and digital communications. As such, those personnel flying on RC-135 missions—out of Kadena or wherever—were and are answerable not to the Air Force, but to the National Security Agency.

RCs are often found circling around the edge of potentially hostile fronts. One such patrol has become part of the essential folklore of late cold war hostilities between the 'superpowers' in a story the full truth of which seems unlikely to be exposed for some time and could well fill several more books much fatter than this.

The mission in question is still shrouded in mystery and the US government has never admitted whether RCs were involved in the way that's been suggested.

So, let's say that the 'alleged' patrol occurred at the edge of the northern Pacific region on the early morning of September 1, 1983. Four days later, it was alleged that one or more RCs was or were involved in the shooting down of a Korean Airlines flight—KE 007.

The Korean Airlines Boeing 747 strayed off its scheduled course between Anchorage, Alaska, and Seoul, South Korea, deep into Soviet territory, where it was shot down by an Su-15 interceptor over Sakhalin, with all 269 on board killed. Though it was flying over the 'front line' of confrontation, air route R-20, it's always been claimed to have been a routine passenger flight.

One of those on board was a veteran cold warrior, Rep. Larry McDonald, chairperson of the John Birch Society. He was on his way to attend the thirtieth anniversary of the US–South Korea mutual security pact and in those days South Korea was still in the hands of the now-discredited military dictatorship.

According to Marshal Nikolai Ogarkov, chief of the General Staff of the Soviet armed forces, in his account of the incident, the RC and KE 007 flew for about ten minutes at the same altitude in what appeared to be a rendezvous of some kind in the Bering Sea to the east of the Kamchatka Peninsula. An hour and 17 minutes after this odd conjunction, KE 007 was shot down just west of Sakhalin Island.

The Soviets claimed the KAL flight was on some kind of covert spy mission in cooperation with RCs and other US spying operatives, but then disclosed that once the two planes separated, their out-of-date ground radar could not differentiate the civilian KE 007's 'blip' from the military RC-135. The Soviets claimed the intrusion was deliberate.

A few days later, two former Kadena-based RC-135 fliers, T. Edward Eskelson and Tom Bernard, wrote to the *Denver Post* revealing that the US National Security Agency had a hand in the when and where of RC-135 patrols. The pilots claimed the NSA would 'adjust the orbits of RC-135s' so they could 'penetrate the airspace of a target nation' to enable the NSA to analyse that country's air-defence systems and any 'potential flaws' in US procedures.

US authorities admitted that at least one RC-135 did fly close to the Korean jumbo but denied there was any connection. They did not reveal where it came from or whether there was more than one. We can perhaps safely assume the RC in question flew from Kadena, as the northern Pacific is part of the assigned territory for surveillance from Okinawa.

It is known that the Soviets were testing a new generation ICBM, SS-X-25 that night, which would account for their increased sensitivity to the intrusion of any foreign plane, let alone an American spy plane like the RC-135.

In fact, according to Marshal Ogarkov, the radar showed at least seven blips on the screen which adds to the suspicion that there was more than one RC in the vicinity that night. The US authorities have not responded to this report.

The mystery deepened three days after the downing when Rep. Jim Wright was quoted after hearing eight minutes worth of tape-recorded Soviet communications that he heard RC-135 mentioned twice. Also intriguing: the pilots of the jumbo didn't send out May Day calls as they were losing altitude, but their recorded voices sound as if they were trying to communicate with somebody in the air close by.

Most of the official accounts of what happened were based on observations and reports made by the Japanese SDF surveillance units at Wakkanai and Nemuro in Hokkaido and released through the US government. One detail reveals another major unexplained discrepancy. Although the official Soviet account identifies an Su-15 as the #805 interceptor—code for the plane which shot down the jumbo—observations made by the SDF suggest that it was more likely to be a longer-range MiG-23. However both sides now accept it was an Su-15.

The Americans might know the truth. Apart from the RC-135 the US government admitted their radar site on Shemya Island and the 'Elephant Cage' on Adak Island in the Aleutians—like the one at Yomitan—could well have been listening in throughout the entire drama.

And to finish off this tissue of conspiratorial glimmerings: almost immediately after the KE 007 catastrophe occurred, President Reagan was able, after a long period of resistance and obstruction in the Congress, to secure the passage of his immensely controversial and destabilising MX missile budget allocation. In Europe a similar effect occurred when the NATO allies quickly agreed to install cruise and Pershing missiles, while in Moscow the Soviet Politburo decided that the USA led by Ronald Reagan was impossible to deal with.

By the way, you may find some confusion regarding the code names and numbers in this story involving the RC-135 and KE 007. Most newspapers wrongly named the doomed Korean Airlines jet KAL 007—and that's how a lot of people still remember it.

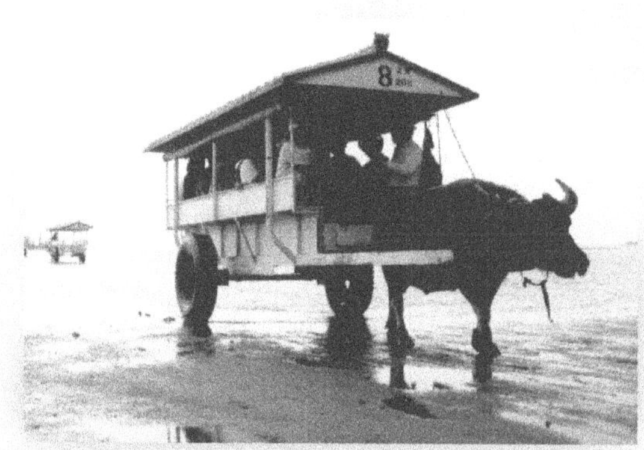

Okinawa is where I want to be

Paul Newman

Paul Newman, Kina Shokichi's manager, is an expatriate Englishman who still speaks with a slight West Country burr. You might be surprised to find him sitting on a stool in Kina's bar. But that's Okinawa.

Paul has an interesting history himself, as a long-time resident who also served in the US Marine Corps in Okinawa.

Paul may not be the first to find himself poised between cultures—military and pacific—but his own particular blend of a military calling and a career in Okinawan music is extraordinary. The how of why he got to be there and what he's doing now is best left to him.

What's your official title?

My official title? It's er—what is my official title? I am manager—actually, there are two managers—I'm the international manager for the band—Kina Shokichi's Champruse.

How did you get a gig like that in Okinawa?

I first got involved with the band through Shokichi's youngest sister Keiko. I met her about ten years ago, we dated and eventually we got married so, in actual fact, I'm his brother-in-law.

When I first came to Okinawa I was part of the US Marine Corps. I actually asked the Marine Corps, when I first contracted with them, to send me to Asia. They offered me Japan and originally hearing that, I thought I'd be going to Tokyo or somewhere like that but they sent me to this small, secluded island in the middle of the ocean, which was quite a culture shock for me. I expected kimonos, geisha, samurai and all that stuff, which is the image I had from watching TV back in the States and Europe, and when I got here it was entirely different.

I look at the Okinawans now, and their culture and values are not the same as mainland Japanese values, so in that sense Okinawa is part of Japan, but culturally and spiritually it's separate.

Do you look at the rest of Japan through Okinawan eyes?

Basically, yes. When I first got to Okinawa I thought, 'This is what Japan is', and then from taking trips up to Tokyo and Osaka I found an entirely different world and it took me a year or two to get used to the fact that it was totally different. Now I look at Tokyo and Osaka as being Japan in the Japanese sense. I look at them from Okinawa.

What were you doing with the Marine Corps?

I was a nuclear, biological and chemical warfare specialist when I was here.

How were you recruited to do that? Was that your educational background?

No. I graduated from high school in England. My family's company moved to the USA at which time I was in the British Royal Navy, and after my contract was over I decided to migrate to the USA to be with my family, to help out with my father's business.

I like moving around. I don't like staying in one place for a long time, I like to see a lot of different cultures, a lot of different countries and I turned around to the old man one day and said, 'Look, I've got to get the hell out of here; three years in America's fine, but that's enough'. The fastest way to do that was to get into the military and get the hell out. So in that sense I didn't join the military to be a soldier as such. It was an excuse to get out and see the world. I just got caught up in the military system, that's all.

It's an ancient tradition joining up to see the world, but what actually was a nuclear and biological warfare expert doing here?

At that time there were a couple of hundred of us scattered throughout the world in the USMC, and our job was mainly focused on the defensive side of nuclear, biological and chemical warfare. So if we, say, were to go to war with someone else and they were to use those particular weapons, it was my job to make sure our guys were taken care of medically and strategically.

We did a lot of statistics coordination: if someone dropped a bomb of a certain size, what the fallout would be, where it would fall, what kind of impact it would have on the community within that zone, how to take care of those people within that area. And it was our job basically to find out what everybody else had and figure out how to keep our guys alive.

That was because at that time—and maybe still, we don't know—the bases in Okinawa were regarded as nuclear targets?

That is correct. That's not top-secret information. Because of its strategic location within Asia, the military call Okinawa the 'Gateway to Asia'. It probably has the easiest access to any of the major countries in Asia that carry that threat—China, Korea and other countries. It was just the spindle in the wheel. If you need to go anywhere in Asia you go from Okinawa—that was how it went in the Korean War, the Vietnam War, even in the Gulf War. You had easy access from the Asian continent into the Middle East.

That's one of the reasons I feel America is very reluctant to move the bases off this island and there isn't anywhere else to put them right now. For the Okinawan people that causes some friction but at the same time the military bases being here in a sense protect the peace throughout Asia. For Okinawan people it's a threat because if war did blow up then Okinawa is going to be the focal point.

When you were preparing for possible nuclear or biological warfare attacks here, you were obviously concerned with the military personnel first. Did you have to make preparations for what might happen if the civilian population was affected as well?

Yes and no. I'll be totally honest with you. Being in the military at that time—the main concern was military. But because of the consequences, you

OVERSEAS REACTION

A group called Remove Troops from Okinawa Network was established in the USA in February 1996. Upon a visit to the island, an ex-Marine Vietnam veteran and a member of the group said, according to the *Okinawa Times*, 'Okinawa must be a peaceful island for the people who live here'.

also had to take into account the civilian population. But that responsibility was pushed towards the Japanese Self-Defense Forces. We would be there to lend a hand but we weren't there to protect the people on the island.

So the US military was drawing the fire, if you like, but not mopping up the collateral damage.

Yes, if you like, we might cause the fire but we couldn't put it out.

Another great tradition for people posted overseas is that they find they like the country better than their own, or they fall in love with someone, marry them, and then they're faced with the difficult choice of whether to take the spouse back home to their country with all the problems that can cause too. How did you resolve this problem? You're married to an Okinawan woman with a distinguished brother famous throughout Okinawa who isn't showing any signs of leaving. What about you?

I'm of British heritage. My roots are English and they always will be, but I don't think being English means you've got to live in England. When I came to Okinawa, for the first year or two I was a bit homesick. You know you miss the pint of beer, the steak and kidney pie, and the family at Christmas, but slowly I grew out of that. Being around Keiko and Shokichi and the family gave me an opportunity to find out what Okinawa was really about, meeting the people. They're very warm-hearted, easygoing, it's a 'meet them once and you're a friend for life' culture. For me that was very exciting and slowly I've grown into that culture, so that now if I go back to the USA to see my family, I get homesick.

I've grown into the culture so much that if I am somewhere else for any time and people ask me where I am from, where's my home, I say, 'It's Okinawa'. I've become 'Okinawa-ised'. I love the USA and England and other parts of the world, everywhere I go I've enjoyed myself, but for me personally, mentally, physically and spiritually, Okinawa is where I want to be. My 'missus' has said a few times, 'Why don't we go back to America?',

A LACK OF MAC

Gen. Douglas MacArthur was famous for keeping his 'I shall return' promise to the Filipino people—after all, there were always rumours about his commercial and financial holdings there—but he rarely travelled far outside his General Headquarters in Tokyo throughout his tenure as Supreme Commander for the Allied Powers (SCAP) from 1945 to 1951. However, he was well aware of the importance of Okinawa, which he described as follows:

'Now the Pacific has become an Anglo-Saxon lake and our line of defense runs through the chain of islands fringing the coast of Asia. It starts from the Philippines and continues through the Ryukyu archipelago which includes its broad main bastion, Okinawa. Then it bends back through Japan and the Aleutian Island chain to Alaska.'

He was also appointed governor of Okinawa but never showed up there in person.

and I've said, 'Okay, you want to go, fine, I'll wait for you here'.

As an objective observer with strong Okinawan links, what do you think should happen to the bases—all that land, space and facilities?

Before I tell you what I think, let me say that a lot of people worry that if the American military were to pick up and leave tomorrow then the Japanese military would walk in. That's one thing. Another thing is that if the Americans left tomorrow, Okinawa can't support itself economically. Mainland Japan is not now in a position to support Okinawa. Another thing is this place would become a typical resort, casino island, in the middle of—the 'Hawaii of Asia' type deal. Economically that might be good but culturally it would not be good for the people of Okinawa.

I would like the bases to leave. This is Okinawa, it belongs to the Okinawan people. In order to move the bases out of here, you've got to have a totally peaceful atmosphere throughout Asia. And I don't see that in the near future. So until countries like China and Korea and countries in the Middle East get to that point, I don't think you are going to see the American bases leaving here.

Where are you going to put them? Send them back to America? They haven't got the space for them. When you say, 'Let's get rid of the American bases here on Okinawa', I would like to say, 'Let's get rid of military bases all over the world'. That's my point of view.

It's all here [taps heart] and it's how people think and the mind-set of humanity; you know, without them we can't exist and with them eventually we won't exist.

Okay, say we sort all that out. What to do with all that land?

Without getting political: Give it back to the people and let them decide. Usually you have these prefectural governments coming in and saying, 'Okay, we need to support the island so we need all these ideas we've worked out'. They have to give it back to the prefecture of Okinawa but the government should not be the sole decision-maker. Let the people of the island figure out what to do—it's a very small population.

Kina's song 'Hana' is one of the most popular songs. Why?

'Hana' is a song he wrote about thirty years ago. When I first heard it, I didn't pick up on the meaning of it but now when I look at it I think it's probably one of the most simply written songs I've ever heard. And the lyrics themselves:

The river flows, but where does it flow?
People flow but where are they flowing?
All of this flowing will some day come together
and flowers will bloom in people's hearts.

It sounds weird but it's so simple and that's what people seem to catch onto right now. You're getting a lot of political music right now, antisocietal music. The song 'Hana' is not, it's about life in general, it's about what's in people's hearts.

Right now, the song has been to the top of the charts in almost every country in Asia. Up until now in Asia, Europe, America and Japan there are about thirty-three different artists who have recorded it in different languages and released it. Each one of them has taken it up into the top of the chart in their own country. Last year the ASAP Sisters, a Black trio from New York, translated it into English—not literally the translation I would have liked—but it's very well made and tasteful and very close to what Kina wrote and it's doing well. Susan Osborne is recording it, Stevie Wonder's backing chorus is playing around with it, thinking about a release.

In Japan, as far as worldwide big hits are concerned, there's 'Sukiyaki', a worldwide hit; now 'Hana' is very close or at the same level. If you understand what the lyrics are and understand Kina somewhat, it's very easy to catch hold of that song and hang on to it. No matter how many times you hear it, you never get tired of it. The melody is very simple and without

FLOWER POWER

The first recording of the song 'Hana'—said to be one of the biggest pan-Asian hits—featured vocals by Kina Tomoko with musical assistance and production skills provided by Ry Cooder and Kubota Makoto.

Since then various artists in Japan and beyond have recorded the tune. In 1992 a compilation album with the same name as the song itself was released with ten different versions including the original 1980 version and a remake by Champruse featuring Shokichi on vocals. This version also features on bass Morgan Fisher, the one-time Mott the Hoople star and producer of the obscure but brilliant 1979 *Miniatures* album that featured dozens of tracks by scores of artists, not all of them musicians, and none longer than one minute. Fisher has lived in Japan for many years.

The compilation album also sports a karaoke version for singalongers, and versions by a range of female singers who can sing the very high notes which give 'Hana' its appeal: Sandii, formerly of Sandii and the Sunsetz, who is now known as Sandii Suzuki; Otaka Sizuru, who usually performs as half of an ambient duo called Dido; and Indonesian singer Detty Kurnia, whose version was produced by Kubota for her 1991 album *Dari Sunda.*

Kina and Champloose performed 'Hana' live at the AT&T Global Olympic Village Concert at Atlanta in July 1996. For an encore they sang a song Kina composed for the occasion: 'Lay Down Your Weapons and Take Up Musical Instruments'.

understanding the words the music gets you in the heart. That's what I feel about that song.

Kina's got a couple like that, but 'Hana' is the big one. It's been out for nineteen or twenty years and still going strong—in fact, it's getting stronger every year. Everywhere Kina's gone in the world, 'Hana' has gone first, and people know the song first before they know Kina Shokichi. *I don't know why,* it's hard to explain.

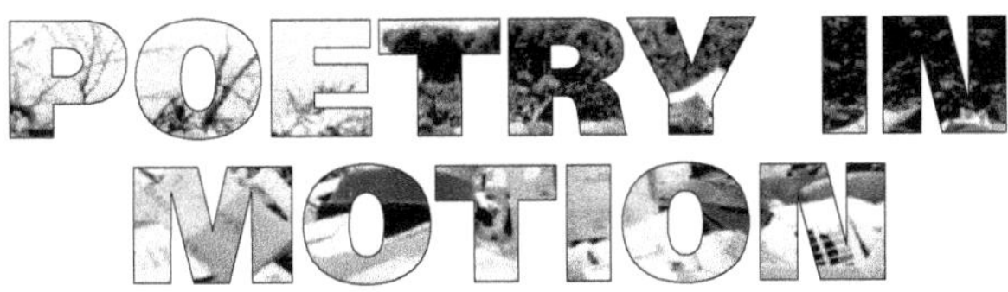

Walk along Kokusaidori street, Naha's main shopping area full of souvenir and army-surplus stores and you'll also find some stunning poetry you can take home. The utopians have been busy thinking up dainty slogans for those who want to remember paradise just as it was intended to be. They've left their wet and waxy messages where they are most likely to be noticed. Yes, the Okinawan T-shirt specialises in promoting happy images of holiday perfection in that special zone of meaning between the Hallmark Xmas message and the advertising homily.

Wake up in the morning
open the window
feel the wind
look up at the sky
listen to
the sound of the waves
Oh! It's a fine day.
Now begin the day.

Okinawa Island Sea Collection Supermarine Resort
Spring Time has come now to the Oceans of Okinawa.

Blue sky beyond brilliant clouds
Green palm shining in the sunlight
White yacht on the pastel sea
Okinawa
I live in a beautiful sea of tropical islands.

How do you come here and play with me?
Okinawa.

Fantastic Okinawan night.

Fantastic
Wonder islands
Okinawa

Marine resort island Okinawa.
Let's go to southern islands.
Go, go Coconut Club

A wonderful wild world of Okinawa.

LIONS, DOGS AND GODZILLA

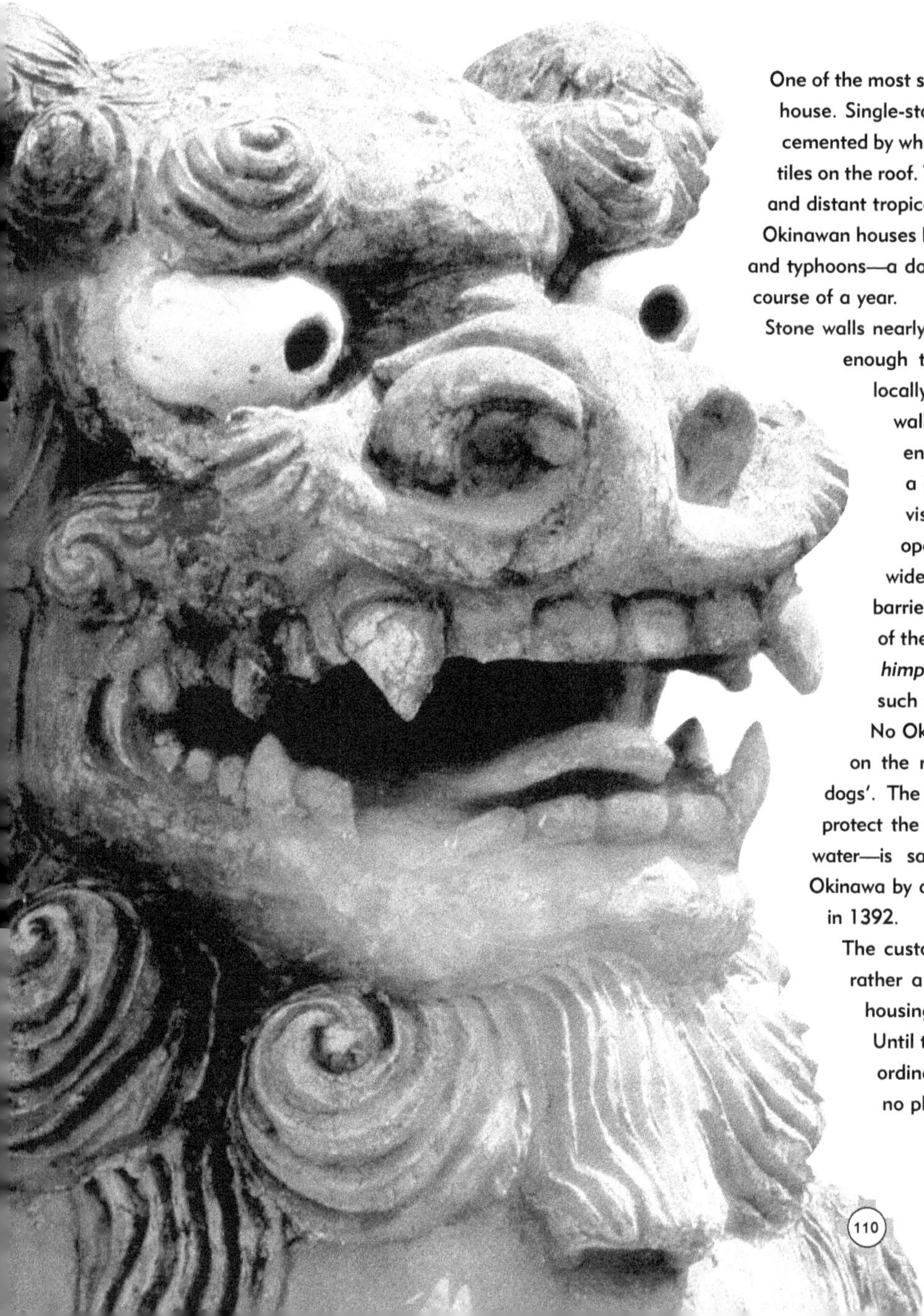

One of the most striking features of the Okinawan landscape is the house. Single-storey houses are built with thick, tall stone walls cemented by white mortar in thick stripes, which also hold the red tiles on the roof. They are a stunning sight against a clear blue sky and distant tropical thunderclouds on the horizon.

Okinawan houses have to withstand severe heat during the summer and typhoons—a dozen or more of which can visit the region in the course of a year.

Stone walls nearly surround the house to make a compound wide enough to prevent fire spreading. Banian trees, known locally as *gajumaru,* spread their roots through these walls and support the structure. The walls don't enclose the house completely. There is an opening, a gap where a gate might be at the entrance, but visitors can't see right into the house through that opening—usually about two and a half metres wide—because set back inside the grounds is another barrier, a *himpun,* a wall inside the walls, right in front of the house. If the outside walls are stone or coral the *himpun* matches them. If it's natural undergrowth, such as a hibiscus bush, the *himpun* is the same.

No Okinawan house-scape is complete without *shii-saa* on the roof—either a single or pair of terracotta 'lion-dogs'. The tradition comes from a Feng Shui concept to protect the house from fire. Feng Shui—meaning wind and water—is said to have derived from Taoism, brought to Okinawa by a group of migrants from Fukien province, China, in 1392.

The custom of having a pair of lion-dogs on the roof is rather a new custom, as the use of wood and tiles for housing was for a long time restricted to the nobility. Until the Meiji days, in the mid-nineteenth century, the ordinary house had a thatched roof, where there was no place for them.

Stone *shii-saa* have inspired other concepts. When the Toho movie company was looking for an idea to celebrate the twentieth anniversary of the debut of Godzilla on the big screen, they turned to Okinawa for a location. Released in 1974, two years after Reversion, *Godzilla v. the Bionic Monster* was a sort of promotion for Okinawa, but is more likely to be remembered as the debut opportunity for a robot version of the beast, known as Mecha-Godzilla, and for some, the fact that it starred a huge, monster-sized version of the lion-dog, King Shii-saa.

The script involves an omen of coming destruction discovered at the half-built construction site for the forthcoming Marine Expo in Okinawa, which opened in 1975. An ancient script predicts the arrival of King Shii-saa to join another great monster in a battle to save Earth from a terrible beast.

It turns out to be a robotic Godzilla, controlled by aliens who have seized a cave in Okinawa as a base for their plans to conquer planet Earth. Needless to say, the 'real' Godzilla and the royal lion-dog team up to see off the aliens.

By the way, according to the Toho promo blurb, the King Shii-saa was 50 metres tall and weighed 30 000 tonnes and was able to emit powerful killer rays from his eyes.

The *shii-saa* has become a popular icon for anything Okinawan these days. There is a groovy Okinawan restaurant in the fashionable Shibuya district of Tokyo called Shesirs (though it's still pronounced 'shii-saa'). There's a pop duo called Shii-saas, whose 1996 CD includes their versions of folk songs and traditional kids' songs they collected in the Okinawan islands.

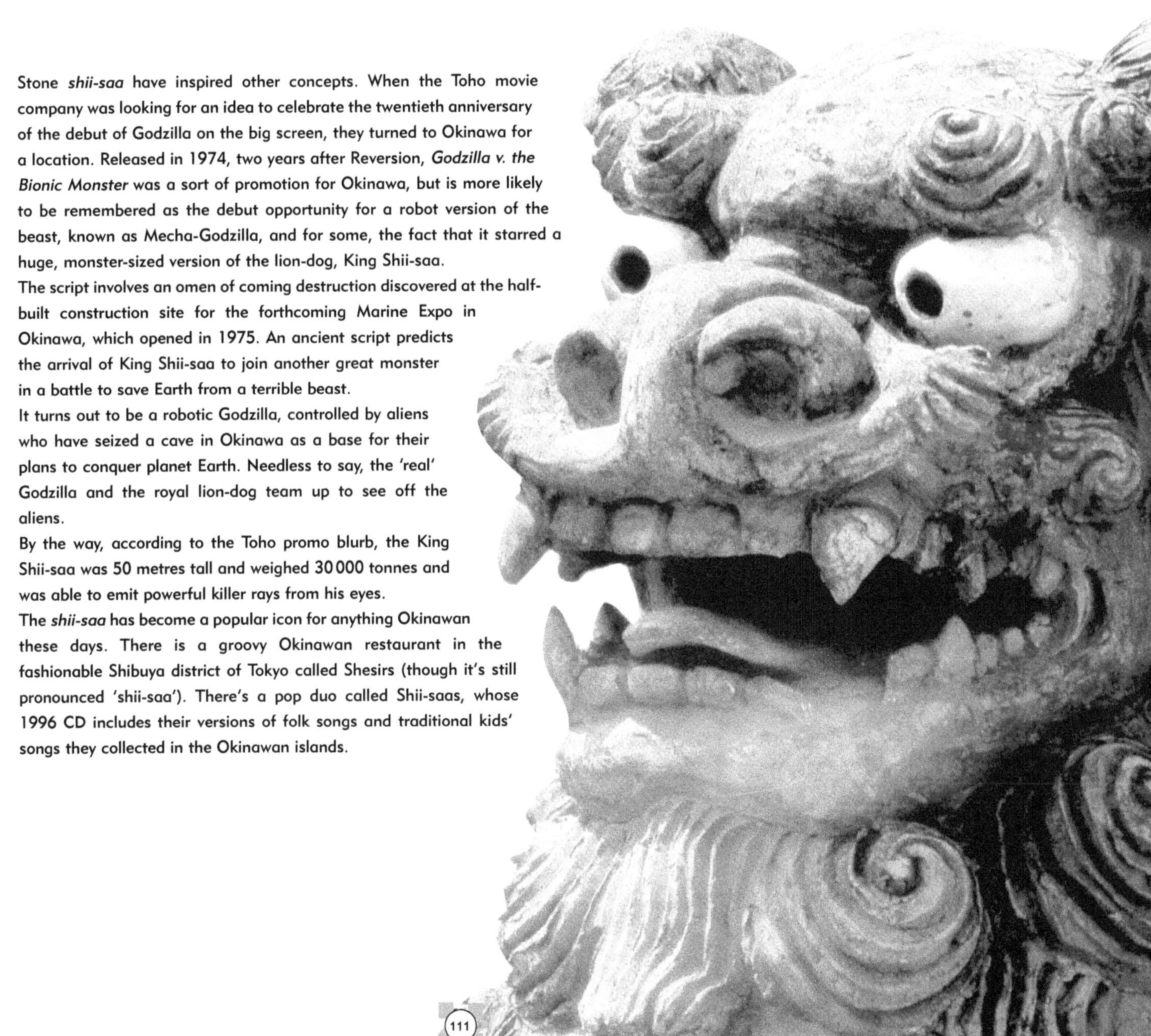

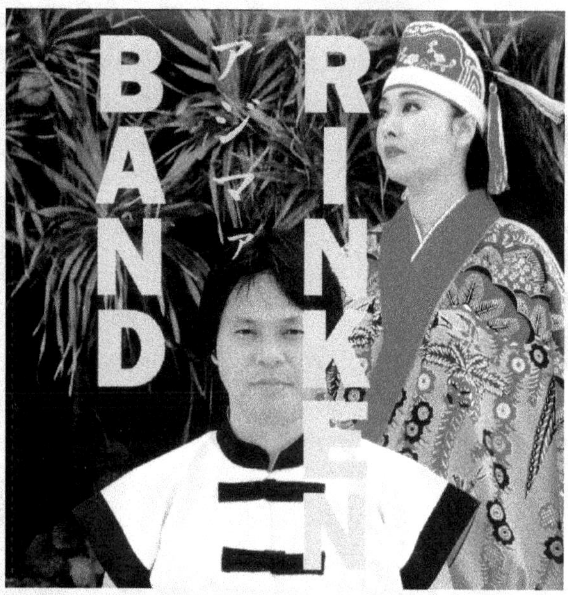

Let nature take its course

Teruya Rinken

We talked to Rinken in his tiny studio upstairs in a small building in Koza city. His studio is close to the entertainment district. This is his territory. He was born not too far from here and went to school here. It was in this studio where many Rinken Band albums were recorded.

The occasion was significant. Earlier that day, April 12, 1996, Prime Minister Hashimoto Ryutaro had suddenly announced that the infamous Futenma helicopter training facility would be returned to its owners within five to seven years. The astonishment was widespread, not least in the Ministry of Defense in Tokyo where they hadn't been informed before the announcement!

Hashimoto's timing had nothing to do with our visit. It was related to the inescapable fact that in a couple of days' time he was due to welcome President Bill Clinton to Tokyo. The Futenma deal was by way of clearing the decks, settling people down and showing the citizens of Okinawa that something good could happen.

It was an offer Hashimoto thought no-one in Okinawa would dare refuse. It was both considerate and self-serving. After all, 1996 was an important election year for both Japan and the USA and it would be mutually soothing if, now that the bases issue had displaced the usual long-winded argy-bargy over 'trade

Cover art from Rinken Band CD.

issues' at the top of the bilateral agenda, the bases didn't create too many unduly fractious interludes as the two great men chewed over their developing relationship.

As it turned out, while the touring press corps from the US might have thought the Futenma offer was an astounding piece of shock diplomacy, nobody in Okinawa was fooled. It was, of course, a piffling concession. When the small print was discovered, it was revealed to be only a 'relocation' and not a removal, which, if the most expensive option was forced through, could cost the Japanese government as much as ¥1 trillion.

Rinken had some things to say about such matters, but was more interested in telling us something about how he and his band have managed to put their own light touch into the big issue of the bases, and the dark side of Okinawan music itself.

It's not really true to say that Okinawan music is all that special. Why? Everybody on this globe has their own music. In that respect Okinawan music is nothing special. What makes it different is that music here is alive and active. If there is anything unique about music here, it is all derived from that fact.

Everyone adds their own elements; what is it that you have added?

I was born into an Okinawan traditional music family. My grandfather was an Okinawan traditional music master and *sanshin*-maker. My father Teruya Rinsuke was a cabaret star who developed his own performance style: singing and chat. He has his own theatre just down the road in Koza city. He's famous throughout the island. My uncle had a *sanshin* shop and used to have his own record label. That's the environment I was brought up in.

'Traditional' music has its own place in the society, yet at the same time you have to understand music in Okinawa is not static or dead. It is evolving and developing. That is why it is difficult to define the very concept of 'tradition', when it is not preserved in a museum. When someone stresses the importance of old compositions, I wonder how old they have to be to be classified 'old' or 'classic', to be classified as traditional. I believe that's what goes with a 'living' tradtional music such as Okinawa's.

Everyone takes a different approach and now it's really hard to say what is truly traditional. Traditional music is very important and there are those who criticise people who try new things. My father was very important in changing things and in many ways opened the doors for others including me.

He was seventeen at the end of the war and started bringing in all kinds of influences to Okinawan popular music—from America and elsewhere—like guitar, samba rhythm and all sorts of things. He translated pop songs from the USA into Okinawan and played them on the sanshin with Okinawan rhythms and so on. Rinsuke really had a huge influence on people like me, but there are traditionalists who abhor any kind of change.

What's your angle?

Because of our tropical climate, it's easy to think Okinawan people are light-hearted, happy-go-lucky island people, but really the music sounds subdued and heavier. I think it's to do with the way the sanshin is tuned and the way we play it. When we hit the notes E and B, we tend to hit the lower end of those notes, which is why I think Okinawan music sounds minor.

We've changed that a bit, lifted the tone perhaps by a quarter, which brightens the band's music. That's our contribution to the development of music here.

Are you involved in politics?

I always believe we can understand why we are here by looking at what happened in the past. In Okinawa, we cannot escape from the past, especially with regard to the effects of the Second World War, and that's how we explain why we find so many bases here. It is encouraged here in this society to learn from the direct accounts from witnesses and survivors of the war and its aftermath.

Our music is not overtly political. We don't use lyrics as a means to directly convey political messages. We don't sing antiwar songs, for example. We sing about how wonderful it is being alive here and now. It's the celebration of life like this which negates war and other acts that involve violence and killing. Our message is also in the sound. We try to give an uplifting and positive sound to our songs.

Do you have an audience beyond Okinawa?

We are expanding our fan base on the mainland. We play a lot of dates there now, and local gigs in Okinawa make up only a fifth of what we play in a year. The bulk of our live dates are played in Japan. We've also been to Manila, so our music is finding an audience outside Okinawa.

Do you have to explain your lyrics to people overseas?

We first played mainland Japan in 1990, and until last year always stuck to

EISA APPEAL

Eisa is a powerful concept. It's Okinawa's version of Obon—the occasion in July when people remember and honour the souls of their dead relatives. It's a day-and-a-night-long festival of singing, drumming, dancing and widespread celebration. The Rinken Band performs an original song about Eisa on their 1992 *Ajima* album and the Nenes sing traditional Eisa songs on *Ikawu*.

performing in our own Okinawan dialect, both in song and our in-between-songs talk. The record company begged us to include some Japanese and last year we performed live with Japanese subtitles at our concerts in Japan. But we don't intend to translate our material and sing in Japanese. It's important to retain your own language.

Is it really that important?

I think it is. Without lyrics, our music does not make sense. I believe the word is important. Often our record company insists it would make our stuff more accessible and commercially popular to write in Japanese, but that's a very shallow understanding of language, don't you think? You can only best express yourself in the language that is truly yours. You can't change that, or get rid of it, or you'll lose the essence of what you are doing. Why we have different languages between Japan and Okinawa in the first place—well, that's another interesting issue.

What's so important and special about the drum sound in Okinawan music—and yours in particular?

Sometimes the sanshin can be solo but it's more often accompanied by drums. Anything with a certain pace has to be accompanied by shimadaiko, the Okinawan drum. In Okinawa we can have fun all night long if we just have the sanshin and drums.

Do you ever use guitar and bass as well as sanshin?

Any stringed instrument is pretty much the same when it comes to the basic concept of its sound structure. You play the strings, stroke, pick and hit or whatever. In Okinawa it's considered to be groovy to play the note a tiny fraction ahead of the beat.

That's the push-pull, offbeat feel to Okinawan music.

Yes, rhythm is very important. I used to have guitar players in the recording studio. Mainlanders they were, and they just couldn't get that rhythm right. We local players are born to it and have no trouble just dropping into it straightaway. We have got that rhythm in our blood—it just doesn't exist in Tokyo.

Okinawan singers use vibrato, almost yodelling, as they move between the notes. It creates a tension because some of the intervals between the notes are so long the attraction for the listener comes when the singer reaches the note—and relieves the tension.

Many songs are written to fit the vocal range of male singers. There's a theory that the way female singers pitch their voices is a result of them trying to sing those tunes. It's a fairly modern thing, they say. But there are many old songs performed without any instruments, which they sing like any other song. I think it is a much older tradition. Actually, there's an island called Henza where there is an annual get together, Usudeku, of women singers. There these old lady singers sing a cappella. They sing in exactly the same way, without *sanshin,* just a drum, yet manage to create great tension in the air, hitting the right chord which only Okinawan female singers can.

Female singing's of interest to me, not just that of Okinawa, but everywhere. I have a collection of CDs of female vocals from all over the world. No matter where they come from, India, Pakistan or Mongolia, good female vocals have a similar effect. You can be taken and captured.

What do you think should happen to the land occupied by the US bases?

It can be difficult if people don't have plans. I hope it does not become a source of community friction or conflict. When some land was returned in Ishikawa to the original owners, the landowners just couldn't parcel out the land to satisfy everyone and it developed into nasty infighting. So I hope the return of the Futenma Air Station doesn't generate that kind of conflict.

My father has a small plot of land within the Kadena Air Base, but it's totally his business what he does with it and I won't interfere. In general, I think the bases should be left for nature to reclaim. I would just leave it, let nature take its course. You know, some beautiful sweet potatoes are grown downstream of Futenma. If the water from Futenma is suitable for sweet potatoes, let's leave it.

Koza's burning

It seems only a trifle can start a conflagration, especially when anger has been accumulating over the years. It's as if it hangs in the supersaturated air like aviation fuel waiting for a spark to ignite the whole neighbourhood; only a flicker is needed and the whole world explodes. The early morning of December 20, 1970, was such an occasion and it was the centre of Koza that burned.

It started with a traffic accident. The US driver was from Camp Kuwae and the injured party was a local base labourer.

Traffic accidents occur every day in Okinawa, and in some cases the offenders get away without getting charged. Only ten days earlier a US military court had returned a 'not guilty' verdict for another US driver for running over and killing an Okinawan woman in Itoman in September 1970. Locals naturally thought the ruling outrageous and 5000 had gathered in protest in Itoman on December 16.

When the US Military Police arrived at the scene of the Koza traffic accident they allowed the driver to slip away. Until late 1995 MPs were allowed to take over any situation and get first access to US personnel involved in a crime. Twenty or so locals who saw what happened criticised the MPs' handling of the situation—only to be greeted with a volley of warning shots which immediately set off a sequence of riots with numbers swelling to thousands within minutes.

Cars carrying yellow plates—denoting they belonged to US personnel—were targeted and dragged into the middle of the road and set alight, as if to say they were all brutal killer machines.

Some shouted 'never allow Itoman to be repeated!', while others danced around the torched cars. The military reaction was aggressive—more warning shots and tear gas while the residents threw rocks.

Some rioters broke down one of the gates to Kadena Air Base and a couple of buildings inside, including the school, were burnt down.

The riot went for about six hours. A total of 73 cars were burned, 23 people were injured and there were 19 arrests.

The riot was not an organised protest but a spontaneous reaction to years of injustice. It now occupies an important place in modern Okinawan folklore and has inspired many people of later generations. Shinjo Taku featured a re-creation of the riot in his feature film *Okinawan Boys* and Takamine Go's screenplay for his new film also includes the riot scene towards the end.

YOU SAY SATSUMAS

Commonly known as sweet potato in the English-speaking world, *Ipomoea batatas* is known in Japan as *Satsuma imo—imo* is a generic term meaning potato. The Satsuma potato got its name in Japan because it was brought from the region in the south called Satsuma, now the prefecture of Kagoshima, in the southern part of the island of Kyushu. Meanwhile in Europe, a satsuma is a large and very tasty mandarin-style orange. But in Satsuma, the same potato is called *Ryukyu imo*. What the Japanese know as the Satsuma potato is the Ryukyu potato in Satsuma and that's how the sweet potato spread in Japan.

The sweet potato first came to Okinawa—or the Ryukyus as they then were called—from China almost 500 years ago. So, in Okinawa it is still largely known as *Kara imo,* Chinese potato. It was brought from Fukien province by Noguni Sokan in 1605. The sweet potato subsequently would save many lives from famine in Okinawa, largely caused by the interference by the Shimazu clan from Satsuma in the economic affairs of the Ryukyus. For centuries the islands' wealth came from trade, which the Satsumas restricted. The general decline of its trading role in the region began the Ryukyu Islands' cycle of poverty, which continues to this day.

Luckily, sweet potatoes are easy to grow in the subtropical climate. They're also easy to store and rich in nourishment, so sweet potato cultivation quickly spread all over the islands and not only saved the population from starvation but gradually enabled islanders to become self-sufficient—until the Second World War.

It was after this early experience that the humble sweet potato began its migration to other parts of Japan, where it also gained a noble reputation for rescuing people from death. Will Adams, the English pilot who consulted and directed the Tokugawa government in the early seventeenth century on shipbuilding, is sometimes credited with being the potato-bringer to mainland Japan. He certainly stayed in Naha in 1615 and took seedlings to Nagasaki but even though he may have coined the term *sweet potato* in English, it never became known as *Nagasaki imo* in Japan.

It was Aoki Konyo, who was sent by the government in Edo, who took it from Satsuma to save people from a nationwide famine. Hence *Satsuma imo.*

The sweet potato didn't originate in China either, but first arrived there from the island of Luzon in the Philippines—some ten years before arriving in the Ryukyus—having been brought by the Spanish, who called them *papas* and *patatas.*

The sweet potato, like the non-sweet one, had been a staple food for thousands of years in South

America. They were taken back to Europe within twelve months of the arrival of Christopher Columbus, who described them as 'looking like yams and tasting like chestnuts'. Columbus's term *aje* did not stay as the name, but a later version, *batata,* was incorporated into the Spanish language for the sweet variety.

From there, sweet potato was spread to all parts of Europe and so have the terms. The word meaning *potato* in many languages is derived from the Spanish word *batata.* Its own *patata,* for the non-sweet variety of potato botanically known as *solanum tuberosum,* is a derivative from *batata.* Portuguese use the word *batata,* however, to describe potato, while sweet potato is known as *batata doce.* The English language adopted *batata,* hence potato, but it soon came to mean the non-sweet potato. In Swedish, potato is *potatis,* while sweet potato is *batat;* and in Danish, potato is *kartoffel,* and the sweet one is also *batat.* In Greek, *patata* means only one variety of the non-sweet kind. More confusing still, *patate* is potato in Brittany, but in the rest of France it means the sweet one. *Pomme de terre,* as potato is known in the rest of France, is adapted from the Dutch word for potato: *aardappel,* earth apple.

Until sometime after the end of the war, the sweet potato remained the staple, subsistence food in Okinawa. A batch was boiled once a day—served hot at one meal and cold at others. Rice was not easy to grow in many places and remained a luxury item until recently. Before the war, two-thirds of the rice consumed in Okinawa was imported. Today, rice is as readily available in Okinawa as anywhere in Japan. Fewer people eat sweet potato now.

Once rice became affordable, sweet potato became seen as a reminder of the old, poor times. During the sixties, conservatives came up with the political catchcry to counter the anti–US bases movement, 'Would you like to go back to the days of sweet potatoes and bare feet?' Many Okinawans seem reluctant to go back to those days, but some took it up as a political tool.

During the early eighties a group of idealistic young 'returnees' who came back to Okinawa after Reversion started a Sweet Potato Association near Nago, on the main island. They dedicated it to twin objectives: promoting organic agriculture and opposing US military bases. One of their precepts is to eat at least one meal of sweet potatoes every day, as a reminder of the heroic history of the *Satsuma imo* and also to break down the dependency on income from US bases that has replaced so much farming and start a return to self-sufficiency in food production. As one of its members, Taira Yoshiaki, says, 'The sweet potato used to be a symbol of poverty. Now we realise what a wonderful crop it is'.

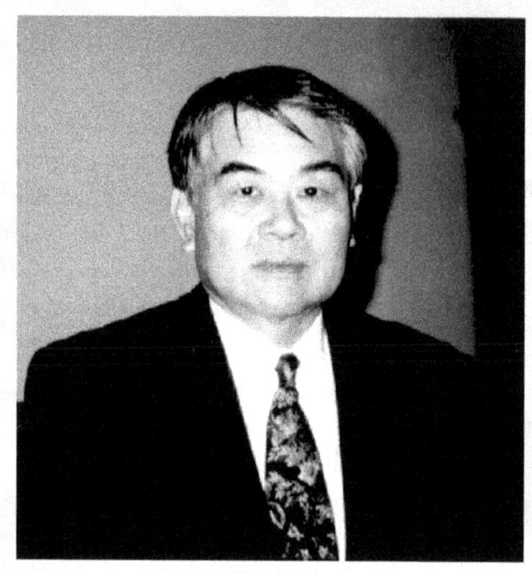

The persuasive voice of development

Inamine Keiichi
Chairman, Ryuseki Corporation

It's unusual to meet people from radical politics, art movements and big business all talking the same language. Maybe only in Okinawa where most people are agreed they don't want bases and they do want a big measure of independence can you hear conservative politicians and chieftains of capitalism saying the same things as radicals and fringe people—almost. The truth is that they are united by a common foe, and the resolution of deeper differences over the nature of sovereignty or the degree of autonomy, both political and economic, can be postponed. There is for now a common purpose—to rescue Okinawa from the military—and to an extent, control from Tokyo. Whether such a coalition of interests will hold after the removal of the bases remains to be seen. The fact is the task of getting rid of them and improving Okinawa's status will take time enough for that problem to be dealt with some way down the track.

Inamine Keiichi is chairman of the Ryuseki Corporation, the biggest local petrol distributor. He has recently become a self-appointed spokesperson on behalf of the local business sector. He is not the typical corporate type you might see in Japan. He is outspoken, frank and straightforward. He was one of the participants in the 85 000-strong rally against the bases held on October 21, 1995, which, for a company man of his status and stature, is a bold and significant statement.

He must have done this kind of interview many times before, so, as soon as we finished our first question we got a twenty-minute-long answer, which he delivered more like a speech, with eyes closed in deep concentration. So our second question was a real portmanteau number containing four headings, which merely gave him guidelines for another speech. In both answers he reiterated in business terms some of the things we heard from people of much humbler position or with more overt political platforms.

Since such corporate entities have so much influence on what our political options are these days, we sought his view on the practicalities of autonomy.

How can Okinawa, with less than 1.5 million people scattered over dozens of islands, hope to survive as a vibrant, self-reliant state?

It's possible to be self-reliant but it will be a difficult task to achieve, because at the moment we are 80 per cent dependent on the central government's handouts—the rest is tourism. More than two decades since Reversion, the state of the economy looks better, but in reality, we are far from self-reliant. It is a serious concern for us business leaders here. But there are possibilities. There are roughly two measures to make Okinawa more economically autonomous.

First, we should look at measures to maximise our geographic advantages. We could be a small-scale Singapore or mini Hong Kong. Okinawa is already occupying an important position in the trade between China and Taiwan. There were more than 1000 boats last year that were customs-cleared here before heading on to their destinations in either China or Taiwan. At the moment the bulk of this kind of trade goes through Hong Kong but 1000 boats a year is significant. Imagine what it would be like when Hong Kong because of its reversion to China is unable to perform at its current level. We believe the importance of Okinawa will only increase. However, I wouldn't be too optimistic about Okinawa replacing the role of Hong Kong because I can see some problems along the horizon already.

The biggest problem we have is with Japan. The central government has a firm policy of one-nation, one-system, which means we can't have a different legal or economic system for this region. This mentality is typical of the centralised command state which is Japan. Changes must be made in order for us in Okinawa to revitalise our economy.

At the moment, the attitude of the Tokyo government is to supply what is demanded. Tokyo has no intention of creating any new demands, let alone a new supply route. To make the best use of our geographic position, we need hardware—infrastructure—set up here to encourage regional traffic:

Oil storage in Kin.

an international hub airport for both freight and passenger traffic, a modern port facility with container-loading capability. These are some of our infrastructural needs.

Then we need to upgrade our 'software' at the same time. This wouldn't involve the massive construction of infrastructure. All we need to do is to turn this place into a business-friendly environment, just like Singapore and Hong Kong. We need to change the financial and economic framework to make it attractive: offshore banking facilities, tax breaks and easier entry for overseas visitors including foreign workers are some of the measures we can implement.

Even though we have a free-trade zone in Naha, it's in name only. We've been asking the central authorities to allow it to have the substance to match the title. Again, we could become a small-scale Hong Kong, which would be able to compete with other free-trade zones in the region, such as Subic in the Philippines or Pusan and Inchon in South Korea.

The second unique advantage we have is a subtropical environment. No other prefecture in Japan can claim to have such a different climate. Our climate is on the northern edge of the tropical and the southern end of the moderate region. Thanks to this unique environment, we have many unique species of animals and plants. We are especially keen to explore marine biology around here. It's said to have lots of potential. We've been approaching the central government to give us permission to set up a comprehensive marine biology study centre to explore its commercial application possibilities. We have been dealing with the Japanese bureaucracies but they seem more interested in holding onto their own turf and tend to resist such an across-the-board research facility.

Okinawa needs a bigger manufacturing sector so that we don't need to rely on handouts and tourism. At present Okinawa's manufacturing sector accounts for only 6 per cent of our total industrial output compared to the average 20 per cent in the rest of Japan. We believe

LONGER BOLDER OLDER

Life expectancy for both men and women in Okinawa is the highest in Japan, which is perhaps the highest in the world. Official figures for 1990 show the life expectancy for men is over seventy-six and for women it's eighty-four, with over 300 people in their hundreds—about five times the rate of the rest of Japan.

So what is the secret of longevity? Some claim it's the weather, but it can't be the climate alone because there are many subtropical climates that are similar.

Others point to the water for keeping the local folks strong—that the coral reef filters Okinawa's natural supplies with the essential minerals and calcium necessary to keep old bones strong. A company called Coral Bio-Tech distributes mineral-enriched coral sand mined from Okinawa. The product is called Coral Calcium—one gram of coral sand packed in a tea bag–like sachet. Once in liquid, all the goodness is supposed to come out and reduce the acidity of water, and, conversely, increase its alkaline content. One bag is apparently sufficient to produce the 1.5 litres of good drinking water you need each day. We doubt this is the kind of stuff you get out of the tap in Okinawa.

It might be the diet. If so, which ingredient? Could it be the tofu or the pork? Okinawans certainly consume lots of both in their diet. Or maybe *goya*—also known as bitter melon—the seed-stuffed cucumber cooked as a vegetable.

Okinawan tofu is slightly harder than the mainland variety and gets eaten at almost every meal. Fermented tofu, a bit like cheese, is a speciality. *Jimami tofu* is made from peanuts.

Okinawans do eat a lot of pigs, and most parts of them, including ribs, shoulders, offal, ears and guts. *Mimiga sashimi* is a dish of cooked pigs' ears, thinly sliced and marinated in vinegar. Testicles and stomach are used in a soup called *nakami. Soki* is perhaps more accessible—barbecued rib—and *rafute* is ribs stewed in *awamori* until almost disintegrated.

Awamori, the local liquor, may also have the answer. It's made from nothing but natural ingredients.

Maybe it's music. After all, most locals sing and dance a lot.

Whatever the secret, today's leaders are set to exploit Okinawa's image as a place that can supply longevity. One plan that's seriously discussed in Okinawa is to turn the island of military bases into the 'island of healing', a sort of New Age international health-care facility where stressed-outs from Tokyo or wherever get cured by the local secrets of long life.

there are plenty of commercial application opportunities in the marine biology area. Health products, cosmetics, medical products are all possible. Construction materials can be mined from the sea.

We have other environmental technology options. The melon fly has been made extinct here and as a result we now have a strong industry exporting tropical fruits and flowers, so that technique would be of some value to other people who have a similar problem.

We have the University of the Ryukyus' marine biology department, which specialises in mangrove planting and coral transplanting, which could also earn us income.

Soil erosion has been a big environmental concern, but we now have new legislation to tackle the issue, a model which would also be of value to other developing countries suffering from similar problems.

Okinawa Electrical Power Co. has been experimenting with alternative power generation sources such as wind power and solar power with encouraging success in the remote islands where connections to the main grid, to the thermal power plant on other islands, are difficult and costly.

I believe the fruits from Okinawan studies and experiments could be really useful and can be easily transplanted to neighbouring countries. As you know, Japan has been the biggest Official Development Assistance donor nation for awhile, but this aid from Japan seems to be spent on nothing but building infrastructure—roads, dams, bridges and other concrete structures. Isn't it about time we give people something better than a hollow concrete box?

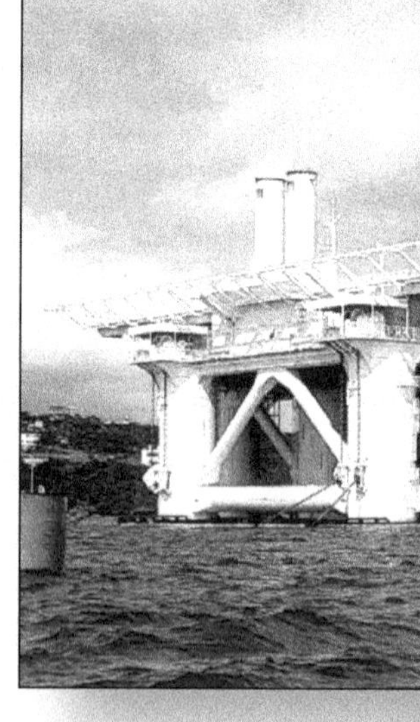

There is a worry, of course. Once the environmental management technology is transferred to less-developed countries where the labour costs are cheaper, jobs will be lost from Okinawa. So we have to remain competitive, otherwise others will easily catch up. Anyway, these environmental-related industries will be the key industries for Okinawa, not just in terms of earning money. They are also the sort of export commodities which would really help local people. We have an international convention centre building where we run various training programs for students from developing nations, which will be useful to them and would enhance Japan's national interest.

Tourism should be opened up to more Asian traffic. Until now, tourists meant only mainland Japanese. We have to widen the horizon and encourage visitors from neighbouring countries. Taiwan and Korea should be our immediate targets. Their annual per capita income has now surpassed $10 000 a year. Mainland China as well as Hong Kong should not be ignored, and our full potential market does not end in East Asia, but should include Malaysia, Indonesia, Singapore, Thailand, Vietnam and other countries.

At the moment, Okinawa is enjoyed as a tropical resort. Tourists also appreciate our traditional culture. We should also look into health-tour prospects. After all, we have a reputation for longevity which does really mean something to people and should be used. We can market traditional and unique herbs, food and drink to our visitors. There are already various plans for health resorts where visitors can enjoy seawater therapy. We should make the best use of what we have—our reputation for longevity, our abundant nature, our sea water—everything.

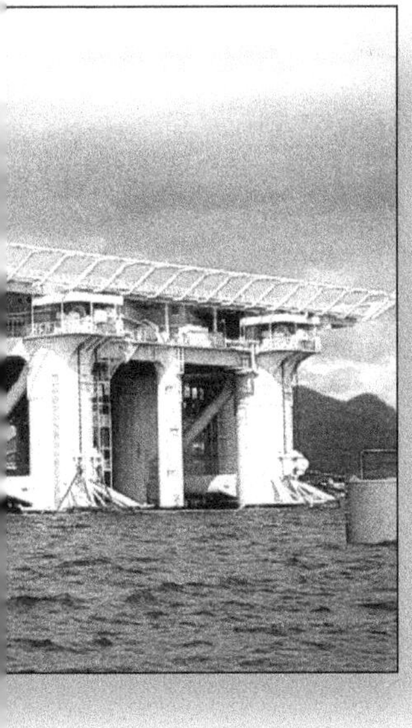

The city of Naha needs to have a focal point, so we are talking about recommissioning a disused structure called the Aquapolis. It was built for the Marine Expo we had in northern Motobu in 1975. Our plan is to give it a fresh coat of paint, refurbish it and tow it to Naha port. We are hoping this could become the icon of our port, rather like the Statue of Liberty in New York and the Opera House in Sydney.

Looking back on the history of our economic development, we realise those successful industries are the ones that make best use of our advantages and of what's special here. I talked about our geographical advantage earlier. Other uniquenesses have not yet been explored, such as our skill in international communication. We have more contacts with foreigners and foreign cultures than anyone else in Japan. We have over

PLANE FACTS 4

The P-3 Orion, the US Navy's main anti-submarine aircraft—developed by Lockheed as a replacement for the P-2 Neptune—is based on the L-188 Electra passenger plane, and is now equipped with the latest computers and sensors to detect most suspicious movements in the deep. The Orion is still one of the world's most effective air-to-undersea surveillance planes. It can control operations as a flying command centre or act as a submarine monitor for another command. The latest version has a huge radar disk on top of the body which gives it an AWACS capability.

Licensed to various friendly US allies, such as Canada, Japan, the Netherlands and, at one time, Iran, sales were aided in some places by money handed to influential purchasers to firm up their enthusiasm. Grease to the palms put a whole tribe of Japanese politicians and bureaucrats on the skids, including the late Tanaka Kakuei who, through an intricate chain of middle men who also got nabbed, took money from Lockheed for use by the Liberal Democratic Party in the 1970s.

400 000 overseas emigrants, which is the biggest proportion of all Japan. We could use this unique experience and ties to become a gateway to the rest of the world. Our experience is unique so our skill should be utilised.

To sum it up, we have the potential to be self-reliant. Whether we can be or not depends primarily on us, but also on the politicians and bureaucrats in Tokyo. Unless we can convince them and let them allow us to operate in a different legal framework from the national one, we may not succeed.

What are the legal constraints to becoming more independent, what's the timeframe for the removal of bases, what should be done with the land and how can Okinawa avoid neglect in the future?

As for autonomy or decentralisation, no consensus has been reached on this yet. Some want a 'special administrative zone' for Okinawa but that would mean one-nation, two-systems. Most seem to feel that would be too radical to win a consensus. The best shot is to set up the free-trade zone properly and gradually expand it.

As to Kadena Air Base, no-one knows when it will be handed back so we are not in a position to draw up a concrete plan to convert it to something else. We have not really reached a consensus on what to do with it but a majority seems to favour turning it into an international hub airport. However, if what we want is an international hub airport, the quicker way might be to work on the extension of Naha airport. The only thing stopping Naha from becoming capable is the fact that it's shared with the Japanese military. So if we could separate its military and civilian functions out and extend the civilian, we wouldn't need to wait until Kadena was returned to fulfil that function. I said this option would be quicker but it would still take probably twenty years to finish the extension of Naha airport.

I cannot see Kadena being anything other than an airport and be economically viable. I am aware there are landlords who oppose any airport there but I just cannot come up with an alternative idea which is also economically feasible.

As regards Tokyo's attitude, this is the first time that we have been taken seriously. The change of attitude is only because the current problem is a serious one which might undermine the whole security arrangement the Japanese government has with the USA. We've been raising the issue for years, but they always turned a deaf ear. Only now do we feel they are taking our requests seriously. While they are listening to us we should take advantage of it and press hard for change. However small the progress, it is still vital for us.

MANGROVE MATTERS

Two of the most interesting people we met on Okinawa were not locals but Japanese environmental scientists working at the University of the Ryukyus. They were Prof. Koda Yoshihiro and Dr Baba Shigeyuki, both leading lights in the International Society for Mangrove Ecosystems, which has a database in Okinawa and is now exporting its knowledge about mangroves.

Iriomote is especially valuable as a mangrove resource. It has several rivers with large estuaries which are ideal breeding grounds for the plants. No-one is allowed to plant mangroves in areas designated as national park land, but it was clear from our observations at various spots around the coast that mangrove culture and maybe cultivation is alive and well and spreading in certain parts of the island. So is mangrove consciousness.

The attraction for these scientists to the mangrove is its essential ambiguity; it's a plant that needs to have its feet in water and its leaves in the air. It reproduces by sending out pods which float around the coast until they find congenial spots in shallow salt water in which they can root themselves. If they successfully take hold they can generate a miniature shoreline forest up to two or three metres tall which can act as a buffer between the breakers and the shore and then, as its root complex consolidates down the centuries, can turn into a significant land mass. Many island chains which are now habitable, from Okinawa to the Florida Keys, started as natural mangrove settlements.

Mangrove roots are host and home to a myriad of fish and crustaceans, ideal for prawns or shrimp and small fry which head out to sea as they grow. Mangrove provides a habitat more nutritious than the brackish ponds that have been dug out all over South-east Asia to supply Japan's insatiable appetite for shrimp and prawns. There's even one on Taketomi.

As well as offering food and shelter for growing seafood stocks, mangroves hold the line against erosion, which is why they are so valuable in places where fragile coasts are battered by high tides or tropical storms. The ubiquitous 'protective' barriers built from concrete 'tetrapods' dumped in bays and off beaches all over Japan—and increasingly in Okinawa—would be unnecessary if mangroves had been retained as a natural barrier. Unfortunately the mangrove isn't 'tidy' and doesn't fit in with beach-resort culture.

Dr Baba said that Okinawan expertise in the study of mangrove culture is now being applied in other countries. He was off to Pakistan the day after we met where he is involved in a river estuary mangrove planting program. He told us of an old Okinawan proverb he's spreading around to help secure the mangrove message: no forest on the land, no fish in the sea.

As he explained, people have known for ages that nutrients gathered up by trees and other plants on land gradually find their way down through the food 'web'—the term he prefers over the usual 'chain' because he says the reality of interconnectivity between species is more intricate and not at all linear—via rivers and creeks that run into the sea and this is an excellent source of food for fish. Many a fisherman has gone broke simply because a plot of forest land was cleared for 'development'.

The mangrove is a forest that is neither land nor sea. Until recently none of Japan's central ministries would take responsibility for mangrove matters. Agricultural officials said it was outside their scope because it was 'marine' while the men from Fisheries shrugged it off as 'land'. Things are changing thanks to the efforts of Koda and Baba and other members of the ISME: there is now recognition that mangroves have to be taken seriously as an essential ingredient of survival.

A British university concluded a study of mangroves along the coast of Vietnam by recommending that tropical countries plant mangroves instead of building concrete breakwaters to protect their shorelines and the people who live there from storm damage.

Researchers at the University of East Anglia say mangroves build up the slope of the shore so that the power of breaking waves is diminished. They also point out that in Vietnam the amount of time is comparatively well spent planting mangroves because not only do mangrove roots foster consumable crustaceans and fish, the wood itself is also useful and so is honey from bees living in the trees.

Increased regional awareness, including Dr Baba's little exercise in planting mangroves in Pakistan, suggests that the Okinawan dream of marketing its unique knowledge and expertise is not so crazy and that such small-scale niche industries could cultivate a measure of economic autonomy for Okinawa.

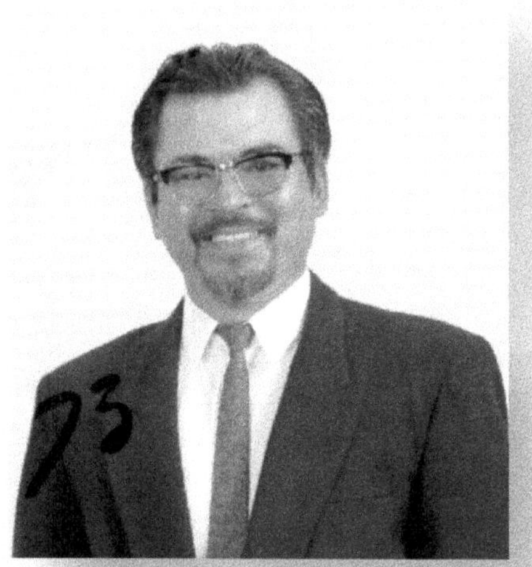

Inject the fun factor

Tamaki Mitsuru

We first came to know Tamaki as a singer with the Rinken Band, which made it big on the mainland during the early nineties. He left them in 1993, so we wondered what he'd been up to since he forsook the glamour and strain of the music-tour life.

We soon realised he's a big name in his own right on Okinawa—indeed his face is all over the island on posters. He's gone back to the theatre as a comic artist in the traditional style, which he spices up with contemporary references and a mischievous sense of irony. One of his characters, 'archetypical salary man' was so spot-on that a local bank hired him for its promotional posters. He's shown surrounded by equally 'typical-looking' family members, and in true po-mo tone, it's not possible to say who's fooling whom.

When he was with the Rinken Band, it was Tamaki's singing, as well as other 'exotic' Okinawan elements, that sounded most refreshing to mainland audiences. Although the band's record company, Sony, tried to persuade them all to speak and sing the mainlanders' 'Yamato' tongue, they never did. Their decision has been proved correct because Tamaki and the Rinken Band have found a substantial audience who appreciate the difference and like them for what they are and do.

Tamaki's satire and farcical renderings are centred on his comedy group Shochiku Kageki Dan, a mix of vaudeville, sketch comedy, cabaret and

dance—a very *champru* unit.

We visited him in his own neighbourhood. He was born and brought up around the central district of Koza and we were told to catch a bus there and meet him at Dunkin' Donuts at the Goya intersection. The area has some naming ambiguities. It seems the name Koza comes from the Americans' attempt to say Goya, but the area has been officially renamed Okinawa city, although we heard no-one use that while we were there.

We decided that lovely though the location was, it was too noisy for a taped interview so we walked with Tamaki through a busy shopping arcade to the tiny shop where he sells musical instruments, Okinawan clothes and souvenirs. Not that this was a quiet venue either; it's just that with its shoppers, bike bells and the ever-running *minyo* sound coming through the arcade PA, it seemed to us to be more 'authentic'.

Half-way through the interview, Tamaki stopped talking about important things that matter to show us some videos of his troupe's recent performances. Even without a clue about what was going on, we could see the attraction and noticed that audiences at these live shows were falling about—and in the end so were we. Tamaki is a very funny man.

Tell us why you think Okinawan music is different and how it stays different without being taken over by US or Japanese culture?

One strong reason is that our music and song relates to daily life. We have lots of festivals here, celebrations and weddings and so on. People will, on these occasions, always pull out a sanshin and play it. It's always part of the proceedings. That's what our so-called new champru musicians, like Nenes, the Rinken Band and Kina Shokichi draw on—it's part of their roots, always connected with day-to-day goings on. It's actually more or less in our blood. From a very young age, I grew up with the sound of the Eisa festival's drums in my blood, and every time I hear that sound now I feel my blood running to the rhythm.

You have preserved your culture, but not enjoyed the benefits of growth like the rest of Japan. In a way, the thing that prevented you from gaining wealth has been the reason why you've kept your culture!

Look, I'm the kind of person who if I was offered a job in Tokyo with big money and all the trimmings, or the choice to stay here for a pittance, I'd stay here. A lot of others have made the same choice. I think Okinawan people share my way of evaluating life's values.

When you look back at our history you can see we've been invaded and occupied by China, the Japanese, the USA, and it's amazing how many musicians and entertainers we still have of our own. We developed humour to counter difficult times. You can say adversity has helped our culture to partially develop and survive, yet we have always had a strong will to survive through those hard times.

Do you have influence in Japan too?

It's the same thing. What we do comes from our life itself, drawing strength from the strong roots it has in the community. Some of our bands do water their stuff down a bit to be accepted in Japan, but we didn't do that when I was with the Rinken Band, when we went to Japan. In our shows there, I even talked in local dialect without explaining what I was saying. I suppose our audience in Japan were so used to the notion that good music comes only from the West, that they were really shocked to discover something as strong and genuine pumping out from their backyards.

Okinawan music is similar to Irish music and reggae in that people everywhere pick up on it and use its forms.

Yes, maybe. You can keep on developing traditional music to today's audience as long as it has strong roots in the society. The recent popularity of music from Okinawa on the mainland certainly reflects that.

What do you do in dialect now that's different from what you did with the Rinken Band?

I remember when I was twelve years old—about three years before Reversion—there was a systematic campaign at school to suppress our language. We had a 'dialect penalty card' and you were given one if you used an Okinawan word. If you collected three of these cards, you would be sent off to the 'sin bin', cleaning the toilets and other forms of punishment.

This drive to the Japanisation of the language lasted well after Reversion in 1972. But it could never kill our language. Ten years or so later, there was a strong swing back to Okinawan things, Okinawan

SOBA TRUTH

To the ears of outsiders, locals pronounce it more like 'suba', or 'soo-ba'. While on the mainland, *soba* means a buckwheat-based thin noodle, the Okinawan variety is wheat-based, fat and chunky. Mainland *soba* can be served cold, dipped in strong sauce, or hot in weak broth. Okinawan *soba* always comes in soup that is made from pork stock. It situates somewhere near wheat-based *udon* noodles but the soup tastes more as if it was inspired by its Chinese cousins.

***Soba* in Okinawa usually comes with pickled ginger (in a very intense pink), a piece of fishcake and shallots. Additional toppings can include pork rib cooked in *awamori*—to achieve that soft texture to the max.**

You need chopsticks to eat *soba* and it helps if you suck it up with real enthusiasm and energy. Nobody cares if you make a lot of noise with your slurping. But, whatever you do, try not to accept those disposable chopsticks—*waribashi*—that so many restaurants provide in Japan. In Okinawa many restaurants have durable bamboo chopsticks painted in red and yellow, but pull'n'snap disposables are taking over.

culture, including the language, because people realised they couldn't really describe what they felt in the mainlanders' tongue.

I have experienced that process myself. When I lived in Tokyo studying theatre between age nineteen and twenty-two, I was under constant pressure to speak the Japanese language properly. That was the bottom line requirement to getting acting roles. I had a real difficult time then. So I tried to be Japanese, but could not and came back home. When I came back here, I became more confident about my origin and less ashamed of my Okinawan heritage. As I got more involved in local theatre and research into the history of entertainment in Okinawa, I appreciated our culture even more.

Some Okinawan people use 'Yamato' language—standard Japanese—especially when they greet mainlanders. However, more often than not, they realised they can't really explain themselves in an acquired tongue. I now believe only in your own tongue can you make other people understand. This is how I speak and I am comfortable and happy about my delivery now, which is sort of a mixture of both. I could not become a perfect Japanese-speaker, but I don't have any regrets now.

How different is the Okinawan language from that of mainlanders?

When I first got there and tried my version of Japanese, people couldn't really understand me. They didn't think I was speaking in Japanese. Maybe we speak too fast.

If you hear us locals speak in Okinawan, I bet you wouldn't understand.

Go ahead and try us.

¢∞§¶•ª¨ˆ§¶´´Australia∞∞ºª•¶welcome§†–"ø¨¨æ…˙∆ƒßto ∂ßå£™Okinawa¢∞@$%*&^ºª•

You have to remember though, there are many different dialects spoken even inside Okinawa. We have in our repertoire a comedy sketch in which we take a bit of laughter out of the different dialects of mainland

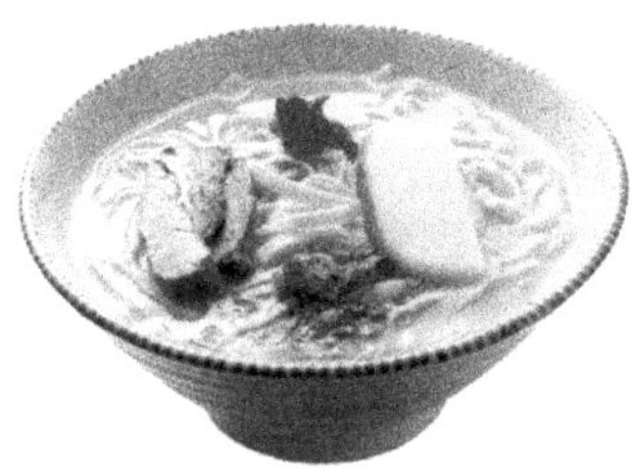

The timber industry will tell you they are only made from throwaway wood anyway, so it doesn't matter if you add yours to the pile. But even if that were true, a visit to your local tip will easily show what a scourge they are: whole forests so people can have a fresh set of eating utensils for every meal they sit down to—more than 1000 pairs a year if you eat out three times a day. Imagine if the idea catches on in China and the rest of the noodle-eating universe.

As Friedemann Bartu says in *The Ugly Japanese* 'Every working day Japan goes through well over 100 million pairs of disposable chopsticks, or some 20 000 million pairs a year. This is equivalent to 200 000 cubic metres of wood—sufficient lumber to build 15 000 homes.'

Nobody uses them at home in Japan and if you take your own with you, there's always something to talk about; much easier than carting your own knife and fork around and you get a nice little box with them too.

And when you have eaten all the *soba* and want to get at the soup, it's perfectly cool to refuse a spoon—and drink it straight from the bowl.

Okinawa and Miyako. It's that different. We have always assumed that the right way to speak Okinawan is the way it is spoken around Shuri. It is regarded as the standard—King's Okinawan. But forcing the other islanders to speak a 'standardised Okinawan', which is really only Shuri dialect, is just the same as standard Japanese was forced on all Okinawans in the past.

Why did you leave the Rinken Band to go it alone?

Well, I was doing both the band and theatre for awhile. But I got really busy with both and I reached the stage where I had to choose one. So I decided to pursue my original interest, which was the theatre. We parody popular culture: film, TV. We aim our humour at people to make them laugh at themselves. The troupe was set up twelve years ago.

We had difficulty deciding on a name. We had a deadline for the poster, you know. Just then, we saw the name Shochiku Kageki Dan (Shochiku musical group) from the mainland touring here. We thought, hey, we can pinch the sounds *shochiku kageki dan,* but use different characters, which literally mean extreme troupe creating laughter. It was meant to be a temporary one-off idea, but the name has stuck with us now.

Some bureaucrat thought we were political extremists and demanded we change the name when we applied to book a public hall. You know, that was the time when extremists were coming in to disrupt the presence of Self-Defense Forces men at public gatherings. Yes, we are extremists, but we use the weapon of laughter.

Do your jokes travel outside Okinawa?

We go to Japan once or twice a year. At home we sometimes get criticised by hardline traditionalists who say we denigrate traditional stuff because we don't follow it strictly. We often make jokes on the Okinawan language itself but we don't do it out of spite. We encourage people to lighten up and to review our reality by laughing.

What do you think of traditionalists?

Different strokes

It's widely believed that two streams of the Japanese language developed separately from each other for some time, but they came from the same root with the time of their separation estimated to be around the third to fifth century BC. Just how this took place is not known, but it is quite possible one group of people migrated south, perhaps from Kyushu to Okinawa, and the other went north through the rest of Japan.

So, in the language 'tree' Ryukyuan dialects developed from the same roots as mainland dialects. Thus:

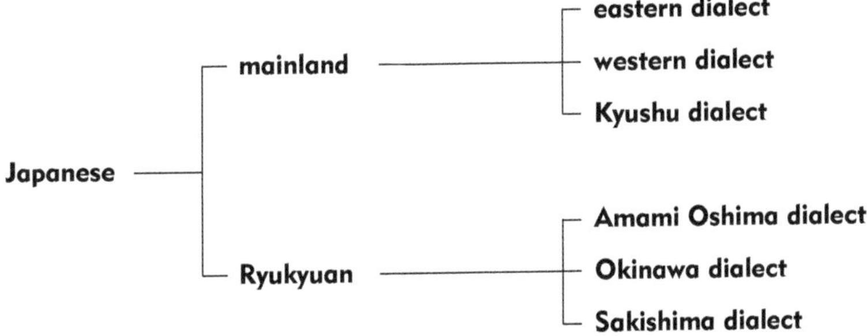

When Okinawans talk amongst themselves at normal speed their Ryukyuan dialects sound very foreign to mainland Japanese speakers. If you listen carefully though, most of the words used are pretty much the same. It's the intonation and particular pronunciation of words which makes the dialect sound so different.

The main difference in pronunciation is the number of vowels used. In Japanese there are usually five vowels: a, i, u, e and o. But in the Ryukyus only three are used: a, i and u. There are many consonants used in the Ryukyuan language which don't exist in modern Japanese. Vocabulary is pretty much the same.

Words like *hana* (flower) are pronounced the same way, while others such as *te* (hand) is pronounced 'ti' (as in tea) and *kome* (rice) is 'kumi', *ame* (rain) is 'ami', *sake* is 'saki', *yuki* (snow) is 'yuchi' and *toki* (time) is 'tuchi'.

Some verbs have a unique set of conjugations which differ from their mainland counterparts and there are adjectives that cannot be found in today's mainland Japanese.

Well, the classic hard-core traditionalists should coexist with radicals who defy every rule. Only with a careful balance of these extremes do we have a good dynamic tradition which keeps strong. Unless you have space for both extremes, it ends up producing stuff only museums appreciate—or total shit.

To me some classic traditional music stuff sounds too slow and boring. But you need them, as long as there is a breathing space for experimentalists. It's a balancing act—it's coexistence.

Curiously, the popular bands today, Nenes, Kina Shokichi and the Rinken Band, all come from this town, Koza. Koza is really a new town, erected after the war—and around here there's a new-town feeling that you need to do something new to survive. You know, there is an atmosphere of going against the established schools and traditions of culture. This town didn't really have tradition. Teruya Rinsuke, Teruya Rinken's father and my master, who has revolutionised Okinawan theatre, is based here.

Do younger Okinawans relate to you?

They do. What I feel from the younger generation is this enthusiastic energy, vigour. It seems to me that they are saying they can better us, or they can do something new that we have not seen before. I think that this energy is a dynamic driving force behind Okinawan culture. For example, young people, no matter how impressed and influenced they are, don't try to imitate the Rinken Band. Doing it your own way seems to be the Okinawan way.

What about the effect of imported cultural forms?

It is possible to incorporate all sorts of influences from outside. The important thing is to maintain tradition. This is where hard-core traditionalists come in. We need to maintain local culture, which distinguishes us from the rest of the world. Okinawa won't be Okinawa when there is no distinction with Tokyo. We won't be Okinawan if we become rootless internationalists with nothing of our own. Historically speaking, Okinawan people are good at maintaining a good balance of keeping our heritage and accepting and incorporating new culture.

Are there young Okinawan rappers?

Yes, it's great. You can adopt any form, provided you have roots. You know our dish *goya champru?* Okinawan culture, especially Koza culture, is often called *champru* culture. See, the ingredients of *champru* are not selected at random. They're all mixed together, but with careful thought. If you ate the *goya,* or bitter melon, on its own, you'd find it too bitter; but together with everything else it's delicious. That's our culture. It's in the mix. We take things from all over the place and mix them together and make something of our own.

Kachashi is a word for dancing, which involves everyone dancing together. It is another example of the Okinawan way of mixing everyone. You get a great feeling going and an occasion, weddings, parties or anything would not be complete without people dancing *kachashi.* Everyone in Okinawa can dance this one.

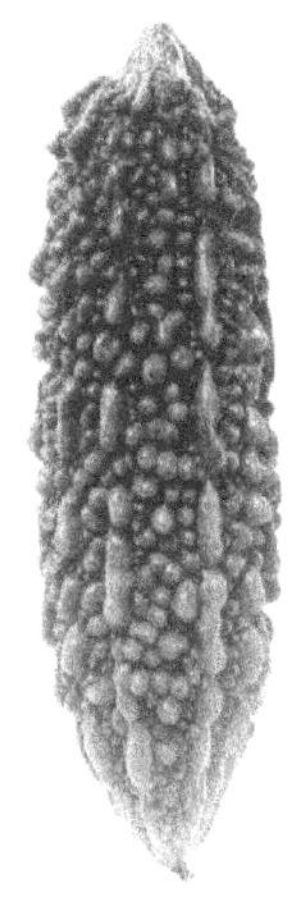

GOYA DAY

On May 8, 1996, a group of 120 Okinawans gathered in Naha to declare it Goya Day, to promote *goya,* the bitter melon, for nationwide consumption. May 8 was chosen because in Japanese *go gatsu* means May and the number 8 can be pronounced 'ya'.

[He starts chatting about the video he was playing.]

This character is called James Taruganini. Taruganini is a traditional character in Okinawan theatre. My adaptation is a true representation of Koza and Okinawan youth. I put on an Okinawan wig, an aloha shirt and sunglasses for this. And this character speaks in Okinawan but with an American accent. So it's a depiction of Okinawa.

This wig is only meant to be used in the traditional theatre. But I use it on a character dressed in a suit, rather like a typical salary man, you know. The type that would say on coming home from work, 'Dinner first', or 'I'll have a bath'. This character has the look of a typical salary man, you know. But when he arrives home, instead, he goes all theatrical, in Okinawan dialect, going on like this, introducing himself, walking through. The audience gets shaken up by this mix'n'match adaptation of traditional stuff into a modern setting.

Have a look at some of the video recordings of our performances. Most of the scenes are set in the present but some characters are dressed in real time-warp traditional clothes. Here, they are talking about the great tradition of 'Okinawan time'. It is based on mainland Japanese complaints that we Okinawans are very loose about appointments. Being half an hour late is considered to be a common thing here. According to them, we never keep appointments, you know. But as explained in this piece, the essence of Okinawan time is to be relaxed and patient about appointments. You need to be trained to be good at waiting without getting upset.

How often do you perform?

We perform about every two months now. We used to play more frequently but now every member becomes busier with their own stuff, such as in radio. We make sure we put on at least one big production a year. Last year, we had three new productions. My theme is always fixed on looking at the past, present and future of Okinawa. People sometimes ask me about the need to stress the question of local difference in these times of internationalisation.

Sure, we have already come as close to being a Tokyo as we can go. Perhaps so much so, I'd say we need to be local to survive. Our future is often said to be hinged on how well we can promote that difference to the rest of the world. But it is one thing to promote the fact our language is distinctive, and how many of us can speak that very language is quite another. The number of Okinawan speakers is definitely on the decline, bit by bit, every year, for sure. Once language goes you can't say we are Okinawan.

What would you do with the land left by the US bases when they withdraw?

Well, lots of people have been involved in Okinawa to get rid of the bases and get this land back but, surprisingly, there's not much discussion about what should be done with the land. I've got this plan to build an Asian Hollywood. I know we can match Hong Kong's claim easily. We have plenty of room at Kadena. You could shoot two or three Die

Hards all at the same time. Those aeroplane hangars are perfect for filming. Plenty of outdoor locations to choose from. That's our resources.

We've got the right climate. We would give a tax incentive and lure clients from all over the world. We would offer filmmakers, directors and actors plots of prime, seaside residences around Onna, cheaply, you know, and encourage those people to take up residency here. This would solve the unemployment problem, not just for Okinawans but also for all those soldiers, who would have nothing better to do back at home in the USA. They could stay here, you know, and there would be plenty of work as extras in the movies instead of being in the military. There would be jobs for security guards as well.

I'm taking this seriously, even though people think I'm joking. I'm putting together a team soon to do some serious planning to come up with a real package. If Kadena is turned into an international airport as planned, film people would pass through and see great potential here. You know, it is much cheaper to make a film here.

Okinawa is a land of arts and entertainment. It's full of entertainers, musicians and theatre people like me. Koza is the centre of all that. It's the right place to set up a centre where people can come and enjoy themselves and get in touch with genuine Okinawan culture.

I'd say the biggest problem is that there has been too little discussion about what to do with the bases. Too much energy is spent on the political process, very little on future planning. There are officials working in high places in a project team, planning what to do with the bases, taking it all very seriously. Especially since military bases have such negative connotations, I'd say we should brighten up the issue with extreme suggestions like mine.

Remember, Okinawans are singers, dancers, writers and all entertainers. Let's draw strength from our cultural tradition and make the best use of it. We should definitely inject some of the fun factor into discussions, otherwise it just isn't going to work.

OK TO ME, RYUKYU TO YOU

Placenames are never singularities. People have names for themselves which may never be heard outside their shores. Others are obliged to live with a term imposed by colonial powers or the 'international community'. Many 'Bosnian Muslims' are neither, and what is a 'South African'?

Disputed territories in particular, and especially those far away from the great media centres, are often known by a variety of names. For example, the group of islands known to Koreans as Tok-do is what the Japanese call Takeshima. The ocean in which they are floating is known to the Japanese as the Sea of Japan while the Koreans call the same pool of water the Eastern Sea.

The name Ryukyu had existed long before the island of Okinawa was politically unified, but most of the rest of the world came to use Okinawa as the name for the main island of the Ryukyus. The group of islands around it is known as the Okinawa Shoto. Okinawa is now the name of the prefecture which was created when the Meiji government abolished the Ryukyu Kingdom in the late nineteenth century.

The name Okinawa first appeared in Japanese literature as Akonaha in an eighth-century publication called *Todai Wajo Toseiden* (The record of a T'ang monk's expedition to the East). The monk was Chien-chen, known in Japan as Ganjin. It was he who brought to Japan from China the teachings of a Buddhist sect known as Ritsu, or vinaya in Sanskrit. He made several attempts to make the crossing and one of them is thought to have brought him to the place he called Akonaha.

The locals in Okinawa now identify themselves as Uchinan-chu so it may be right to assume that something like Uchina was the indigenous name which predates all the known 'foreign' terms.

From the other side of the water Chinese people seem to have always called it Ryukyu and the first written version appears in a seventh-century work called *Sui Shu*—although it's not absolutely clear from the text that it means exactly the same islands we now know as the Ryukyus. Texts from the late Han period also talk about islands in this vicinity but these seem to include other islands off Taiwan where the Tawu people now live—who are known in Japan as the Yami.

Taiwan itself was described as the Small, Little or Lesser Ryukyu while Okinawa was the Big or Greater Ryukyu.

The spelling of Ryukyu using two Chinese characters as is done now was standardised during the Ming period of the fourteenth century and because most of the rest of the world—East and West—learned about the archipelago through their contact with China, it was known by various versions of its Chinese name: Ryukyu, Luchu, Liukiu, Loo Choo or even Roo Choo.

For centuries Chinese was the lingua franca of trade throughout East Asia. Navigators from the West sailed through and hired Chinese readers to act as translators in the eighteenth and nineteenth centuries. Thus, Westerners also picked up the Chinese view of this part of Asia.

Even though Okinawans or Ryukyu people might think of themselves as Uchinan-chu they too are used to the terms used by outsiders—just as many nations today live with English or French versions of what or who they are. The irony is, however, that slowly and surely the Chinese name has been replaced by the Japanese preference, which is why the majority of outsiders now use Okinawa as the generic term. Okinawa is in such common use now it seems the Japanese version has been both internalised and internationalised.

Still, Ryukyu is widely used when the locals talk about their relationship with the outside world, especially China. The realisation that the Japanese model—Okinawa—has become the standard has seen a revival of the term Ryukyu, especially amongst those talking about more autonomy for the islands.

The retrieval of Ryukyu reflects both nostalgia and loss: a once and future yearning for something better that might be on the way.

Japanese maps call the stretch of islands between Kyushu and Taiwan the Nansei Shoto, the south-west group of islands, with Ryukyu Shoto as a subgroup that includes Okinawa and the Sakishima.

The term Nansei was introduced in the late 1880s by the Meiji government and clearly indicates where one is looking from—Tokyo. It was never a term used either by locals or the Chinese and it includes the Senkaku group of islands, which are not connected to the Ryukyus geographically.

By the way, the standard textbook in English to present a comprehensive history of Okinawa is *Okinawa: The History of an Island People,* published in 1958 by American George Kerr. It's mostly about Okinawa's relations with Japan up to Reversion and is currently in print through Charles E. Tuttle of Tokyo.

Kerr suggests people may well have come to the Ryukyus from a variety of places north, west and south and that they probably shared a culture with people living in Kyushu, the southernmost of Japan's larger islands. Kerr says vestiges of that culture survive 'underneath' Japanese culture and can best be seen, or even heard, in the use of some words including some of the terms used by the late Showa emperor, Hirohito, when he spoke in public.

Various ways.

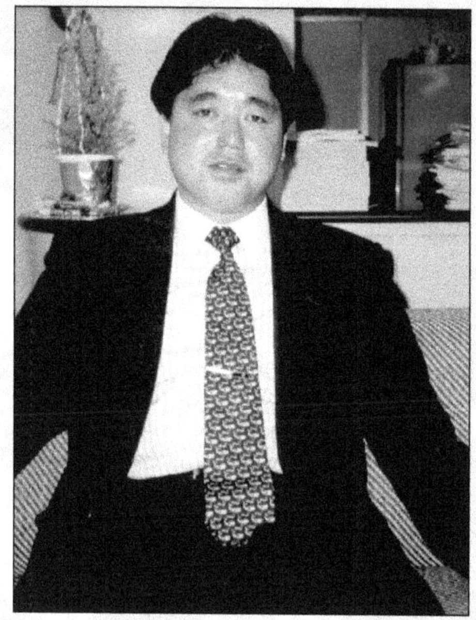

What this place needs is a fun park

Shimoji Mikio

When we first met him at the time of the big upheaval in September 1995, Shimoji was talking about the revival of the great Ryukyu tradition of being a trading nation, and he emphasised how improving the relationship with immediate neighbours such as Taiwan was essential to future development. Although he's part of the Liberal Democratic Party, the conservative coalition that ruled Japan for so long and developed its cold war strategy, he is a young enthusiast who feels untrammelled by ideology—except of course he wants freer markets. The second time we met him, he came up with an even more surprising and controversial option for Okinawa's future.

What future would the people of Okinawa have without the military bases; has Okinawa been too dependent on the USA for its livelihood?

Well, it's not really the USA, it's the Japanese government that's been paying for the bases' upkeep and the rent to the original landowners. You won't understand the situation here if you think of Okinawa as part of Japan. I believe we are different and unique, and we are dependent—almost totally—on Japan.

Can you develop a measure of economic autonomy in the next twenty to thirty years?

Political independence may not be possible, but some kind of change must occur because the current situation is not right. I went to Tahiti recently—as part of the protest movement against French testing of nuclear weapons in the South Pacific—and noticed the similarity of Tahiti's situation compared to ours in Okinawa. In Tahiti they exist because of handouts from the French government. The local population is divided over that—there are people who justify the nuclear testing as the cost of their handouts.

We get handouts from Japan for letting out land to the US military. The kind of change I am talking about has to take place, because at the moment it is killing our uniqueness, what makes Okinawa different. The Okinawan soul is what needs to be revived. Twenty-four years after Reversion, fifty-one years since the end of the war, we have lost our identity. I call for cultural autonomy rather than political independence. But there's a definite need for us to develop our own economy so we can depend less on these handouts and bear the cost.

What can Okinawa do to sustain itself?

Well, at the moment we are protected and we get subsidies. For example, we get a 95 per cent grant from the central government for all our public works construction, whereas the rest of the country gets 60 per cent. We also have import barriers to protect our industries. We can't develop self-reliance and local industries which will stand on their own two feet if that situation continues. We need strong competitive industries of our own to be genuinely self-reliant.

What's the future without protection?

No company as it exists now could survive without that protection, but no-one wants to face this reality straight on, and talk about an 'independent' and 'self reliant' Okinawa. Contradictions in terms. They talk about idealistic dreams but in reality none of them could survive without the protection. It's like biting the hand that feeds them.

Why has Okinawa been held back for so long?

Well, even the issue of what to do with the US bases and our economy is one connected issue. But the same issue, if seen from the central government's viewpoint, is the relationship with the US and its security. That's why there is a wide gap between us and the central government. It is an economic issue to us, but the Japanese government treats it as essentially a security issue.

What would be done if the bases go?

Let me give you some figures on the role of the bases in our economy now. There are 28 000 landowners who agree to lease their land to the government for the bases and that brings in about ¥70 billion. There are 7800 workers employed on the bases and that brings in ¥50 billion. There are 35 000 US service personnel who spend another ¥50 billion and the Japanese Defense Ministry spends another ¥150 billion on various programs such as noise reduction, security, etc. All in all, that amounts to about ¥350 billion. It is not insignificant.

Loss of job opportunities now provided at the US bases would have significant impact. The latest unemployment figure for Okinawa is 6.6 per cent while the rest of Japan is 3.2 per cent. When a new figure becomes available for April, after new graduates and school leavers hit the job market, it will be 8 per cent. Figures like this would cause a riot on the mainland.

The unemployment rate among the 15–20-year-old group is about 24 per cent and 17 per cent of 20–24 year olds are jobless. It's bad enough already and the loss of bases as an employer would make it even worse. Overall, the unemployment rate without the bases would go up by 1.8 per cent—to near 10 per cent.

The rent paid to landowners is not taxed, so that's like having an industry worth altogether about ¥2 trillion.

The base issue has become very emotional, especially since the 1995 rape case and everyone is talking about immediate removal. I am in favour of removal of bases. But rational discussion of just how to get rid of them is almost impossible. People especially don't take up the economic impact of the bases at all. I am not making a value judgment on the bases, but without seeing how influential the bases have become to our existence in economic terms in the past fifty-one years, we cannot come up with a proper strategy. I am in favour of a phased removal of all the bases.

How would you generate enough income in a post-base situation?

Well, that is precisely the point. What shall we do without bases? As I suggested, bases are still discussed only in terms of war and peace rather than what can be done with them. It's time to work out a real evaluation

BUILD UP COVER UP

If you look back at the history of Okinawa, it's easy to see how it's been treated more or less as a colony, a peripheral opportunity, rather like Hokkaido was in the last century, and later, during Japan's great imperial sweep through Asia, like Taiwan, Korea and Manchuria. It was a place where pioneers could go and make their fortunes, and where the army would follow to protect their interests—in the classic colonial model.

Taiwan, Korea and Manchuria were abruptly prised away from Japanese control in 1945, but even though Okinawa never was part of 'Japan' it is still a de facto colony. The special *AMPO* journal survey of Okinawa's predicament, published in 1982 by the Pacific–Asia Research Centre in Tokyo, described Okinawa as Japan's 'concealed colony'.

Both Okinawa and Hokkaido are overseen by the same kind of bureaucratic institution in Tokyo, where the Okinawa and Hokkaido development agencies provide financial assistance in more or less the same way as Official Development Assistance is sent to countries further afield—as aid.

These funds end up the same way too, in a pattern replicated everywhere governments deem a region or lucky overseas nation is in need of infrastructure—bridges, ports, roads, drains, dams and anything made of steel and concrete that cost a lot to build—they pour in. As well as being in the public interest, these public works are the profit domain of the construction sector, and the biggest beneficiaries in Okinawa are the companies that get the contracts to build them—private construction companies.

For the past fifteen years there's been something of a construction boom in Okinawa, fuelled by ODA-style funds. The realisation that Okinawa was greatly in need of such a spending spree came at the same time the central Japanese government was being pressured by outsiders, and its own economic reformers, to spend more on upgrading its public works everywhere, especially in places deemed to be backward, such as Okinawa or Hokkaido. The result has been a massive Okinawan Big Project surge that has yielded great profits to those big companies. Okinawa now has highways, tollways, improved port facilities, beach preservation programs, tunnels, pipelines and concrete breakwaters everywhere. There is no beach not protected by a phalanx of huge, ugly four-footed lumps, known as tetrapods, dumped offshore to assuage the assault of the annual typhoons.

And there is another similarity with the ODA phenomenon. Even though local companies get lots of contracts, a large amount of the government funds tend to flow back to the centre—to profit-takers on the mainland.

A DAY TO REMEMBER

June 23 is a public holiday in Okinawa; but not anywhere else in Japan, maybe because the occasion is too local. Okinawans take this day off to commemorate the end of the Battle of Okinawa, which was really the end of the Second World War for them.

The day was chosen because leaders of the Japanese 32nd Forces on the island committed suicide then. Many locals are not happy about the choice, simply because all fighting did not end on June 23. The generals may have gone but they failed to leave behind orders to their troops to surrender. Battles and mopping-up operations continued. The girl with the white flag was photographed on June 25. The official cease-fire was not signed until September 7.

Any trend towards glorifying the sacrifice of Japanese soldiers is now seen by many Okinawans as implicit approval of Japan's Self-Defense Forces.

They argue the very existence of the army in Okinawa brought them the war, that the Japanese army prolonged the battle in a futile and bloody attempt to preserve the Japanese empire from collapse, that Japanese soldiers failed to defend the civilian population, killed them for speaking in their local dialect, and used them for their own protection.

Talking about empire and commemorative public holidays, Estonians also have a public holiday on June 23 called Võidupüha, or Victory Day. It marks the decisive battle at Võnnu (Ceisis) in northern Latvia in 1919, which ended Estonia's 800-year struggle against Baltic-German forces seeking to re-establish German control over the land and its people.

Following this victory, Estonian and Latvian forces cooperated to ensure the fall of the puppet regime which had been established in the Latvian capital Riga. Latvia regained its freedom and Estonia's borders were secured. However, the Estonians were also fighting their war of independence against the Soviet Red Army at the same time as the Germans were pushing into northern Latvia. In early 1919 the Red Army almost reached Tallinn, the capital, but the Estonians rolled them back with help from Finnish volunteers as well as the British navy and its arms. In 1991, after fifty years of occupation by the Soviets, June 23 was restored as a national holiday. So June 23 has become a symbol of Estonia's struggle to be rid of the Soviet domination imposed in 1940, as well as the 800 years of German domination that ended in 1919.

June 23 is also the National Day in another small nation, Luxembourg.

Closer to Okinawa, June 23 is also the date that Japan's security treaty with the USA was renewed for ten years in 1960.

of the bases as economic entities and then plan to replace them in the economy. It has to be planned from that perspective. I have to say it is simple to ask for their return, but difficult to face reality.

What are your plans to get back to the kind of economic independence Okinawa enjoyed hundreds of years ago?

There are specific ideas around, such as the extension of our free-trade zone at Naha port. It will be some years before Kadena is returned, but Futenma base will be handed back soon. I am promoting a plan to turn Futenma into a sort of Disneyland-style fun park. Because we have so many typhoons, up to eleven of them every year, it would have to be built indoors with weatherproof protection to be feasible as an all-year-round tourist attraction.

You know, so many of our people are now employed in the service sector, including tourism—about 70 per cent—and you can't expect them to go back to farming or manufacturing when the bases are released. So tourism has to be the backbone of the local economy and the bases have to be used for that purpose.

Don't you want to emphasise Okinawan folk or cultural traditions rather than copy an American idea like Disneyland?

I don't mean that literally. Of course our culture is very important, but if you want more than 3 million visitors here every year and you want to get them to stay longer you've got to offer them something—they won't spend more than three days experiencing Okinawan culture and enjoying Okinawan food and drinks. You know why Kyushu is attracting so many tourists recently? We need something like they have in Kyushu: the Fukuoka Dome, hot spas or the Dutch village historical reconstruction. They are all indoor and so have no special season. I believe what this place needs is a special attraction, a focal point, a place to spend time and have fun such as a theme park.

WHAT'S THE THEME?

The Dutch holiday village in Kyushu admired by Shimoji is called Huis Ten Bosch, the house in the woods, and located on Omura bay. It's a complete reproduction of a Dutch village of the seventeenth century with canals, brick-paved streets, a replica of the Dutch Royal Palace and a computerised visual display that simulates scenes from the old country, including the breaching of dykes after a terrible storm in the North Sea.

The Dutch connection to Kyushu goes back to the time when it was the base for the activities of Dutch traders who, although they had a small enclave in Nagasaki, never built anything like a village. Huis Ten Bosch is a well-promoted honeymoon venue accessible from the *shinkansen* bullet-train terminus at Hakata by special red-painted trains.

POLL IT BUREAU OPENINGS

Political re-alignments of seismic proportions have for the past decade been routine to the point of mundaneness in the national politics of Japan—a local variant of the post–cold war political re-alignment which is happening on a global scale.

Japan's response to the cold war materialised as the so-called 1955 system, by which the conservative LDP was in power and the Socialist Party was in opposition for most of the period between 1945 and 1993. It began to collapse when the LDP was edged out of power by mass defections of its members and continued when the Japan Socialist Party relinquished its traditional oppositional role and actually joined hands with the LDP in a coalition and then changed its name to Social Democrats. They jettisoned most of their long-term ideological baggage, including opposition to the security treaty with the USA in exchange for a taste of power. For a long time only the Communists continued in their opposition to this grand confection but, despite the 'problem of China', it seems unlikely that the old cold war confrontation can continue in Asia when it has collapsed elsewhere.

Nevertheless, while the US–Japan treaty remains as the focus of strategic thinking for a majority of Japanese politicians, Okinawa will stay at the centre of the wider issue of regional 'security'.

On the ground in the bearpit of parliaments, however, things are undermining even that.

There are some strange contradictions in this. The new alignments of Japanese politics haven't been taken up in Okinawa—because they are already there. There are strong political groups in Okinawa quite separate and different from the old Left-Right divide, groups which have the potential to change the political landscape throughout Japan. On the other hand, the 'old' parties still exist in Okinawa. This is probably because there is still plenty of mileage in the old ideological divide simply because the treaty between Japan and the USA is still seen as being in place to protect the free world from Communist threats in Asia, and the strength of that conviction is planted right there in Okinawa for everyone to see every day. It's impossible to ignore the Left-Right divide in Okinawa. So the re-alignments that fascinate Diet watchers in Tokyo have yet to alter Okinawa's basic political structure where Socialists and conservatives have resisted the winds of change and the old cold war agenda and the security rhetoric about the clear and present danger posed by China and North Korea actually means something to people—the possibility of conflict and catastrophe.

What is different is that while the 'old' parties seem not to be changing in Okinawa, something else that was always different there, namely the existence of 'other' parties outside the centralised party divide, indicates one way in which Okinawa is in the vanguard of political changes in Japan.

The most significant of these differences is a

'new' political group called the Social Mass Party (SMP). It isn't really new at all but its position clearly represents the same kind of stance taken by so many 'new' parties in the rest of Japan, it must seem to be one of them. Like so many things 'discovered' by outsiders it seems to have been recently invented!

The SMP derives its ideological heritage from somewhere between the Communists and the Socialists, and was formed in the wake of the gubernatorial elections of 1950 when the prefecture was well and truly under US jurisdiction. Its main policy platform in those days was Reversion. When that was achieved in 1972, SMP members considered dissolution but decided to continue. Most of the other parties simply became branches of the major Tokyo-based groups. The SMP never did. There never was a mainland 'mother' party for the SMP. That means the SMP is unique to Okinawa and Japan, but its regional existence is far from an anachronism.

During the Occupation period the extraordinary irony was that although Okinawans had no autonomous political power they did develop a faith and skill in the democratic process. The election of members to the prefectural assembly was taken seriously by politicians and voters alike so that Okinawa developed good democratic mechanisms and habits while many of Japan's other prefectural assemblies were not taken seriously and fell easy prey to dictates from Tokyo.

It didn't mean that voters in Okinawa elected that many 'progressive' SMP majority governments—far from it—but the process has stood them in good stead in the recent drive for a bigger measure of independence.

The election in June 1996 gave Governor Ota majority support from a coalition of parties in the prefectural assembly—Communists, Socialists, SMP, Komei and independents. On the mainland, Komei, a political party fostered and backed by the Soka Gakkai Buddhist organisation, dissolved itself into the Shinshinto conservative opposition group but in Okinawa it maintains itself as an independent entity—in a coalition with Communists!

Political parties in Okinawa have already developed independent trajectories and as regionalism now manifests a stronger consciousness in Japanese 'mainland' politics, more and more groups feel confident about making challenges to the centre. The re-alignment of the major parties and the subsequent development of strong new parties not connected to the established ideological split is proof of this movement.

Despite the temptation for some to see Ota as a national figure with the potential to draw all the regional elements together, Okinawa's role in all this has been less to lead than to demonstrate. It's as if people in Japan now realise what has been going on in Okinawa has been there for decades and as such must be strong, effective and well worth replicating.

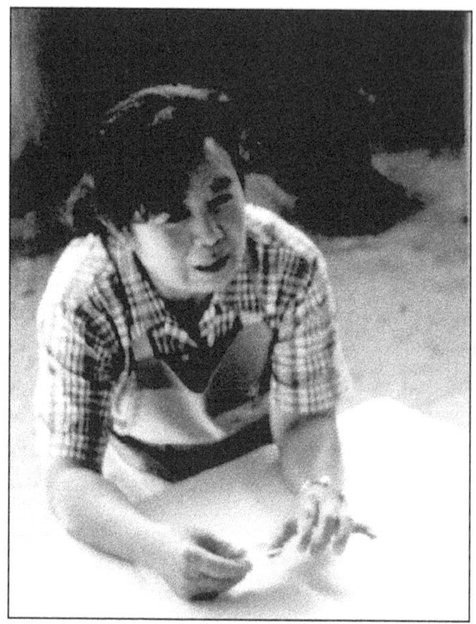

Taketomi Special

Kohama Haeko

The impression of any place will be different depending on the people you meet—not just the people you choose to speak to, but the 'ordinary' people you have contact with in shops, buses, restaurants, hotels, stations and ferry ports.

When planning this trip, we decided to avoid 'international hotels'. They have their own universal 'culture' which fails to reflect or relate to local culture of whatever kind.

In fact, we never made any arrangements or advance bookings before arriving in Okinawa but just fronted at the Naha airport information desk and asked for a list of hotels, business hotels, ryokan, Japanese inns, and minshuku, guest houses.

After a couple of phone calls we found a minshuku, a small ferro-concrete apartment block with three flats on each floor, near the port. Right next to a car park, it provided a friendly enough space, with two adjoining tatami mat rooms, each with a TV set, our own laundry, shower and kitchenette and, as a landmark for navigation home, a couple of gigantic silos owned by a local flour mill company. Hardly a handsome or pretty location, but it was within walking distance of the centre of Naha city, the price was right and the innkeeper provided a solid Japanese breakfast—plenty of rice, a plain omelette, a piece of grilled fish, a slice of bacon, pickles and a bowl of miso soup—and, if we'd wanted it, dinner and conversation into the night. The other guests were construction and maintenance workers, young backpackers and travelling salesmen on tight budgets.

It was typical of the minshuku experience anywhere in Japan but more so. On most nights we would pass by the dining room and see our host chatting to his guests after they'd eaten dinner. One night we went downstairs to tell him our travel plans. We were planning to come in and out of Naha a lot and he was happy for us to leave our bags in his care at no extra charge—and he had quite a lot to say about most things. He used to work on the US base at Naha port, spoke some English and was eager for us to share his personal bottle of awamori.

In the peak season he told us the place would have been packed and our mini-apartment would have housed maybe two families. It was modest, no-frills hospitality and we enjoyed his understated, matter-of-fact generosity.

★★★★★

Arriving on Taketomi was the same but different. We landed at the pier on the ferryboat from Ishigaki, again with no prior accommodation arrangements. There were about a dozen microbuses waiting to pick up guests and a couple of drivers asked us if we needed accommodation, but we had decided to walk about a kilometre to the centre of the island and have a look around before committing ourselves. Not something we'd do in the high holiday season, but in springtime we got away with it.

It was a fifteen-minute walk from the pier, but took less than ten to walk through the 'main street'. There are no hotels on Taketomi, just minshuku, and the first we found was completely deserted. We could have walked in and taken anything, but we passed it by for another place a few steps up the coral laneway, where we found Kohama Haeko.

The amenities at her inn are basic: a traditional house with tatami mat floors—the rooms we had were size six—and there were only two other guests. There isn't much to do on Taketomi after dark, so dinner at the minshuku is pretty central to the island experience. Kohama's daily concern is to make sure it's interesting enough to stop her long-term stayers from getting bored and make sure the recidivists who have fallen in love with the island keep coming back. After one of her plain but delicious and wholesome spreads, she told us about herself and Taketomi.

When are your busiest times here?

People generally follow the holiday seasons and school holidays. Most people come here around the New Year holiday period in January. Students come in late February and March. Then there's an influx during Golden

Week in May, and July, August and early September during the summer holidays. Our other peak time is around October when we have the Tanetori festival on this island. It's observed according to the lunar calendar, so we don't know exactly which date we are celebrating this year.

Summer is the busiest time with an average of fifteen guests staying every night, so I call in some help from the village. Since my parents died last year and the year before in succession, at all other times I look after this inn all by myself. My niece gives me a hand at dinnertime after she comes home from work. I don't want to employ anyone else on a full-time basis, so I don't have any plans to expand. I like to run the place myself, so it won't ever get bigger.

There aren't many shops on Taketomi. Where do you get things from?

I catch a boat to Ishigaki for all fresh food supplies. That's what I did yesterday to get some fish for you after I learned that you don't eat meat. I just hopped on a ferryboat, visited the fish market for about twenty minutes and was back within an hour. The ride only takes ten minutes. Once you decide to go shopping it doesn't take long to get to Ishigaki.

We used to be able to buy homemade tofu here, but that comes from Ishigaki now and there's no locally made awamori either. The old people use the local shops but if you run a place like this you have to go to Ishigaki to get enough supplies. We get a 'locals only' discount deal on the fare. It normally costs ¥570 one way, but we pay only ¥970 return. I don't know if that is cheap or expensive, but we have no alternative. Compared to people who live farther away from Ishigaki, we are better off.

Why is there no commercial fishing here?

My father used to do lots of fishing. He would get lots of squid, and octopus too. My father loved fishing—he was always on the water when the sun was shining. We had to freeze some of his catches. The problem is the demand here isn't big enough to sustain a business. There are fish, but there is no incentive to go out and get them.

Do you know the woman who comes down here from Hokkaido during the winter? She more or less supports herself picking seaweed and through the fish she finds.

There is a prawn farm on one end of the island. It's been going for about eight years. My niece works there. The prawns are sent all over Japan and we eat them here too. We didn't serve them to you because we had them the night before! Sorry, but we have another guest who's been staying here for awhile. We couldn't feed him prawn two nights in a row. They're very delicious, juicy and sweet. Best grilled, with a touch of salt. There were some in your salad last night. Did you like them?

They were delicious. Do people grow rice here?

Because the island is so flat, agriculture is very difficult. There's hardly any water. Until fifteen or sixteen years ago, some farmers from this island grew rice in rented paddies on other islands. We buy all the rice we eat here. There are no serious farms, just gardens really. I grew the vegetables you ate last night. I'm afraid we are nearing the end of growing season though. We can only grow vegetables during winter here. It gets too hot during the summer and we can grow only vegetables like pumpkin and bitter melon.

Were you born and brought up here?

I was born in Taiwan and lived there till the end of the war. I began my primary schooling there, but because of the war, we did not have any classes. I had to restart here after the war. After I finished my compulsory education, I worked briefly in Ishigaki, then in Naha, where I stayed for about twenty years. I've been running this place for twenty-two years. Before that, my parents ran it.

There were twenty-plus minshuku on Taketomi at one time. Some of them had to close their doors when no successors were around to take them over. There's only a dozen now, all shapes and sizes. This is one of the smallest. But as I said, I have no intention of expanding. There's nobody to take

NUMBER ONE VISITOR

The first American bigwig to visit Okinawa was Commodore Matthew C. Perry. He came with four black US Navy ships in May 1853, on his way to Japan. He used Okinawa as a bargaining chip to force the government in Edo (now Tokyo) to take his demands for Japanese port access seriously by threatening to seize Okinawa which, at the time, the USA did not recognise was necessarily 'part of Japan'. His ploy was successful and when he came back again the following year his request was met. When Gen. Douglas MacArthur accepted the surrender of the Japanese Imperial forces on the deck of the USS *Missouri* in Tokyo Bay in September 1945, the ship had the original Stars and Stripes flag from Perry's ship framed and displayed on the ship's superstructure. Shots of it were included in the US cinema newsreels that covered the epic event. MacArthur is reported to have said that US forces 'fulfilled Perry's promise'. MacArthur did not visit Okinawa.

it over from me so it's up to me alone to decide when I quit.

Both my parents came from Taketomi, but they actually met in Taiwan. It was part of Japan then, so lots of people went there to work—now they go to Ishigaki, Okinawa and Tokyo. They had five daughters, including me, in Taiwan.

Do you get visitors coming here from Taiwan?

Yes, a few. They are beginning to come on group tours. Since the year before last, quite a few of them come on day tours to this island on big boats. I think more people from Taiwan will be coming here. Just recently a local ferryboat operator announced the number of services between Taiwan and Okinawa was increasing to three a week. So there will be more traffic and maybe more visitors.

Where else do your guests come from?

You may be surprised to know we get very few visitors from Okinawa's main island—one in a hundred of our guests. Most are from mainland Japan, and some of them come back again and again. The most frequent visitor must have been here fifty times. There's another guy from Tokyo who comes here six times a year. He only started coming three years ago, but since then he's made twenty visits. There are a few addicts like them!

Why do they come here?

They come to relax. They think of it is as a 'home town', a place where they can come and relax after all that stress from work, to be rejuvenated. They come here to immerse themselves in an environment which is totally gone from the cities. Some say they can only get through life because they can come back here. There's quite a few people like that. They consider this place as their adopted home town.

Digging for History

Iriomote is almost the total antithesis to the feel of 'Japan'. The island is full of natural rainforest, white beaches, coral reefs, waterfalls, mangroved rivers and rare species of animals, including the deadly *habu* snake and a wild cat found nowhere else. More than 80 per cent is national park. Tourists come here to experience jungle wilderness.

The island forms part of the Yaeyama group. In terms of size, it's the second largest island in the prefecture, yet it is the least developed part of Okinawa. The island is about thirty kilometres east to west and twenty kilometres north to south.

Iriomote is the only Ryukyu island with known coal reserves. The existence of 'burning rock' was long known to the leaders of the Ryukyu Kingdom. In 1853 it became a matter of international concern when members of Commodore Perry's expedition were in the vicinity looking for coal to fuel their black ships. An important objective of Perry's visit was to find coal in Japan for American whalers. The Ryukyu government's response was to send written orders down to Yaeyama telling people to conceal their coal from Perry. Even if they stumbled across it, they didn't 'discover' it, which some storybooks like to tell you.

As the Meiji era brought full-steam-ahead development all over Japan, the Mitsui company was given a mining concession on Iriomote. Mitsui started operations in 1886 but they lasted only three years. It was too hard mining coal in malaria-infested hilly rainforest. Mitsui was allowed to use convicts as miners. What coal was dug was sold mainly on the Hong Kong market.

After Mitsui's failure, new operators came and went, trying their fortunes. Much later, in the 1930s and 1940s, Japan's war drive into Asia revived demand, but transport became too dangerous; impossible towards the end, and mining was abandoned at the end of the war.

However, before it was all over, it had its own little niche in industrial history, which has almost been totally concealed as nature reclaims its territory.

The most accessible coal mine relics survive at the most recently developed mine on the Urauchi river. It was used from around the turn of the century and lasted until the end of the war. Local islanders were very circumspect in their dealings with the mines. No-one had any illusions about working there, which is why mine workers had to be recruited from other parts of Okinawa and further afield. Initially, miners were recruited with the promise of good pay in a tropical setting, with plenty of food and women. The reality was slave labour and malaria. Working conditions were appalling and there was no way out. Miners were punished heavily if they were caught trying to escape.

Locals would rather go elsewhere for work but they did supply miners with food—fresh vegetables and fish—while the coal company store provided other supplies at hugely inflated prices, which is why so many miners ran up debts, and another reason why they couldn't escape.

When Taiwan became part of the empire in 1895, people were brought over from there to work, basically as slaves, and later, when Korea became an imperial slave-provider, Koreans too came to work Iriomote's mines.

It takes twenty minutes to get to the ruin from the pier where you catch sightseeing boats that go up the Urauchi. There's not much left to see and it's hard to imagine there was a miners' village there housing 300, together with a theatre and a brothel. The land is steep, densely wooded and there are no roads in and out.

Fifty-plus years after the closure, all that's left standing is a few brick pillars and footings. There are no monuments, nothing to acknowledge its heritage, no hints of what went on there, including the fact that many people who died of overwork or malaria were not given proper burials at all but thrown into the river where, maybe, their bones still lie.

The boat people who take you past the mine upriver to look at mangroves, tree ferns and cataracts ignore the place. As far as they are concerned there is no reason why anyone on holiday would want to be reminded of murky realities from the past. Other locals we spoke to had only vague information and no interest in talking about the coal mines of Iriomote. However, if a plan devised by Itokazu Keiko succeeds that may be already changing.

IRIOMOTE INTERLUDE

On one of the long, empty stretches of Iriomote beach we met some young travellers living in the jungle at the edge of the sand. We were alerted to their presence by the sight of a lone hitchhiker making for what looked like impenetrable rainforest near the coast at the southernmost tip of the island. The road runs parallel to the beach for some kilometres, separating a fifty-to-eighty-metre strip of vestigial rainforest between the sand and the road from its mountainous origins further inland. The hiker disappeared through a gap in the jungle and we followed at a distance to discover not only the great white sandy stretch of Haemida beach but also several young travellers camping under the cover of its edge of jungle.

Some told us they'd been there a few days, others planned to stay for months. Hippies, drop-outs, travellers, whatever, they were endeavouring to survive without making too much impact on their surroundings, and from the edge of the water the only visible sign of their presence was the occasional scrap of blue plastic tarp draped in the trees. Most came from much further north.

Osaki Chizuru is from Nagoya. She told us she kept returning to Iriomote because she felt 'time stopped' there.

She and her friends showed us their little tented camp, nestling in the bush, filled with and surrounded by all kinds of utensils, some found, some bought. They were making bread, the basis of that night's meal, to which we were invited.

One young guy said he was a seasonal migrant, who'd been in the jungle for a month and, before it got too hot, would be heading back to his home town in Hokkaido. He was a bit afraid he wouldn't be able to fit back into society if he stayed on Iriomote much longer. He'd already spent two spring seasons there because he thought the island had been 'calling' him. He was never homesick for Hokkaido but thought maybe it was time to move on.

'Yesterday', he said, had been 'a typical Iriomote day—canoed in the morning, had lunch, collected seaweed, did nothing, ate dinner, had a drink, went to bed'.

Osaki took time off from helping knead the bread to tells us her Iriomote story:

'I heard there were about thirty of them on the beach at the moment. The population fluctuates according to the season. Except for high summer when it gets too hot, there's always about this number living on the beach.

'People arrive from all over the country by all modes of travel: on motorcycle, on bike and on foot. I arrived here a couple of nights ago, spent the first night at a *minshuku,* then moved to this beach camp yesterday. I travel on foot. I am planning to stay here for a week this time. This is my fifth visit.

'Here you can forget everything, where you are, and what you are. Time stops; sometimes you wonder that "this cannot be right", but it is real. The days pass by without you realising it.

'The first time I came was because I'd heard of the famous Iriomote wild cat and I wanted to see it. When I found this beach, it captured me forever. I got sucked in.

'The reason I like Iriomote best of all the Okinawan islands I have visited—Kohama, Hateruma, Taketomi—is because it's the only one that has mountains and jungles. The geographical contrast is incredible. Last time I was here I went into the jungle bushwalking a lot.

'People get their groceries at a village shop. At certain times of the year village people come around here looking for extra hands to work in the sugarcane and pineapple processing factories. You sign a contract to work for a certain period of time. They pick you up for work and at the end of the day bring you back here. Some long-term beach dwellers spend a month working in a factory and just camp out here for the rest of their stay. It's officially illegal to camp but nobody makes a fuss. The locals come and swim here during the season.

'We have a good community feeling among beach residents. People come to know about this place by word of mouth. Those who come are on the same wavelength. We often bump into each other at various other places all over the country. Sometimes we make arrangements and appointments to meet at other places. There's a kind of network of like-minded people. Meeting people you share that with is another reason for coming here.

'We get together every now and then and have a party. Life here is not too difficult. There is a fresh-water tap at the end of the beach. We can pick edible seaweed. We can fish. The sea water is warm and lovely. Sometimes I wonder that I may not be able to get back to the hustle and bustle of urban life, but I don't know if it matters all that much.'

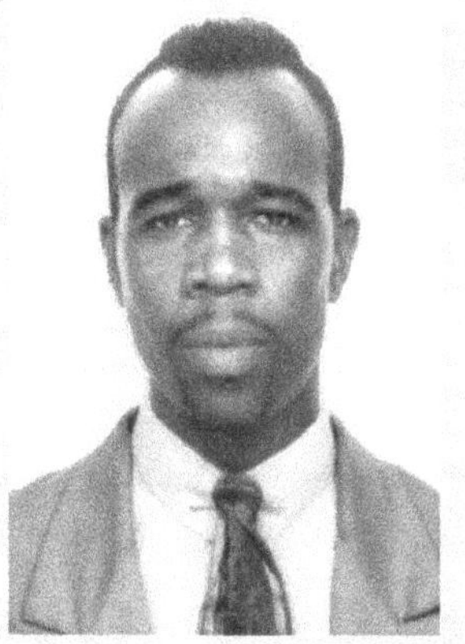

First-generation Okinawan

Byron D. Jones

We met Byron through a friend of ours in Naha who said he was maybe one of the most unusual foreigners living on the island—he is a young American born in Virginia, in his mid-twenties. Byron's *meishi,* or business card, offers his various services, including sanshin performance, English consulting: business and personal, freelance writing and video production. He uses the traditional Ryukyu motif of three connecting Yin and Yang–style symbols set in an eye.

He was brought up on base where his father was a commander. These days he makes a living at various media activities and is learning to play *sanshin* and sing *minyo.* He has been befriended by singer and band leader Kina Shokichi, and the day we met he was helping two other young guys move some furniture into the building occupied by Kina's swish bar and performance venue.

Byron didn't want to do the interview there because he wanted to play *sanshin* for us, and since he likes to do that down by the sea, we scrambled into his car and drove to a headland close to the end of the runway at Naha airport where, between jet take-offs, he talked and played several songs including a couple of Kina's hits, 'Hai Sai Ojisan' and 'Hana'. Before he started the interview proper, he told us, 'My heart is now in Okinawa so no matter how many times I leave, I always got to come back. A lot of people catch that bug'.

Hey, you guys ever heard of a guy named Nishie Masayuki? He's an anthropologist, teaches at Waseda University, he made an

Okinawan dictionary. He does work in the Caribbean. He's a cool guy. I don't think he plays sanshin though. [chuckles] If you're ever in Tokyo go see him. He's a sensei, teacher. I met him at a colloquium organised at Waseda together with the University of Oregon, and they were comparing American and Japanese culture. I got involved with that because I was going to graduate school. I was the only Black American guy there.

You know, everybody had all these ideal statements about America, about how 'everyone has a chance'—you know the stuff—and most of the kids there were from private schools and they had a little bit of cash, you know, and I was saying, 'Well, that's true for some people', but that things were a little bit different. Then these Japanese guys were there saying, you know, 'Japan is homogeneous', and I said, 'Wait a minute, wait a minute', like I was the only guy from Okinawa! So I gave them the Okinawan side too. I finally realised, like I'm in the middle of nowhere!

That was about four years ago. Nowadays they'd probably have a better idea. I got into an argument with a professor of literature from Waseda because she was saying, 'Okinawa is Japan' and I was saying, 'No, it just happens to belong to Japan right now'. Like this was the first day of the colloquium and I was saying all this stuff about Okinawa having its own language, but it was cool and we got to be good friends. I sent her my poems, to translate them into Japanese and she was cool. She's like my mom: real strict—like my mom.

What's this place?

It's Senaga-jima. Today you've got cloudy skies but the water's pretty much blue. It's always like that except at typhoon time and even then it's okay. There's another place we could go, up next to Okinawa city right next to the ocean—Senaba—right by Kadena Air Base with a big, long seawall like the seawalls they have everywhere around here. It's a very cultural place. They used to have graffiti on it, but now it's art, so they left it all there. A lot of it's in English. Couples go out there, have a little barbecue, look at the ocean, do a little scuba diving, do a little surf. I go out there and play my sanshin all the time.

There's one lady, her name was Sumie; she was ninety-seven and she used to come out and listen to me play and give me advice. I haven't seen her lately. I hope she's still genki, healthy. My grandma's ninety-seven too.

The old Japanese air base used to be here, where the new airport is now. It's nice around here. Little niches where you can bring a little honey. Lots of kids come here out of the way of their parents.

I find a lot of similarities like that. My mom's from Alabama. It has that rural atmosphere on the farm, like here in Okinawa, sugarcane too. Lot of people have that similar rural mentality—though not so much in Naha—with the strong female ruling the household, with the contemporary and traditional—like with African-

Americans. People are people, you know. They know about each other.

How did you get involved with all this?

I like music. When I was fifteen I went over to my friend's house, and her mother was like third-generation Okinawan—American that is—from Hawaii. Her mother played *sanshin,* and I asked her to teach me and she said no because she figured she didn't have the time and didn't feel like it, but anyhow, I always wanted to play one. What happened was that being a Black American guy—most of whom get involved in learning about their ancestors being from Africa—I was never able to do what Alex Haley did with his *Roots* thing, to find out what country, what language and what culture those particular ancestors had, but I was raised aware of that kind of thing.

So when I came over here and went to high school from fifteen to seventeen, I got into the culture—I had an Okinawan girlfriend at that time, which helped my appreciation—and I realised that people here had been discriminated against by people on mainland Japan and it was a little different. It caught me in my heart because I realised the same thing had happened to me. People everywhere really, I mean you can be white and Irish and get discriminated against and have an idea what it was like, so I had a clue what it was about: people who had their own culture that was still alive, and a history that was rich and a language that was still being spoken by the older generation—and they're still around—so you can't lose that kind of thing.

Before I started trying to play the music, I started learning the language, because it's here and hasn't been totally lost yet. Anyway, I'm here and it's home and even though my ancestors didn't come from Okinawa, people aren't only what their ancestors were and did. They're also what they are doing now.

How did you get here in the first place?

When I was fifteen, my dad was in the Marines. Either he was going to retire as a lieutenant colonel or he was going to get promoted. He got promoted and we came over. I graduated from Kubasaki High School, right here in Okinawa city. We moved to a lot of other places. When I went away to college in Alabama they wanted to find out about Okinawa and I realised I didn't speak the language—I'd always wanted to play the *sanshin* of course, but didn't—so after a year of having a lot of cultural experiences in the rural South, I came back to Okinawa, saved a little bit of money and bought my first sanshin for 300 bucks. My dad thought, what am I doing spending all that on a piece of wood! But it seemed to me to be a good investment, because people now always say, 'Oh, you play *sanshin!*'

Anyway, I was trying to learn the language so that I knew what I was singing, and use the language too, so that was my first purpose. Then, over time, I actually started to like the music. I still haven't much of a clue about what it means, but I'm working on that. But now the feeling comes through a lot more. I get a lot of supportive people who see me around and say, 'Keep up the good work'.

A lot of the old records start the first track off with the sound of the sea on the shore; is that why you brought us out here today? You like to play out here and hear the sea?

They have a word, *uminchu,* a person who likes the ocean. Well, there's a lot of ocean around and that's where I like to practice and play. I used to work up around Henoko, a little village up in the north of the island. I got an appreciation for the sound of the leaves of the sugarcane down by the ocean there. I used to hang out down by the sea with my friends, hear the wind blowing and the rustle of the leaves—that's like the ocean too. It moves back and forth like the sound of the waves. So when I sit down by the ocean and play, I consider myself to be playing with the waves.

Do you write your own songs?

I used to write poetry when I was younger, and that was all about love and being with your girlfriend, and I'm getting back into that and I write a little bit—but that's my plan for the next few months—get into that Okinawan grammar dictionary.

PRIZED GUEST

Oe Kenzaburo, the Nobel laureate, wrote a book about his visit in 1970 called *Okinawa Noto* (Okinawa notes). Along with Hiroshima, Oe took up the cudgels on behalf of Okinawa's plight. Oe has championed a few such causes but, his critics argued, seems selective in his choices. He is against nuclear weapons but silent on nuclear power and has been criticised for being interested only in issues which portray the Japanese as victims. He has neglected to say anything about the Rape of Nanking by the Japanese Imperial Army in 1937, but he's got no friends on the Far Right because, after he'd taken the Nobel Prize from the king of Sweden, he refused to accept a medal from the emperor.

His books, by the way, are mostly published by Bungei Shunju, part of the Fuji Sankei media group. Bungei Shunju's flagship monthly of the same name occupies the right of the political spectrum in publishing and has supported the 'revisionist' view that the Rape of Nanking wasn't as bad as all that, if it 'happened' at all.

Do you have mixed feelings about the US presence here?

Yeah, of course. If they were never here, then I wouldn't have had a chance to be part of this wonderful place. It's strange. A lot of Okinawan people think that Okinawa is just basically in the middle of nowhere—it's a humble point of view—and they'd be surprised to know how many people in the world know of it. I mean, even in the States there's a thousand at a time coming in and out of here. And you know how in America everyone can say they know someone in the Marines—you know, 'My uncle's brother's friend is in the Marine Corps'—well, everybody knows somebody who's been to Okinawa. A lot of people get a chance to come and live here for a little while.

There is a benefit for people coming here, looking for positive things when on a short stay, but now it's really all about how Okinawa can be more autonomous, and personally, I think they should be able to have their own country. There have been benefits from the bases, more thirty or forty years ago than now, and people do have jobs on bases—but if the bases weren't here, there'd be more jobs in those spaces.

You have people getting paid rent, which is good, and that gets used here in all the projects, in addition to the construction project money that comes from the Okinawa Development Agency. So that money is all going to good places, but besides that, the base land is just sitting there and in terms of being economically autonomous, a lot of people in Okinawa see it as a hindrance. I mean it's like, 'Here, take this money now', but what kind of investment is that?

What's frustrating to me is I have my friends here who study abroad, learning different languages, getting fluent, then come back home here and what are they doing? Flipping burgers on base or selling ice cream. That's upsetting, but I'm going through a very hard financial part of my life right now, so I know that if you've got a job and you're paying rent and making money to support your family that's a good thing. But in terms of personal dreams and aspirations, and what kind of person is a benefit to society—I know everyone does something,

Give 'em enough interoperability

The name Okinawa is derived from two Chinese characters, *oki* and *nawa. Oki* literally means off the coast and *nawa* is rope—what in English would be a 'string' of islands.

When the announcement of the removal of the Futenma base was made, it caught everyone by surprise. Local newspapers printed extra editions that evening. The Clinton administration had already made up its mind and was using Futenma as a trump to diffuse any anger which might undermine the security arrangement system, the cxornerstone of the US–Japan relationship. The Japanese government quietly agreed to be more 'interoperable' as far as its defence commitments in the Pacific area were concerned.

Technical stuff perhaps, this interoperability, but it's a code, a way of concealing a more strategic role in what seem to be merely functional, practical military matters that help guys driving planes and guns to work better together, with less fuss and mismanagement from interfering political fools. Let the boys who know what they are doing get on with it—whether it's 'coalition' manoeuvres, peace patrols or police actions—they work better when people are speaking the same military language. This was what President Clinton and Prime Minister Hashimoto agreed to at their meeting in April 1996. The Futenma carrot was supplied to keep Okinawa quiet.

Bill Clinton's predecessor, Richard Nixon, did just the same. In a summit meeting with Prime Minister Sato Eisaku in 1969, he set the tone for such deals. He assured Okinawa that it would be returned to Japan and from then on its citizens would be covered by Japan's laws and conventions—including policies which prohibited the deployment of nuclear weapons in Japan as a whole.

No-one will ever say that Okinawa has never been used for storing nuclear weapons before or since Reversion, but it is generally thought it must have been. Major Memi at Kadena told us that as far as nukes on the island were concerned, 'All laws were complied with' and wouldn't say anything else. It's the new version of the old 'neither confirm nor deny' answer to whether or not US forces deploy nukes.

Anyway, in return for getting Okinawa back in 1972, the Japanese promised to stop flooding the US market with cheap textiles—the trade friction terror topic of the time.

All this was neatly tied up in a Japanese saying, 'Could we have it please?', which means that the Japanese got the rope—Okinawa—at the cost of cotton thread—the textile industry. We wonder what's at the end of the rope this time.

even the guy who fills you up with gas—it's a waste of talent. The guy selling gas is getting paid but he could be running his own company, that's a very frustrating thing.

The other thing is that if the bases go in about twenty or thirty years, that's going to mean they're going to be fifty or sixty years behind Hong Kong, Singapore and the other 'dragons'. I mean it's not just a question of Okinawa being 'just a little bit more autonomous'—it's not just Okinawa, it's part of the timeline with the rest of the world. So if the bases are going to go, every day that the transition doesn't start, without some kind of plan like Ota and those others guys are putting up, then it's going to be harder and harder for Okinawa ever to become autonomous.

What's your overview of the base issue?

Well, in the USA a lot of people get sad when the bases leave their area. The bases bring a lot of economic stability to every community they're in, but obviously the community there is part of the community to support and protect it; but with the protest about the rape case [in 1995], I don't believe Okinawan people are questioning whether or not American bases would defend Okinawa if aggression came. One part of the Okinawa thing comes from World War II. If Japan had never invaded Okinawa in the first place, and put the Ryukyus in the military thing, they would never have been attacked in the first place in World War II.

George Kerr quotes someone in *Okinawa: The History of an Island* People way back saying that if Okinawa ever got to be part of Japan and Japan got in an argument with another country, then Okinawa would suffer. That was like a prophecy some 200 years before 90 per cent of everything got totally destroyed. Until the time Japan took over during its isolation period, Okinawa was a flourishing kingdom. Nagasaki got rich because they were trading through Okinawa, which was still allowed to trade out. All the money was going to mainland Japan and Okinawa was missing out.

Okinawa became more and more part of Japan. The king was kidnapped in order to bring that about, and from then on Okinawans were second-class citizens. The taxes people in Okinawa were paying up to World War II were more than the government was returning to the prefecture, so there was a minus flow even before the big military build-up here. And after the war, Japan didn't even ask for Okinawa back and a lot of people here weren't too happy about that either.

People on mainland Japan are using Okinawan people for their benefit. There are some areas where there is common good, but not in this case, where the burden of 75 per cent of the military is here. The unique strategic benefit of this island says why, but why does it have to be that way?

I believe that what happened with the rape thing is a perfect example of the people in Japan looking after themselves or ignoring or minimising what's going on in Okinawa. I don't think it had so much to do with the bases themselves, but just that Japan is not looking after Okinawa, so Okinawans have to look after Okinawa and that's what they are trying to do—we're trying to do.

People had a chance after the war to take advantage of American education opportunities. They opened Ryukyu University, that's where Governor Ota was working and he got his education through the American program, and I believe people in Okinawa are grateful, but you want to use that knowledge.

In 1972 a unique thing happened in Okinawa. There was this big Revert to Japan movement. I don't see that as a pro-Japanese movement at all. People now in their fifties and above are pro-American. People younger, in their late thirties, are not so much 'American' and not so in favour of the Japanese either, and with the much younger people there's the whole spectrum like everywhere else, like the US or any place else. But you do have some people who care.

Those who were adults when the Americans came and saw the benefit and good-heartedness of the people, and the way that they weren't trying to discriminate against the way the people in Japan were, whereas those who were young then, or were babies or hadn't even been born, and were growing up in the fifties and sixties and saw basically the oppression—the way the United States government had been dealing with people everywhere else in the world—against all the talk here of democracy.

And then the landowners organised themselves and didn't want to get the rent—they were only paying about one-third of what the people thought it was worth anyway, and then it was fixed by the High Commissioner at that level—all these people wondered whether this was 'democracy', so they thought maybe they would be better off back with Japan. That's when the Revert to Japan movement started and that went all the way up to 1972.

Then of course another unique thing happened. The American government and the Japanese government were talking, but there was no representative from Okinawa there at that whole process. There'd been a surge of the independence movement and there was no time for it to be heard because Okinawa was not at the table. That's what happened from my perspective anyway.

It may all be very significant from an Okinawan perspective, but in the wider context we're all supposed to be moving towards a 'global society', so if you're an independent country, or you're part of someone else's country, probably in the next sixty or seventy years it's probably going to matter less and less, if world bodies like the UN have more and more influence over what happens.

These are precious times, when we have to decide what can go by the wayside and what we're going to keep.

Assume the bases go, there's a lot of land—what would be a good thing to happen to it?

Well, places like Camp Kinser and Camp Foster, the Marine bases, and Kadena, which is like a whole town, just sitting there—well, and they're all right the way they are now with high-rise buildings that can be used—

there's nothing wrong with them. But over there at Makiminato near Naha city there's a whole plot of nothing, it used to be a whole housing area that went down eight or nine years ago and it's still not used. They bulldozed it.

Really it's not feasible to get them back all at one time unless they can use them as is, which they probably could do. But if you're going to have all that barren area and all that billion dollars of loss for a period of time, it's going to be that much harder to get everything back up. So probably they'll do it one piece at a time with transitional periods, using buildings for various purposes.

You know how the rest of Asia has the benefit from industrialisation, how industry has been moving out of Japan and the USA into South-east Asia and places. Well, with the cost of living here being what it is, I don't know—textiles wouldn't be feasible—but if they wanted to make some cars here, put a few factories there for some immediate benefit, well the space is there, right next to the road. That would be good.

Ota and those guys have some good ideas like trying to have a 'new city'. That would be good. There's a whole bunch of land, you could do a little bit of everything. You've probably noticed people here can do a lot with the little bit of space that they have. Everywhere else on Okinawa you've got houses here and businesses there mixed up together, so I think they could make a slow transition to do that on the bases.

If Okinawa is really looking towards making an independent-type movement, it has to use them as industrial places making cars and stuff. If they put about 15–20 per cent of the land aside, it would be a good thing.

When I was back in school I used to think people should put aside a proportion of the rent money. It would still be their money, but it could be used for the future development of the land so that, in the case of it being given back, the money would be there already earmarked. So it would be in their best interests to get the next development up and running.

Can I say something else? I wanted to come back here and work as a government guy and do something that would benefit people. I like what Kina Shokichi does. I heard of him when I was in Oregon from an Okinawan buddy who loaned me a CD, and I thought it was so cool that some guy was actually using the Okinawan language. I didn't know what the words meant but I had this feeling from it.

So I listened to his songs and practiced them with a few Okinawan guys up there in Oregon and we'd play Champruse songs, or whatever, and then I came down here and had an opportunity to listen. And that's when I got involved with them and they were very supportive. Actually, the sanshin I'm playing now is theirs. They let me borrow it so I could study its structure properly. They've been great.

People who aren't so fond of Shokichi, well that's just a typical 'home town' thing. Like Jesus, you know. They weren't particularly fond of him back home either.

Me and Shokichi aren't like 'the best of buddies' because he's a really big guy, but I am like 'the rest of the family', I'm really close to them and Shokichi has put a lot of energy into what I'm going to do. You saw that little Hopi symbol in the middle of the floor at the club, with the white, yellow and red thing. Well, we're trying to get that *eisa* thing. You know, where they got a hundred Native Americans, Europeans, and white guys and Asian guys all do eisa together, so I'm just trying to help out with that. He's a really cool guy, definitely a human being. He's a straight up-front kind of guy.

A lot of people can't deal with up-front honesty. I know that he's trying to do things that help benefit the world and as long as he's doing that, I'm with that. He's a special, unique individual. If I can emulate those things that's fine. It's been a blessing in my life to get to know those guys. Even his parents took me in at Thanksgiving. Some people see me as his kind of *deshi,* student. We never talk about that on a formal level but he said, 'Byron, you can come to me for advice some time'. I think that relationship will get a bit closer.

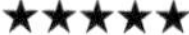

Byron concluded his interview with his version of Kina's song 'Hana'.

BYRON D. JONES

Always there

Traditional Okinawan music—*minyo*—is almost always accompanied by the three-stringed instrument called a *sanshin.* Singers—and that includes all kinds of people who sing and play for their own pleasure and their friends' entertainment—have their instruments within reach at all times and if they feel like it they start playing and singing a tune. It might be a classic, a derivative of a well-known traditional song or something completely new. Whatever it is, the *sanshin* is always there. It's a piece of Okinawan identity and when Okinawans left many took their *sanshin* with them.

Players do not strike chords on a *sanshin,* only melody—or a line played as on a bass guitar. Other ingredients for *minyo* are the *shimadaiko,* a pair of drums with the smaller one placed horizontally and the bigger one vertically, and *samba,* three pieces of wood tied together with a piece of coloured cord and held among the fingers of one hand to be plucked and hit with the other hand, rather like the Spanish castanet, for additional rhythms where needed. The *sanshin* itself can be quite rhythmical.

It was brought in, like many other things, to Okinawa by Chinese migrants who settled in Kume village on the main island in the fourteenth century.

The original Chinese version is believed to have had a much longer neck and the body was snakeskin-coated. The Okinawan version was not just shorter in the neck, but often replaced the snakeskin with a special local paper. But the snakeskinned *sanshin* is still widely used. In the end, what makes a good *sanshin* is not the body but the pegs that hold the strings to the head and are used to tune the instrument.

It was Teruya Rinsuke who first electrified a *sanshin,* though in fact his version had four strings. The electric version is widely used by younger-generation Okinawan acts.

Shamisen, as it is known in the rest of the country, is derived from the Okinawan version but with a longer neck. You can pick up a decent *sanshin* for around ¥40 000.

THE USUAL SUSPECTS

When we spoke to veteran campaigner Ahagon Shoko in 1989, he made it clear that despite the fact most landowners on his tiny island of Iejima were happy to take the rent from the bases, the rest of Okinawa would, in ten years, develop an effective protest movement that would pressure the Japanese government to take it seriously. The prefecture-wide support given to the governor in 1995 revealed the truth of his prediction.

On October 21, 1995, the biggest crowd since Reversion—85 000— gathered at Futenma for a rally protesting the rape. The rally also called for revision of the SOFA and was attended by farmers, unionists, business managers, women's groups and nonaligned people of all kinds. They passed an anti-base resolution, which Ota forwarded to President Clinton before his scheduled visit to Japan in April 1996 as 'indicative of the Okinawan people's consensus of opinion'.

The character of the protest activities we saw at three demonstrations during our brief 1996 stay in Okinawa is worth commenting on. The first was at Kin city, where the US Army has been using public airspace to 'test' its artillery for many years. In April 1996, a public road called Prefectural Road 104, a short, two-lane paved road connecting the east and west coasts of Okinawa island was closed because the US Marines were doing some exercises there. The roadblock was manned by a lone Japanese policeman who signalled to us to turn around. We heard no detonations ourselves but they were very much on the mind of folks who gathered at Kin to protest.

We'd been alerted to the possibility that there might be a big turnout to protest and this seemed to be confirmed when, while were we slurping up a quick bowl of noodles in one of the only places open in the late afternoon, we saw hundreds of children marching with their teachers up the main street towards the venue—the municipal athletics field.

We quickly finished our meal and followed. They were seated in rows on the grass near a stage. A pack of Outside Broadcast vans was parked nearby. It was a bitterly cold evening and proceedings were very slow to start but it soon became obvious that the kids would not be joined by many other people. Dozens of reporters roamed the field filing stories via mobile phones live to radio stations, rehearsing and recording pieces to camera or scribbling into notepads. As it happened the rally made top billing in the evening news and in the next day's papers.

We moved amongst the children to ask them what their views were. None that we talked to had any idea why they were there. Even their teachers seemed ignorant of what was happening and the English teacher coyly refused to talk at all.

Eventually one staff member explained that the children were there to be 'educated' about the issue. The word 'mobilisation' was used and we had the feeling that although it was right and proper for children to be told the facts of the military threat to their own environment another reason they'd been brought was to make up the numbers. Okinawa's daily papers—both strongly anti-base—reported a crowd of 1000 but made no mention of the compulsory attendance of 350 students.

Such 'educational' opportunities seemed almost counterproductive. Save for one women in her forties, the meeting was addressed by a group of elderly men who all spoke at length. The kids shivered and wriggled with boredom as darkness approached.

Later in the week we went to a bigger meet, called by a group of unions at Yogi Park in Naha to protest the offer made by the Japanese government to move the US helicopter base from Futenma to another location on the island. This was attended by professionals and middle-class people as well as office workers, university students and unionists. We spoke to a small group of elderly nuns who said the Japanese government was to blame for Okinawa's problem. However, the feeling we came away with was that this was another 'mobilisation'—more groups and factions but somehow exclusive of the wider population.

We encountered an extreme version of the same syndrome one evening around 7.30. A loud and angry chant coming from a hand-held bullhorn attracted us to about thirty protesters screaming at the Japanese Defense Facilities Administration Agency building in Naha city. They were from a radical Left faction and were surrounded and outnumbered by a squad of riot police armed with shields and batons, two armoured buses and a vehicle equipped with water cannon. There were also a couple of dapper plain-clothes police in chinos and golf shoes who talked continuously into mobile phones.

The group had no permission to stop anywhere en route let alone outside a government building. As we watched a couple of police and protesters tangled in a short jostling match. There was no more excitement and the march eventually set off down the street on its prescribed route to Yogi Park. This march was a very private gathering of like-minded activists with no participation possible from anyone else.

It seems that if the movement against centralised control and bogus international security agendas is to have any real success in Okinawa or anywhere—as those other signs we saw of genuine grassroots commitment would indicate—the struggle can't be left to the usual suspects.

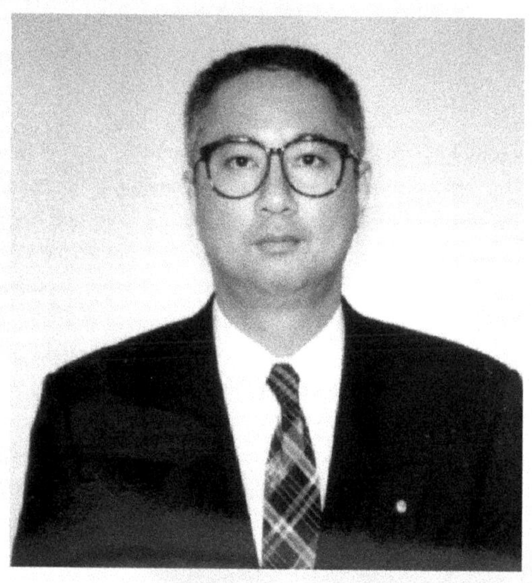

Spirit from the land of peace

Higa Masakuni

Awamori is a special drink. It's strong but not hard, elusive but unmistakable, sometimes clear, sometimes faintly hued, but always different. Drinking it is definitely not an historical exercise. Any bar in Okinawa is filled with *awamori* drinkers of both sexes and all ages and they aren't doing it to preserve their heritage. You don't drink awamori because it's cute. It's much too powerful, real and right there.

Awamori is extraordinary. It's distilled from Thai rice. It has the power and texture of vodka, the fire of slivovitz, or maybe Scandinavian drinks like brenvinn or aquavit, but is much more subtle than all of them, more like malt whisky, perhaps, but nothing like it at all. The atmosphere of the Higa Distillery at Itoman in the south of the main island was reminiscent of an Estonian vodka distillery we've also seen, and the procedure is not all that different.

No brand or label of *awamori* tastes like another, but they all taste like *awamori*. It's the wine of spirits, to be drunk young and rough, or aged for years from huge and ancient textured jars. Its admirers outside Okinawa are a select community of connoisseurs with a very special knowledge that's about to spread. Okinawa's secret is coming out. *Awamori* is set for a burst of international 'niche marketing'—you heard it here. You'll drink it there.

There used to be hundreds of independent *awamori* distillers all over the Ryukyu Islands, but despite economic interference, poverty, war and other constraints the old craft—or art—of *awamori*-making has survived and been strengthened and seems set to grow again. There are still forty-six distilleries all over the Okinawan islands.

Along with so much other Okinawan heritage, many of the old distilleries were destroyed by the bombardment of 1945. The distillery we visited is an unglamorous ready-made factory sited in a light industrial zone. Nevertheless, the Higa Distillery has its own history and is right on the contemporary package-tour itinerary. It's a user-friendly establishment set up to encourage visitors who are fascinated by the unmistakable allure of fermentation, who want to see and smell for themselves just how a bag of Thai rice becomes such a potent vat of unique distinction.

No-one leaves without a bottle of *awamori,* or maybe a clay pot, a jar, a china *shii-saa,* or more likely a litre-sized tetrapak just like a milk carton, which is how a lot of the sacred brew is sold these days.

Also on display is the history of the drink: all kinds of bric-a-brac used for storing, transporting and most importantly drinking. Our guide was company president Higa Masakuni, a suave and articulate advocate of *awamori's* difference and Okinawa's history with a shrewd and surprising marketing angle on how his unique product can be positioned to take advantage of Okinawa's unenviable strategic predicament.

★★★★★

Here you see a picture of a horse carrying huge barrels of awamori in prewar days. That's how awamori was distributed in those days. After the war, as you see here, all sorts of vessels including beer bottles were used to bottle it, because there was a shortage of everything, including bottles. Everyone in Okinawa used to drink *awamori* and before the war it was the only place it was drunk.

What is the source of its unique taste?

Awamori is a spirit distilled from Thai rice and the process is similar to all distilled drinks like vodka. Like whisky and brandy, it matures and gets smoother with age. Good awamori does not hit you straightaway. It should taste smooth and come in slowly, even if you drink it straight. Awamori matured longer than three years is called kusu, matured sake. Often, awamori acquires the colour of the earthenware jars it matures in, giving it an amber colour.

What is awamori?

There are basically two types of alcohol drinks produced and consumed in the world. One is brewed from fermented fruit juice, cereal, or potato. Japanese sake, beer and wine are all this type of drink. The second kind is a drink distilled from the first sort. Just like cooled steam from 'wine' makes brandy, malt-based 'beer' turns into whisky and rice-wine 'sake' becomes *shochu*. Awamori is distilled. The difference between rice *shochu* and *awamori* is in the kind of malted rice used in the fermentation process.

Awamori was originally introduced to Okinawa from Thailand in huge clay pots more than 500 years ago and soon after was made here. Our company is 113 years old and I'm its fourth president. At the time of our centenary, this new factory was built with visitor-friendly facilities. Here visitors can see how awamori is made and learn the history and culture of this uniquely Okinawan drink. We had more than 20 000 visitors through here last year.

Why is it called awamori?

There are three theories why this drink is now called *awamori*. It used to be called many names, including *saki*, believed to be the same word as Japanese sake. The name may derive from *awa*, millet, and some Japanese–English dictionaries do give 'millet brandy' as a possible translation of *awamori*. It might be because of the other *awa*, the bubbles that occur in the liquid during fermentation—when that black yeast is active. The bubble theory gets its support from the fact that the bubbles were used as a kind of measurement of the strength of the finished product. Retailers observed the bubbles as *awamori* was poured; the stronger the drink, the more bubbles appeared, and the longer they stayed. The third theory for the name *awamori* comes from the fact that the Shimazu clan, of Satsuma, needed to call it something distinctive as it became increasing popular when they sent it off to Edo as gifts to the ruling clan.

What kind of rice is used to make awamori?

We first started importing rice from Thailand during the Taisho period. Until then we used rice produced in Japan. We used to grow Indica rice in Okinawa as well.

The Japanese didn't like Thai rice when it was imported some years ago, but in Okinawa it has always been treasured. Japonica rice is soft, it has

Awamori essentials

The quintessential Okinawan experience is drinking *awamori*. It was imported from the Thai kingdom of Siam about 500 years ago when the Ryukyu Kingdom was at the height of its powers. Its ancestor is said to be called *lao-rong,* but there is no production of distilled drinks in Thailand today.

Awamori can be distilled from any cereal. In the old days they used millet, or a mixture of millet and rice, but since the turn of the twentieth century, it has been made solely from imported crushed Thai rice. So, while the rest of Japan argued about whether or not rice should be imported at all, Okinawa was, for years, allowed to bring it in from Thailand.

It tastes nothing like sake, Japan's rice wine. *Awamori*'s close cousin in mainland Japan is a drink called *shochu,* mostly distilled in Kyushu and drunk throughout the rest of Japan. *Shochu* is close, because it was derived from *awamori,* but it can't be favourably compared to the distinctive subtlety of the original.

Awamori can be matured, sometimes in a clay pot, for longer than twenty years. Some of the pots also come from Thailand and a few of them are 500 years old.

We saw a bottle of twenty-year-old *kusu* with a price tag of ¥20000. There is a distiller in Kin who will keep your *awamori* for you in their own ancient pot to mature in a cave. There are many distillers throughout the islands, so you can try out local varieties as you travel, but some islands like Taketomi don't make it any more and have to get it—like their fish and tofu—from nearby Ishigaki.

Good *kusu,* like good vodka, makes a good, quick shot. Just one or two. The most popular way is to drink *awamori* with water and ice cubes. And there are plenty of watering holes, from cheap cafes and restaurants to trendy clubs or karaoke and *minyo* bars in which to taste it.

Some people claim *awamori* is another reason why people in Okinawa live so long.

Interesting to note that one of the first of a long series of crimes against Okinawan women by US servicemen occurred during Commodore Perry's visit in 1854. William Board got drunk on *awamori* and broke into a house and raped a woman. He fled the scene but was drowned in the Naha city harbour.

too much water content. The drier Indica has proven to be more suitable for making *awamori* successfully in our subtropical climate.

In the fermentation process we use a black yeast, which produces more citric acid than the yellow, malted version used in mainland sake production. This citric acid helps stop unrefined *awamori* from rotting in the hot, humid climate. The use of this black yeast is crucial. It's the agent which turns the rice hydrocarbon into alcohol. Mainland sake production uses a different variety but for the same purpose. It produces next to no citric acid, which means it's susceptible to attack by other organisms. That's why they can only make sake during winter in mainland Japan. Thanks to citric acid, we can produce *awamori* in the middle of summer in Okinawa.

Nothing else is added to *awamori.* Rice, water and black malted rice—all natural ingredients—make *awamori.* We use water from Yanbaru, in the north of the main island, where the natural environment is still preserved. It is not spring water, but soft water. It takes about two weeks to make unrefined awamori. Its alcohol content is about 60 to 80 per cent. This base liquid is filtered and we add water to adjust its strength. It's then left for about five months before we bottle it.

Is it really unique?

Yes. Okinawa is now the place where real *awamori* is distilled. It's part of our tradition. The Thais stopped making *awamori's* ancestor a long time ago. It's distilled alcohol and is different from Japanese sake, even though both are made from rice. I want to make sure the *awamori*-making tradition is handed down to the next generation.

They used to say it would not be popular because of its distinctive smell, but these days that doesn't seem to matter so much. I've always thought if Scotch whisky can be appreciated by so many around the world, why not *awamori?* We have had some success making it into an international drink and some of our products have won a few awards overseas.

Okinawa has long been associated with its strategic position as the

AWAMORI TO THE RESCUE

During the Second World War, the Japanese army enlisted five *awamori* specialists in Okinawa to travel to Burma. The Japanese occupation forces had unsuccessfully tried to produce alcoholic drinks for the battle-weary soldiers there for some time. After their failure in brewing beer and sake, some suggested maybe *awamori* might work. Sure enough, they successfully produced *awamori* in Burma, just before the war ended. It is no longer made there, but is now produced in Mongolia as well.

'keystone' of the Pacific, but it's always in the military sense. I would like to use that same word, but turn it around to mean the complete opposite, so I've registered the name keystone and one day, I hope, we can market *awamori* to the world market and call it the 'keystone of peace'. *Awamori* is a spirit from the land of peace.

We have a tradition in Okinawa to use brand names to broadcast our beliefs and messages. In our display there is a brand of *awamori* called Nuchi du Takara, Life is precious, named after the Okinawan belief that life is most important. It's the lesson we learned from our experience during the war and living with the US military. There is a bottle to commemorate the Reversion.

Do young people drink awamori?

Like everything else, *awamori* is tending to lighter and lighter versions. Traditionally, it is as strong as 40 per cent (80 proof), so to target those who prefer the 'light trend', we now make a 25 proof version (12.5 per cent) and even lighter versions. They are popular with the young. The young used to drink whisky because they thought it was hip—they saw soldiers drinking it—but now they're back drinking *awamori,* our traditional drink. You'll see them enjoying it in the local bars. Women drink *awamori.* It's back in fashion.

Are you exporting to the rest of Japan?

Only 5 per cent of our total output from Okinawa is exported to mainland Japan, so we're really only just beginning to penetrate the market. But the people who have tried it there like it. They like it more than *shochu,* the closest drink to *awamori,* which comes from Kyushu. We are marketing the lighter 25 proof *awamori* in Japan and some big whisky producers are taking up its distribution over there. We work through a mainland company that markets and distributes our *awamori.* We just shipped one hundred cases to our wholesaler. I think there's a huge market in mainland Japan and the rest of the world, don't you ?

Aren't you worried about others stealing your recipe and making it like they make whisky?

It has happened already. We Okinawan people think awamori can be produced only in Okinawa, but it has been produced in Kagoshima. Recently awamori made in Mongolia was imported to Okinawa! As with Scotch whisky imported to Scotland, everybody knows the difference between copies and the real thing. People know real *awamori* comes from Okinawa, but it's flattering that they want to make it elsewhere.

Is it important that it comes from Okinawa?

Yes, it's important. That's where distillers in Okinawa have the advantage over other *awamori* producers elsewhere. When it comes to awamori, we have a long heritage and tradition, which they don't. It is part of our local culture. We're proud of our drinking heritage and that's why we've set up this visitor centre to promote it.

Aren't you worried people who come here will discover your secrets?

Not really. We don't let them know the real hidden secret. It's the place that has the secret. Okinawa is the secret. To make good *awamori,* it has to be Okinawan.

Tracing the grain

Early migrant settlers on the Ryukyu Islands must have arrived with their own food cultivation technique. Most likely they brought rice with them, but it's not known exactly when it arrived, or where from: south or north? Ethnologist Yanagida Kunio has suggested one of the many ways rice got to Japan was from China by travelling up the Ryukyu chain of islands, 'the ocean road'.

Watabe Tadayo, professor of rice cultivation history whom we met once in Kyoto, said he agreed with the direction but thought the origin was more likely to have been South-east Asia. He found out the kind of rice grown until seventy to eighty years ago in the Yaeyama region, the southern islands of the Ryukyu chain, was identical to a Javanica variety called *bulu*—widely grown today in the Philippines, Taiwan, Hainan and the Indonesian islands. The variety grown in Yaeyama was believed to be a primitive kind, which could grow both in wet paddies and dry fields.

According to Watabe, Javanica cultivation must have reached as far as southern parts of Kyushu island and even some parts of western Japan. In Japan, Javanica cultivation was replaced when another group arrived, perhaps from the north. They employed a different kind of rice—Japonica—and a different method of cultivation. Typical of southern cultivation is the use of beasts to stomp the fields, compacting the soil to better hold water. Japonica growers don't employ this technique.

Rice is generally a summer crop, but in Okinawa rice and millet were traditionally considered to be winter crops, which suits its weather pattern and water supply.

Monsoon water was the main water supply. On the islands in the south of the Ryukyu chain, rice has two growing seasons per year and sometimes the farmers push for thrice.

The Ryukyu Islands experienced the arrival of many different varieties of rice. It was common to see different varieties of rice grown in one island. Indica rice arrived during the Ryukyu Kingdom days and became very popular on the Okinawan main island. The island of Amami Oshima, for example, would have had *bulu* rice, then the Indica variety arrived, and as Satsuma took over, Japonica was introduced from the north.

Cultivation of Japonica was accelerated in the 1920s when the Ministry of Agriculture introduced a tropical-weather-resistant variety specially developed in Taiwan for Okinawa. It replaced almost all the traditional varieties from most islands.

Rice is still grown on many islands, but it is important to note that Okinawa has never been a rice-producing country in the same way the rest of Japan has. Rice is merely one of many edible plants. Today close to 60 per cent of cultivated land is dry fields, whereas the bulk in mainland Japan is wet rice paddies. In the economic statistics given out by the prefecture, rice is bundled together under 'rice, tobacco, sweet potato, etc.', accounting for ¥11 600 million and 11 per cent of total agricultural output in 1992. Sugarcane, other cash crop vegetables and flowers for the metropolitan markets of the mainland are the main crops.

LOVE IT BUT LEAVE IT

Okinawa has a huge diaspora. Almost everywhere in the Pacific region it's possible to find people who originally came from Okinawa. They may be descendants of pearl divers in Broome in north-western Australia or sugarcane farmers on Saipan but they moved there in relatively recent times.

Many centuries ago Okinawans, whether they were from the main island or the islands of the south, were very successful navigators and roamed the region looking for trading opportunities. They weren't however known for permanently leaving their own islands until recent times. Before they were absorbed or annexed by Japan they made a good living out of 'third-party trade'—buying goods from one country and selling them to another.

In the last hundred years or so, however, like other poorer people living in remote parts of Japan, they were encouraged, obliged or even forced to move out of Okinawa. If they didn't want to go somewhere else to work they could prove they were really 'Japanese' by joining the Imperial Army and fighting in its wars with China and Russia at the turn of the century. But they were more likely to prove their worth as migrant workers to populate and develop Japan's new empire in nearby Taiwan or the faraway Mariana Islands, taken from the Germans during the First World War.

Most of the civilian population in Saipan was from Okinawa and those who survived the terrible battle of June 1944—where many died by suicide as did their kinfolk in Okinawa a year later—returned home after the war was over and Saipan became a US trust territory.

Like other Japanese they also found their way to Hawaii, California, Canada and Brazil. The first recorded official migration party from Okinawa left in 1899 for Hawaii. A group of twenty-six migrants was organised by Toyama Kyuzo, a former schoolmaster and member of the Okinawa Club, a political organisation set up to obtain the right to vote. Another group of forty-five was sent four years later. Migration from Okinawa to Hawaii seemed set to grow until the US government imposed a restriction in 1907. Toyama was also responsible for the first group of migrants to the Philippines in 1907. The economy was so bad at home that more than half the annual income of the prefecture came from funds sent home from these migrants.

Some Okinawans who migrated to pearl-infested waters near Broome, Western Australia, still have businesses there. In the early days a decompression chamber was brought there because many divers—including Okinawans—died of the bends. Their remains can be found in Broome's Japanese cemetery.

In an October 1945 *National Geographic* article, the writer cannot suppress his amazement at finding so many Spanish and Portuguese speakers in Okinawa. Many were, of course, returnees from Peru, Chile, Argentina and Brazil, and any brief visit to any part of Okinawa will soon reveal a citizen who has spent time outside his or her own island in other parts of Japan or the rest of the world.

In postwar years, migration to overseas destinations was all the more necessary because of the wholesale destruction of the war. Systematic migration programs were agreed with Argentina, Bolivia, and the USA. Emigration peaked in 1958, with later movements to more 'domestic' destinations taking up the majority.

Japan's indifference to Okinawa's needs in the years following the sixties forced thousands of Okinawans north to factories in Osaka and the Kansai, with which Okinawa had long had regular passenger boat connections.

Today, a total of 300 000 Okinawan descendants including *nisei* and *sansei*—second and third generation—live abroad. The biggest registered Okinawan populations are in South American countries—120 000 in Brazil alone.

Okinawa is the only prefecture in Japan to hold a gathering of expats once every five years. More than 3000 returned to Okinawa from all over the world to take part in the second gathering in November 1995.

There is also always a steady flow of returnees. You will notice many South American restaurants in Okinawa. When Nomo Hideo became the first real export from Japan's professional baseball to the 'major league' in the US, it was the Okinawan band Diamantes that provided his theme tune. It made them a household name throughout Japan. The song has the same tune as the 'Banana Boat Song'.

What is truly *champru* about this; the band was put together by Alberto Shiroma, a Peruvian-born Okinawan, whose family left Okinawa three generations ago. There are two other Peruvian-born Okinawans in the group. Their music is best described as a mixture of Okinawan and Latin American traditions. There are about 600 Peruvians of Okinawan descent living in Okinawa.

French map of Pacific, 1748.

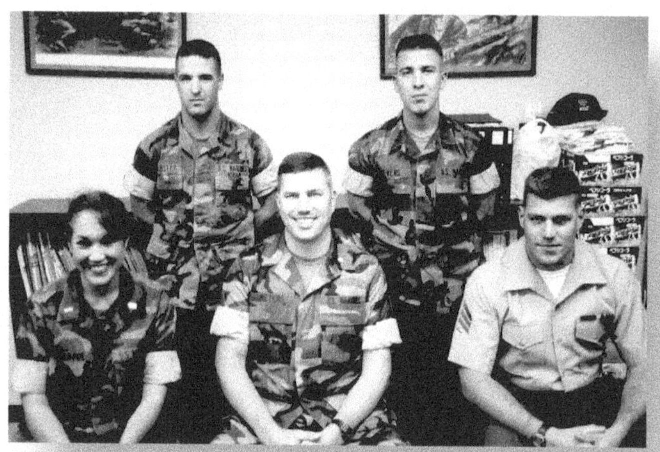

Semper Fi

US Marine Corps

We interviewed five youngish US marines at Camp Foster, each with a different degree of experience on Okinawa. One had been there a few weeks, another had done two tours. Others were hoping to re-enlist. The interview was conducted under the watchful eye of a senior sergeant who scrutinised the events from the corner of the room. Outside, it was typical low-rise functional military architecture, probably from the late 1960s. After rejecting the first choice of a lecture theatre—it was too noisy and nobody could find the air conditioning switch—we moved to a large conference room with oak-panelled doors and leather chairs around a heavy, hardwood conference table, which we quickly moved out of the way.

Marine Headquarters at Camp Smedley D. Butler is perched on the high point of a piece of waste ground cleared long ago of any local vegetation to make way for a great bald sweep of park planted only with flag poles, whose original function was to fly all the state flags of the United States of America. The orientation of the building meant an insidious whistle behind everything, as a howling gale, which had blown up from the sea that morning, buffeted the island like a mini-typhoon.

The tone of the talks was not exactly rigid, just careful. But between the predictable homilies about interacting positively with the host nation's

culture, other views did creep in. At the end there was a brief off-the-record exchange when two marines started talking about how they were mindful that during the 1940s the approach of the invading US forces was presaged with a major propaganda effort by the Japanese military characterising the Marines as 'bloodthirsty savages'. Instead of fighting harder, however, the population was terrified, which is why so many of them died, as one put it 'too afraid to resist'. Marines were not monsters, then or now, they reassured us.

Our first contributor was something of a surprise: a thirty-something-year-old female journalist, Lieutenant Da Capo.

★★★★★

What's it like being a US marine in 1996?

As a woman marine, I've found that we're given much more opportunities than what I've heard about from women marines in the past. I'm happy to see that one of the changes that will be happening is that our physical fitness test is changing. They're holding us to higher standards. We're given the opportunity to do a lot of things that the men have done in the past but that women did not. On a personal level, my experience has been outstanding. I've been treated completely equal in the Marine Corps, and overall it's been a wonderful experience and I hope I'll be able to stay in for as long as they'll keep me.

What sort of roles are you expected to perform on this stint in Okinawa?

I'm here on a three-year tour because I'm with my husband. I'm in charge of the Okinawa Marine newspaper here, so I'm very much aware of what's going on in the host country sensitivities area.

You mean interacting with the local community is part of what you do in your newspaper?

Yes, we try to highlight and focus on the good things the Marines do on the island. They do a lot of community relations, interfacing with the Okinawans. Our dependents and children are interfacing with Japanese and Okinawan children and marines actually go out doing community relations with the Okinawans. We highlight that a lot. Typical relations would be orphanage visits, repainting orphanages and homes—a lot of community activities you would see back in the USA as well.

Do you get involved in finding out about their community, their culture, traditions, music, stories?

Very much. It is different. It is a completely different way of life and it is a big adjustment. It takes about a couple of months to get adjusted to the driving, the different music, television, but it's a fear of the unknown. Once you come over here you see how receptive the Okinawans are to Americans—they're very friendly people, always smiling. I think a lot of Americans may get the perception that it's very hostile over here, but it's not at all. It's actually been a wonderful experience for me.

So a lot of what's been going on in terms of the anti-base movement—you don't feel it's directed at you?

I've found the Okinawans to be very interested in Americans and accepting of American culture. They're very pacifistic people, and so far my experience has been wonderful. It really has and I hope to stay and extend it if I can.

Some US service people end up marrying Okinawans and living here. Is that the kind of story you write about in your paper?

Not really. We mainly focus on what different Marine units are doing on the island and in the Pacific region and what the dependents and family members are doing.

KEEP LEFT?

Under US rule, most of life's framework was organised the American way. Though auto traffic in Japan has always kept to the left-hand side of the road, in Okinawa it was changed to the right-hand side when US military rule was established.

When Reversion came in 1972, many things changed back to the Japanese way, but it took six years for traffic to switch back to the left. There used to be an argument among Japanese that Japan, not Okinawa, should change its traffic flow to correspond with most of the world—where right-hand traffic is more common. However, from July 30, 1978, traffic in Okinawa again flowed like the rest of Japan.

These days even inside the bases the traffic keeps left, which many marines we spoke to said was the first culture shock they felt on arrival in Okinawa.

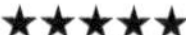

Colonel Myers

Do you enjoy Okinawa?

I love it. This is my second tour here. I was here for a year in 1984 and this time I volunteered for three years and brought my family. We're having a delightful time. Okinawa is a tropical paradise. We get to go to the beach, to tour the island and the little islands all around it. You couldn't ask for a better place to be stationed in the Marine Corps.

Does this 'tropical paradise' interfere with what you are supposed to be doing here?

Well, it works the other way around. I'm the lawyer for the Marine Corps bases here and I've been terribly busy recently with a number of incidents that have occurred, so I haven't had as much time as I'd like to go ahead and tour both Okinawa and mainland Japan. I'd like to see more of the Far East, to go down to Australia for instance.

What's your job here?

I'm the Marine Corps base staff advocate, which means I'm a legal adviser.

That means if US servicemen get in trouble with the Japanese authorities, it's your job to represent them?

My office is responsible for making sure we coordinate those activities with the Japanese prosecutor's office.

What's your assessment of the situation in light of the rape case?

I think any crime is always unfortunate and tragic. The Marine Corps tries its best to do the right thing. We all expect each other to be good neighbours and occasionally there are people who just don't follow the rules, and that's unfortunate, but that happens.

What's the overall reason for the Marine Corps being here?

It's part of our commitment. We've had a treaty with Japan for fifty years. It's a mutual security agreement and it's part of the United States' global commitment to being a force to assist countries in need in the Pacific rim area. In order to do that we have to have troops available to support humanitarian missions, relief efforts, whatever it may be, at relatively short notice and that's what the Marine Corps is very much expert at. It really helps to have that advantage of a number of days advance in the Pacific region rather than having to relocate from the USA.

The Marines were probably the first ashore in April 1945 not far from here—at Yomitan—and they encountered no resistance at first. Then there was a hell of a battle that lasted for months, until June; are you very much aware of that history, heritage, tradition or tragedy, whichever way you see it?

It's very important to marines. We spend a great deal of time involved in our own history and tradition. The battle for Okinawa was a very important one—there are a number of battles that occurred here in the Pacific that all marines are interested in. Most marines who come to

Okinawa end up reading some of the books—*Tennozan* and some of the other ones that are actually histories of the battle—and we consider that an important part of being here. There are a number of tours so that we can see the different battle sites on Okinawa and get a first-hand experience of what it might have been like.

When you went home after your first tour, was that battle the most lasting memory you had, or was it your time in the service and your experience of the island?

I think I've always enjoyed the opportunity to go overseas. I brought my wife and my son, and for them it was the first time that they'd had to live overseas and we found that probably the most enjoyable part of being on Okinawa. The people here are friendly. We made many good friends and we're making lots of new friends this time around and we're really having a delightful time here.

What would happen if the US volunteered, agreed or was forced to abandon its commitment in Okinawa and transferred somewhere else; what would they do with all these bases?

You're asking me to speculate about what the government would do. I think the prefectural government would like to see Okinawa turned into a large tourist site and some light industrial activities brought in to support the culture and the people.

Okinawans had a pretty raw deal, apart from the war, because they didn't enjoy the rest of Japan's boom while they were being administered by the United States, which was less concerned with building up the economy than running the bases. Do you think they would go downhill fast without that economic input from the bases?

There's a tremendous amount of economic impact, just from the

FORTS, CAMPS, BASES AND NAVFACS

Land used by the US military is variously described according to which command occupies it. The Army call their territories different names like *fort* and *camp*. The latter is more common in overseas postings. These Army camps are often named after local placenames such as Camp Zama in mainland Japan. The Army was once the main occupation force in Okinawa but now its presence is reduced, with only one significant facility at Torii Station near Yomitan.

The main force in Okinawa now is the US Marine Corps, which also uses the term *camp*, but they are named for their military heroes and in Okinawa, the selection is mainly from heroes of the Okinawan campaign. Hence such mundane names as Camp Foster, which used to be known as Camp Zukeran when it was occupied by the Army. Camp Foster is still known amongst Japanese by its old Army name, as is Camp Lester (Camp Kuwae).

What is more confusing is the Marines also apply the term *camp* not just to a physical facility but also to a unit, such as Base Camp Smedley D. Butler, which is physically situated inside Camp Foster. It is the central command of all Marine camps.

So if you're looking for Camp Butler ask for Camp Foster—which is why we were late for the interview with the marines.

The Air Force call their overseas establishments *air bases*—ABs for short. At home, however, they're AFBs, with an added F for *force*. Kadena's full name is Kadena Air Base.

military presence here in Okinawa. We shop out in town, we do lots of activities out in town, there's a lot of money that's spent on the local economy that I'm sure would be missed if we were told to go someplace else.

★★★★★

Sgt Todd Webster

I've been here going on six months now. Never been here before. I've been around with the Marine Expeditionary Unit. I've been a marine for six years and I've enjoyed it. When I first came in, I signed up for four years but I've re-enlisted and I'm becoming a recruiter.

I'm a photographer and I've learned every aspect of photography in the Marines and now I'm into quality control and video and graphics. I'm loving it. Right now the Marines Corps is in such a position that everything they do is new. I'm on the cutting edge of technology and everything is being fed to me at a rapid pace; I've no choice but to learn it. It's great.

The US Navy doesn't use a generic term to describe its plots. Instead, more technical language in acronym form is used to denote a base's prime use. Hence COMFLEACT (Command Fleet Activities), NAVFAC (Navy Facility) and NAVSTA (Naval Station). Yokosuka is a NAVSTA and Kadena is a NAVFAC.

The Japanese use the word *kichi* to describe all bases occupied by any military forces and just add the particular command on top, so Kadena Kugun Kichi is Kadena Air Base. In English, the Japanese government calls them all 'facilities' or 'areas'.

So being in Okinawa you don't feel you're in some obscure part of the world?

No. I was very afraid of that before I came over here. I'd heard people talking about it and I thought it was very distant and very isolated, but it seems like the Marine Corps has done a lot to do away with that feeling of isolation that people have had here in the past. We're very much united here with the rest of the world. I don't feel a bit lost or left behind.

You haven't had much time to make friends outside the Corps and in the community, but have you noticed whether your friends have done so?

Yes. As a matter of fact, a bunch of my friends have met people out in town and kept very close friendships with Okinawans. Myself, I haven't got enough grasp of the language, that's the only thing that really becomes a barrier. I've noticed that there's that desire for friendship and communication and I can't speak their language, and although they do a better job at speaking mine than I do at theirs, there's still a barrier there.

We have Okinawans that work in my shop and they teach us different words. I suppose I could really learn, but it seems to me that if I'm only going to be here for a year, when I'm just starting to get a grasp on it, I'll be heading out.

We haven't seen many signs of military personnel off base in uniform, how do the rules work about going on and off base?

My experience of the Marine Corps is that we've always been very concerned about our appearance and it's not got as much to do with public relations as a sense of pride. Our uniform is made for the Marines Corps to do our job—not to wear around town and show off—so generally when we go out in town we wear nice civilian clothes, and we have standards for our civilian clothes, too. We have to have belts on at all times if there are belt loops on our trousers. There are very strict guidelines as to what we can and cannot wear. We don't want to look bad. That's the Marines' attitude. We always want to give the best positive image that we can and show as much pride.

What hours are you allowed to leave base?

We can leave the base any time we want. As far as I know, there's only one area that we're not supposed to be at after certain hours because there have been problems there before. It's a bar district, so that kind of thing happens in those areas, but there are no set hours. As far as our being out in town, we can come and go as we please.

You never had any trouble with local people?

No. They've always been very friendly to me. I've always been concerned about going out on my own but this is the only country I've been that they don't preach to you to go out on the 'buddy system'. Wherever you go, you know, they say, 'If you go somewhere take a friend, don't go alone', but here they don't say

CAPITAL RACKETEER

Maj. Gen. Smedley Darlington Butler, for whom the US Marines' command headquarters in Okinawa is named, was 'one of the most colorful officers' in the history of the Corps, according to its official record. He received two Medals of Honor, one of only two marines ever to have done so.

He was quite honest too. According to Jules Archer's *Plot to Seize the White House*—about Butler's exposure of a planned fascist coup in early 1930s America—he made this frank admission in 1931:

'I spent 33 years ... being a high-class muscle man for Big Business, for Wall Street and the bankers. In short, I was a racketeer for capitalism.

'I helped purify Nicaragua for the international banking house of Brown Brothers in 1909–1912. I helped make Mexico and especially Tampico safe for American oil interests in 1916. I brought light to the Dominican Republic for American sugar interests in 1916. I helped make Haiti and Cuba a decent place for the National City [Bank] boys to collect revenue in.

'In China in 1927 I helped see to it that Standard Oil went its way unmolested.... I might have given Al Capone a few hints. The best he could do was to operate a racket in three cities. The Marines operated on three continents.'

anything about that. In fact, a couple of weeks ago was the first time I ventured out on my own and I had a very good time and everyone was very nice to me.

Where did you go?

I went shopping down the Gate 2 area. I walked out into the street and went to shops and started noticing less and less Americans. It was very interesting and they were very nice and helpful.

You felt you were finally getting out there?

Yes. I felt I was starting to touch Okinawan culture and that was nice. I always look forward to that, but sometimes, because of the job, by the time you get home you're tired, and you don't get out as much as you'd like to.

The sort of people you'd meet would be of your own age. What do you think you have in common with them?

The desire to know what each other is about. I think that bridges the age barrier—to know what other people are like. When you meet an individual who's different, you want to know why they are different and why they think the way they do, and then you want to impart a bit of yourself on them and teach them 'This is what we do in America', and you get a good learning experience.

Have you heard much Okinawan music?

I hear it every so often. One of our drivers is an Okinawan national—he plays it in the van a lot. It's not up my alley. It's not that it's bad music, it's a little too folk musicish for me. There's a band that plays near Gate 2 out in the road and they play some of the best jazz I've heard in a long time.

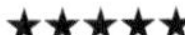

Sergeant Coy

I've been on the island about six weeks and so far I've had a good time. I'm still settling in. Getting around is cumbersome if you don't have a car.

What do you expect to get out of your time here?

Well, you asked what it was like to be a marine. Well, as pat an answer as it sounds, I don't think there's any more honourable, rewarding or exciting way to serve your country. Marines join the Corps for different reasons but I think for most that's a primary one.

Another reason is, I think, to get abroad, experience different cultures and different parts of the world and Okinawa is a perfect opportunity to do that. I wasn't sure how many of the familiar comforts of home that I would enjoy over here, but I've found that many things I am used to at home I can get right here. And as far as those things uniquely Japanese are concerned—scuba diving—I've never done that before. I'll be able to get out and get a scuba diver's licence and do a little bit of that. There's a lot of history on this island and I can't wait to get out and see it.

What about Okinawan food, have you tried bitter melon with tofu?

The only local cuisine I've tried so far is Mongolian barbecue—at an all-you-can-eat buffet. It was very good, but very salty. I woke up the next morning and I thought I had the salinity of the Great Salt Lake in my mouth.

I've travelled a little bit around the world, so I know a little bit about what it's like to adjust to a new environment—and this is not like where I come from, Chicago—and so much the better.

Do you think it's part of your duty here to get to know the people of Okinawa or is that just incidental? That it's not part of your job to create a bond of any sort?

I think it's a duty to do our job and to not step on any toes. As far as getting to know the locals, as much as they would like to get to know us then we can meet them in that respect. But we have to remember we are guests of their country and we have to respect their particular customs and traditions and attitudes. They are very friendly and polite people and they are probably a little more passive than what Americans are accustomed to, but I've only been here six weeks and I've had no problems whatsoever.

Lance Corporal Nevers

What's your situation here?

Well, I'm leaving in about twenty-five days but I'm not counting. I've enjoyed my year here very much. I looked into bringing my family over here from the States to let them experience the culture, but it didn't work out so I'm heading back to the States.

For a family wouldn't it be base culture they were coming to, rather than Okinawan culture? What is base life like?

It's a bit different here than in the USA, where I live off base with my family, but I went on base to work and for the shopping, just like here. In fact the majority of people who come here usually live off base for a year because of the housing shortage here. It's a good thing because they get to be friends with their neighbours, the majority of which are Okinawans. It helps out as far as learning

Lost shopportunities

The old US Military Highway 1 is now classified as National Highway 58 and it's one of the major roads north through the centre of the main island of Okinawa. The southern half of the route passes through country that is almost totally built up, with shops, factories, businesses, car yards and residences. The only 'open' space is occupied by air-base runways and aprons, fuel dumps, parade grounds, military parking zones, golf courses, running tracks and football fields all servicing the US presence. North of Nago you'll find some 'wild' country, mostly degenerate rainforest, some of which is used by the military for various essential preparedness activities, including live-ammo target practice and counterinsurgency training operations. The coast here is mostly taken up by resorts.

As you approach the militarised concentration around the Kadena area, another American 'presence' makes itself obvious along the roadside: dozens of retail outlets aimed at US servicemen and their families, many of whom live off base. Furniture stores and used-car lots, thrift shops, loan companies, bars, Christian missions and clothing boutiques occur at increasingly frequent intervals around the main base area.

In no way do these establishments resemble the bold, colourful image that modern America usually tries to present. This is time travel to downtown nowhere, a transplant from the edge of Western civilisation somewhere between the mid-West, the Deep South and the northern Rust Belt.

This is 'American World', where you can stop off at American Furniture, the Army–Navy Surplus Store, Heroes Used Bikes, Boutique de France and Ye Olde Antique Shoppe, all of which date from the time the presence got its big boost in the mid-1950s, with fascias and fronts picked out in lettering unchanged since the early sixties. There's nothing retro cute about them. This is American culture in slow decline, the peeling, faded, run-down debris of an economy in a trough, persistently outshone by the brash, loud, new neon of the Japanese businesses that have sprung up beside them in recent years. It's a depressing holding operation on which no-one has spent a penny, spared a lick of paint or plugged in a bar of neon for forty years and it shows. The reason seems clear. Nobody ever thought they were here to stay, so why bother? But they have stayed and stayed and stayed to provide nothing but a drab and tragic blight on the Okinawan landscape just as insulting and deadly as the military hardware they came with.

US forces Okinawa badge.

the language goes. It's a lot easier than watching TV commercials that try and teach you the language. It's better to talk to Okinawans who know both languages and can explain what words mean.

I've had the chance to go to town and go through some of the war memorials and the off-the-beaten-path sites, which makes you think a lot about what being a marine is, because of the marines who came through here fifty years ago. I was fortunate enough to get here in time for the commemorative ceremonies they had in June last year for the fiftieth anniversary of the Battle of Okinawa and meet some of the retirees who were still around or who could come back.

To watch them interact with the Okinawans that they interacted with fifty years ago when they came here for the war, you could see the pride they had and watch the expressions on their faces. It was very moving and very beneficial to me to see those marines coming back after fifty years—you know, being by a tree they remembered because they slept there night after night, or maybe their best friend was killed there. It was very moving watching them sit and think back about how it was then.

A lot of Okinawans have mixed feelings about whether they were being liberated or conquered by the United States in 1945; there's still unfinished business here, if not between the Corps and people, then between the two nations, the US and Japanese governments. Does that ever impinge on your daily life? Do you worry about the bigger picture?

I don't worry about it, because what's going to happen is between the two governments to work out. Obviously, I'm here to back my government, and that's what I signed up to do. Whatever they need us to do is what we are going to do. It doesn't affect my daily life.

I can go on and off base as I like and interact with the people here. I don't think it's my duty to do that, but my privilege to get to interact with those people, as opposed to those bases you could be stationed at in the USA where you interact with people who, even though they may be different in different states, are all Americans. Here you're interacting with

GO SOUTH YOUNG MEN

Promising in its 1996 election campaign that it would 'upgrade' Australia's military alliance with the USA, the conservative Liberal–National coalition government has agreed to various measures to boost bilateral ties. The measures were announced at something called 'AUSMIN'—the Australia–US ministerial talks—held in Sydney in July 1996.

Apart from increasing the espionage capability of the 'joint facilities' satellite communications base at Pine Gap, AUSMIN participants agreed to station a US Marine Corps detachment in one of two northern Australian towns: Darwin or Townsville. They will coordinate regular Marine Corps exercises, twice or thrice a year, which will involve up to 2500 marines.

a different culture and it's more a privilege than a duty to experience that.

As far as what's going on with the governments—that's a decision to be made at that level and what they do will be right.

The Okinawans didn't ask us to come here in 1945 and they didn't ask for the mainland Japanese to come here either. Unfortunately for the Okinawan people, they just happened to be where it happened. It's just speculation to wonder what would have happened if we hadn't been here and how the Japanese government would have run this area. They'd been under Japanese control up until then for a long time, and you might say it's just different control having the United States government here, but I think it's benefited them a lot.

If the bases were closed down here—well, as Colonel Myers said, we put a lot into the establishments out in town and a lot of them come here and work on the bases and they are making salaries to support their families.

In the days when the US dollar was worth a lot more than it is now—when the dollar bought ¥360, which it did until around 1972—you'd have been a more privileged person.

Yes, my father was on mainland Japan about thirty years ago with the US Navy and I've talked a lot to him about what is was like at ¥320 to the dollar. When I got here it was 83 and got right down to 73, now it's about even—like a yen to a penny. Well, back before that you were a lot more influential and could afford pretty much anything out in town but now it limits what you do. With the exception of going out to eat, I'm pretty much limited in what I do out in town. What I buy is things that will last for awhile, things that I can take back with me.

Are you buying souvenirs to take back?

Yeah. One of the major things I'm looking for is *shii-saa* dogs. I've been looking for a nice set of those. I haven't found one yet and I'm looking for some nice silk too. I've got a fan, a couple of framed pictures, and a Fuji walking stick, a keepsake from climbing Mt Fuji that I'll take back to the States.

EARTH TO GO

Okinawa is famous for earthenware, ceramics and pottery of all kinds. The tradition dates back to the time when three master potters came from Satsuma, Kyushu, in 1617. They had been brought to Satsuma from Korea at the time of Toyotomi Hideyoshi, the samurai leader who dreamed of conquering the whole of Asia. As a first step, he sent a massive invasion force to Korea, which failed—Japan's last attempt to take over the region until the 1870s.

One of the potters stayed in Okinawa and worked in the Tsuboya district of Naha. There are no pottery kilns there any longer, but dozens of shops sell every kind of pottery, mostly made now in Yomitan village.

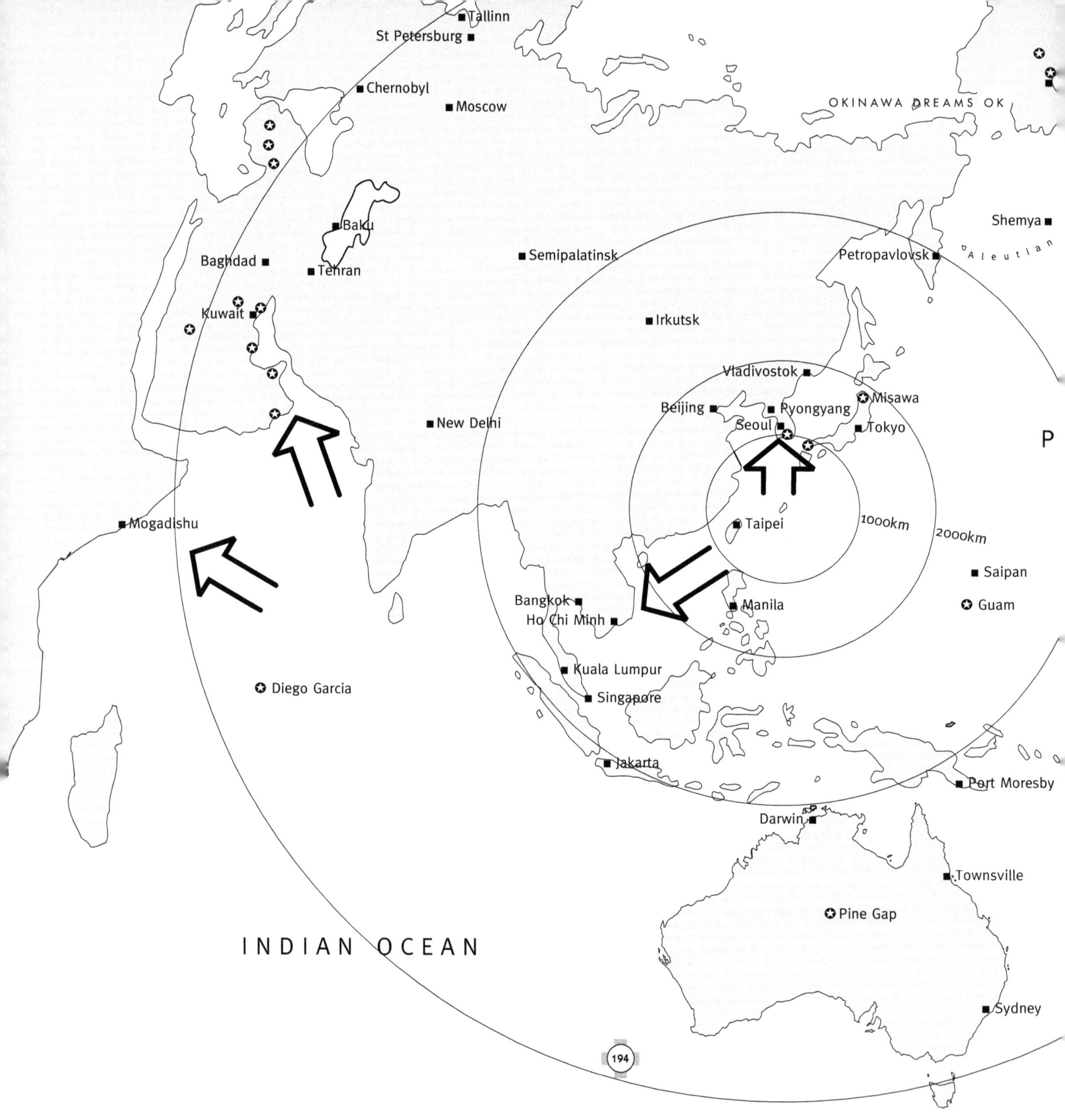
Tallinn
St Petersburg
Chernobyl
Moscow
OKINAWA DREAMS OK
Baku
Baghdad
Tehran
Semipalatinsk
Shemya
Petropavlovsk
Aleutian
Kuwait
Irkutsk
Vladivostok
Misawa
Beijing
Pyongyang
Seoul
Tokyo
New Delhi
P
Mogadishu
Taipei
1000km
2000km
Saipan
Bangkok
Manila
Guam
Ho Chi Minh
Kuala Lumpur
Diego Garcia
Singapore
Jakarta
Port Moresby
Darwin
Townsville
Pine Gap
INDIAN OCEAN
Sydney

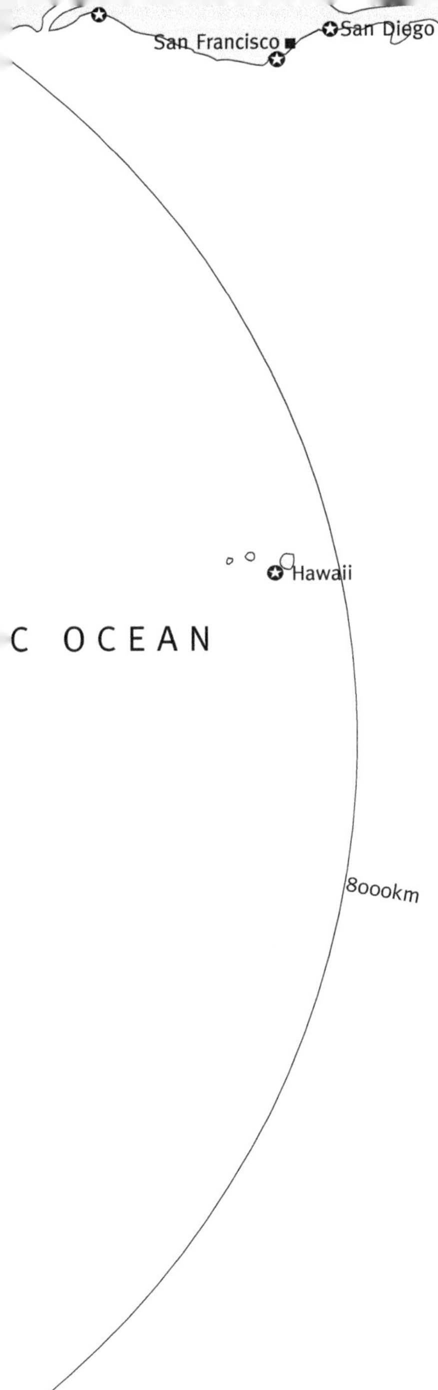

BETTER, AND BELIEVE IT

In general there are less US troops deployed in the Pacific than there were before 1989, the end of the cold war. They are down 27 per cent, from 135 000 to 98 000. US forces deployed on the Pacific coast of the USA, Hawaii and Guam have also been cut back by 15 per cent.

However, in Japan the cut was only 5 per cent, with 58 per cent of US forces deployed in the region stationed in Japan and more Japanese ports now playing host to US warships than before.

The role has changed too. In 1945 it was generally believed US forces in Okinawa had a brief to keep an eye on Japan. Now, their wider role is freely acknowledged, and like all US bases in Japan, they are launching pads for both regional and global operations. Increasingly, the forces in Okinawa are set for global deployment.

A couple of examples: The 31st Marine Expeditionary Unit was born as a result of US global restructuring and its forces in Okinawa are under the same Central Command that covers the Persian Gulf, Red Sea, Egypt, Somalia, Sudan and East Africa. In 1992 marines took off from Okinawa to take part in Operation Restore Hope in Somalia.

The arrows show how the penetration of the Okinawan-based US forces has changed and expanded over the decades since the end of the Second World War.

THE AWFUL COST OF AN AWESOME TASK

Some 47 000 US troops are stationed in Japan as a whole, at about 105 installations, 20 of them 'major'. The personnel breaks down like this: 23 000 US Marines, 16 000 in the Air Force, 6000 Navy, 2100 Army, plus another 10 000 ship-based Navy personnel with the Seventh Fleet, home-ported at Yokosuka and Sasebo.

As US Assistant Secretary of State Winston Lord put it before the US House International Relations Committee, Asia and Pacific Subcommittee, on June 27, 1995, 'Japan provides almost $5 billion a year in Host Nation support to our forces, more than any other ally. This covers approx 70 per cent of the costs of our forces and means that it is less expensive to maintain forces in Japan than in the US'.

The amount allocated in the fiscal 1996 Japanese government budget totals ¥640 billion, or $6 billion—which works out at ¥14 million per soldier.

Around 20 000 marines are stationed in Okinawa and their facilities make up 75 per cent of the land used there by US forces. Their headquarters is in Camp Foster, also known as Camp Zukeran, right next to the Air Force's huge Kadena base. Also in the neighbourhood is Base Camp Butler, famous for huge flags of the host and guest nations, which looks more like a government building than a Marine command centre. It was originally the site of the US High Commission for Okinawa, the all-powerful authority before Reversion, and is still the site of the island's highest military command.

Some land the US forces occupy was directly 'inherited' or extended from Japanese military installations. Others were products of the early 1950s fortification of the island as the military cornerstone against Communism from mainland Japan. It also provided new homes for the troops every time the US government needed to return more land on the mainland islands, usually for political reasons. The pattern began when the Marines moved their headquarters here soon after the Peace Treaty was signed with Japan in the early fifties. The Marines were obliged to decamp from their base at the foot of Mt Fuji and, with bulldozers as well as bayonets, new quarters were found for them on Iejima and at Ginowan.

The same thing happened when the US Air Force had to leave their Tachikawa base near Tokyo in 1958 and Ashiya in 1960. The Army's spy unit was transferred from Saitama, also near Tokyo, to

Okinawa in 1962, and in 1966 the Marines' amphibious brigade moved in from Hawaii. Three years later the Strategic Reconnaissance and Bombing Group came to Kadena and was shortly followed by the Marines' Expeditionary Command, which was obliged to leave South Vietnam, as it was called, in 1971. The most recent forced relocation was when an Air Force special operations unit had to leave the disused Clark Air Base in the Philippines.

While in Japan there has been no major change in troop strength since the cold war ended, there have been big cuts in Europe, especially in Germany where, by 1994, US forces had been reduced by 60 per cent—from 228 000 to 88 000. Reductions in the rest of Europe haven't been so drastic but now troop strength amounts to about 41 000. In Japan, the numbers have remained almost static, although the 'area' on the mainland has been cut by 58 per cent since 1972. Okinawa has lost only 15 per cent over the same period, while troop numbers fell by a quarter—from 39 000 to 29 000.

We're told the reason for Japan's continued importance is purely 'strategic'. Cost must also be a big factor simply because Japan is the cheapest place for the US forces to stay, because Japan pays. Successive Japanese conservative coalitions were sucked in by the strategic argument and agreed to pay up because there was no strategic alternative. They couldn't be seen to be 're-arming' their own military, so they happily paid the USA to 'manage' the region militarily.

Of course, some US facilities are found in the US and some of those have been cut out completely. But if they were all located back home, the USA would have to pay, and if they were based at home, they would have to be shipped and planed to the scene of the action. So Japan's share of the burden makes the 'forward deployment' of US forces in the western Pacific a very cheap option for the USA.

It's been called the 'sympathy budget', words used by the late Kanemaru Shin when he was defence minister in 1978, and the cost of 'sympathy' was then ¥6.2 billion for coverage of local employees' welfare benefit payments. Twenty years later, the Japanese taxpayer foots the bill for more than welfare—just about everything including rent and assistance payments to the local prefectures and councils.

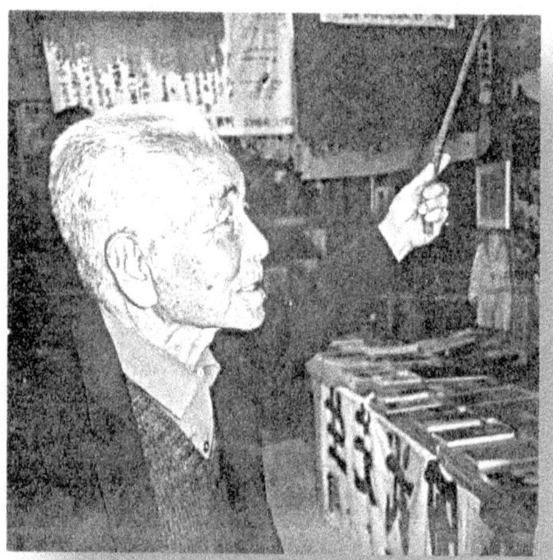

Go home and be happy

Ahagon Shoko

Iejima is a small island to the west of the middle of the main island. You can't miss its distinctive tall cone sticking out just off the coast. It's less than a half-hour ferry ride away from the pier at Motobu peninsula. The island is 22.67 square kilometres and is mostly flat farm and garden land growing corn, sugarcane and flowers. The mysterious volcanic plug in the middle of the island gives the landscape it's only real topography. It takes about twenty minutes to scramble to the top of Gusukuyama and from there the entire island can be seen. Sounds rise up from the ground below and crows fly around at your feet. At the southern end there's yet another US military facility known as the Iejima Auxiliary Facility.

This is really a bombing range. The reason we visited this island in 1989 was because we heard it was the 'birthplace' of Okinawa's anti-base struggle. Ever since US soldiers barged in in 1954 with 'bulldozers and bayonets' to take away the farmers' land for a bombing range, Iejima's plight has been a shared struggle throughout Okinawa.

After their eviction Iejima's farmers had no choice but to wander around the main island begging for food—and letting everyone know their predicament. Their experience set the tone for and offered a strategy to many other places.

Ahagon Shoko was one of the original campaigners who laid down principles for nonviolent opposition. He and other farmers tried to persuade US soldiers to come to their senses. Being an avid Christian and believer in democratic values, he put moral questions directly to the soldiers. 'If you behave like this', he would say, 'evicting powerless farmers with guns and bulldozers, you will follow the same path as Hitler and all the Japanese militarists'.

Once 63 per cent of the island was occupied by US forces; now it's 32 per cent, which has come mainly through Ahagon's persistent efforts. However, in 1996 Iejima was earmarked for a possible host site for some of the Marine functions that will 'need' a home when the Futenma Air Base is returned within five to seven years of April 1996.

Although he had already suffered one stroke when we spoke to him, Ahagon had all the demeanour of a hale and hearty octogenarian. And while we were puffing from a quick climb up Gusukuyama, he strode around his museum showcases with great enthusiasm, a total convert to the shameless promotion of peace. He explained how he likes a modest life. All his clothes are hand-me-downs from donors.

Bear in mind that what he said on this day in 1989 was in the context of then-burgeoning perestroika, but was some months before the Berlin Wall actually collapsed, and the climate of opinion in Okinawa was much more conservative than in recent years, certainly as far as the posture of its prefectural government was concerned.

In some ways Ahagon's campaign is based on similar faith—that, just as one day they knew the wall would come down, so too, the bases would go. Even though when we talked to him he seemed to be a bit of a loner, there's evidence in this interview of the kind of faith and self-belief it takes to persist with long-term resistance in the face of power, apathy and self-interest. The ground swell was revealed, the tide did change, and the earth has moved, which is why this is included with more recent material.

One endearing characteristic of Ahagon's discourse is his frequent use of huge rhetorical questions upon which he then proceeds to expound.

Also of more than passing interest: his campaign to reclaim the Iejima base by stealth and horticulture. He and his friends and supporters have been regular visitors to the base, where they do a bit of planting and cultivation, helping nature take its course, reclaiming the otherwise unwanted parts of the area for more natural or agricultural purposes.

What's the philosophy behind your struggle and the peace museum?

Look at me. I'm just a poor, ignorant farmer. All my clothes and shoes I

ONLY OPTION

Okinawa's strategic usefulness was first proven in the dying days of the Second World War. As quickly as they were captured, airfields on Okinawa were repaired and used to send bombing missions to Japan's mainland. Only a few years later, Okinawa became the only place from where the USA could, according to *American Lake* authors Hayes, Zarsky and Bello, 'launch a nuclear attack without worrying about allied consent'. Before the Korean War, there were no other launch sites anywhere in the northern Pacific.

During the Korean War, the same B-29s used against Japan flew missions out of Okinawa to carpet-bomb the peninsula. The Korean campaign coincided with preparations for the Peace Treaty with Japan—a major reason why the USA was so adamant about keeping Okinawa. Nuclear bombs were not used during the Korean War, but the threats were real and the forces ready. Eisenhower was quoted as saying nuclear weapons would be cheaper than conventional weapons and MacArthur is well known as having advocated their use. Nuclear-capable B-36 bombers were standing by.

It was at this time that the landowners of Iejima were told by the US administrator that their plots were to become a range for bombing practice.

picked up or they were given to me second-hand. One of my philosophies in life is to keep my living standard to that of fifty or sixty years ago when it was enough. I have become very good at sewing, because I have had to mend second-hand clothes. I don't buy any new clothes, gloves, shoes, hats—or even threads.

I'm a poor, ignorant farmer but I have studied a lot. Religions? Christianity, Buddhism, Islam, I've studied them all. History? I have studied everything from world history to the history of local culture.

What is most important? The study of the heart—where you feel right. You have to make others feel happy to make yourself happy, that's the starting point of that study. Peace can be constructed only where everyone is in peace.

I know things about human beings. What is a human being anyway? A human being is human only as a social being. We are made to help each other. Happiness can only be found there.

I'm just a poor farmer but I have fought a campaign against the mighty US military. What is this military? We have to have a global mind to achieve a global peace. We all need to understand that arms don't strengthen you but they destroy you. Both the USSR and the USA are doomed as long as they try to rely on military strength to reign over the world. Both of them.

I'm just a poor farmer in Iejima who has fought against these military facilities for thirty-four years. When looking at the base issue in Okinawa, people further afield, especially US citizens, should evaluate if these bases are really serving their interests. I'm afraid these US bases here are just as bad as the installations the Japanese military had in its occupied territories, Taiwan, Korea and Manchuria—obstacles to peace which are doomed to end in misery. As happened so many times in history, nobody has become happier or even wealthier as a result of war. Nobody. Just look around.

All the warmongers died in misery. There's Alexander the Great, Oda Nobunaga, Toyotomi Hideyoshi, and Okinawan history has Amawari and Gosamaru. More recent pursuits of armed supremacy, Hitler, Mussolini, Tojo and Konoe all followed the same fate. They died in disgrace. We don't want

the USA to repeat the mistake Japan made. We always tell American soldiers this story and that they should just go home, leave us alone, we can look after ourselves, thank you. I tell them, 'Be happy, spend more time with your family instead of wasting time on war'. We need to educate these soldiers to construct a peaceful world.

We have our own way of seeing Japan and the Japanese, and that view has changed over time as well. I have my own ideas but I don't force my views on to young people.

Education during the prewar time was obviously designed to produce good soldiers for the coming war. We don't see the current education as being the same as that but for the preparation for the coming nuclear war.

The nuclear attacks on the Japanese were worse than what the US suffered. The US got involved because of the attack at Pearl Harbor.

We don't just shout, 'Yankee Go Home'. We always speak based on reason. We know that the Americans would not be here if the Japanese hadn't started it by invading Asia.

I thought there wasn't ever going to be another war after the devastation of World War II. Everyone thought peace would prevail. Then this island was turned into a bombing range. It is a place where the military prepare for the next one. One day I found a mock nuclear bomb shell on the range and realised what kind of war it was the military was preparing for. This island, I thought, held the key to prevent that, because if the military could not practice for one, they would not be able to fight one. To stop a nuclear war we needed to stand up.

But how? I became acquainted with people from the UN Commission on Human Rights. They told us if we all objected it would not happen. For the focal point of popular opposition, I set up this museum. We wanted to tell the world what war is all about. About 200 000 lives were lost in the Battle of Okinawa, including 20 000 American soldiers. The museum is set up here to show there is no winner in a war.

People come here from all over the world—almost all schools in Okinawa have paid a visit here. Many from mainland Japan. Visitors have come from more than twenty countries including India, New Zealand and Germany. American Indians too.

We are just poor ignorant farmers but we learned a lot about war. It's basically the act of cheating and stealing and killing, just to obtain some things from others. We have learned about peace too. What we call 'peace' is the condition where we can help teach and help each other, especially the weak or, say, the mentally handicapped; to help us live together, learn from each other. It starts with small groups, the smallest in fact is a couple, and then it moves to larger groups, the community, society, countries and the world itself.

Why can't the US live together with the USSR just as much as Australia does with many South American countries? Can't we all be friends? Peace can be achieved only when we are all friends.

We have campaigned against the US bases for more than three decades but I can assure you that we have never done anything derogatory or to denigrate or harm citizens or leaders of the USA.

> *At one stage 63 per cent of the island was occupied. It's now reduced to 32 per cent. Tell us about your part in the struggle against the bases.*

From the beginning our movement emphasised what is right and wrong for the US. So our starting point was: 'Is the facility here good for the Americans or not? Is it good for the Japanese?'

Our attitude was this: if the USA had been a small, desolate, starving nation we could certainly help them by sharing our land. But the reality was that their country is huge and has more than plenty. They had dollars, nuclear weapons and they'd just won the war. Why on earth did they need this place. 'Go home', I told them. Otherwise what they were doing was no different from all those war crimes committed by the Japanese war leaders in Manchuria and elsewhere. If they pursued the same line, they would be doomed.

'Go home', I told the soldiers. 'Leave us alone. This is our land, where you should not be allowed to walk in without our permission.'

IMPERIAL COCKTAIL PARTY

Other imperial visits include the current emperor, but not his father. As crown prince, Akihito and his wife came in July 1975 to open the Marine Expo. At that time many of Japan's New Left factions were promoting opposition to tennoism, the Emperor system, as central to their ideological critique. That month their activities quadrupled, literally. In Tokyo four Okinawan youths broke into the Imperial Palace and members of the Chukaku threw Molotov cocktails at four places including Defense Agency headquarters.

The young imperial couple experienced first-hand this toxic cocktail of political agitprop when they visited a cave at Itoman, almost on the southern tip of the main island. The cave was one of many in the south where in the last days of the Battle of Okinawa fleeing soldiers and civilians—including school kids—hid themselves and died. Many civilians died in those days—killed by enemy soldiers, caught in the crossfire, killed by Japanese soldiers who alleged they were 'spies'; and many others committed suicide, often under pressure by stalwart tennoists. Four youths who had been hiding inside Itoman cave emerged to throw Molotov cocktails at their imperial highnesses, who escaped unscathed.

The crown prince came back for more in 1987—to open a national athletic meet. This time he was greeted by the famous flag-burning demonstration by Chibana Shoichi, protesting the tragedy at Yomitan cave and linking it with attempts to make the public use of the *hinomaru*, the Imperial flag, compulsory on public buildings, including schools.

Our initial question was why the need to have this facility here. I'd be happy to cooperate with the Americans if their plan was a correct one and acceptable.

They said they had to be here because of their commitments through AMPO, the security treaty with Japan. I thought AMPO was worse than the treaty signed by Japan, Germany and Italy—the Axis alliance—so I told them I couldn't care less about their treaty. I told them: 'If the treaty was signed between the US and Japanese governments, you should go build a bombing range in the backyard of the minister who signed it'. As far as we were concerned, it was such a dangerous treaty and as such we would not observe it.

We told them the US would prosper if they listened to the voice of reason, but they would perish if they pursued the current course of military supremacy. They must have learned something from us because they reduced the size of what they occupied on this island.

We always quoted from Western history and the Bible to counter the arguments made by US forces. It's the Bible that says those who pursue power through swords will perish by swords. Those who pursue strength through the bases will surely perish with them. So too will the people who pursue power through nukes.

We told them. We've walked into the US facility here and 'reclaimed' confiscated land by building houses inside. We told the soldiers who tried to stop us, 'This is not the USA, this is not your territory'. Face to face with them, those soldiers with their guns. We told them they have no rights. 'This is not stateside. This is our land. Pack up and go home!'

Think twice, we told them.

Japan had won the war and did the same thing to

farmers in the US, would you just accept it? Just think about it.' We were asking nothing special. Just common sense.

Those soldiers told us that they were just doing their job, obeying orders. We told them that if they were just obeying orders from above, we would order them as well. We told them to convey that message to their American leaders.

Then we got a written order to remove the houses we'd built because they were 'obstructions'. We told them we thought that's exactly what the fences they had built around the base were, and we asked them to remove them, take them home. They didn't pursue the issue any further after we said that.

We have always had rules in our campaign. We never get upset or speak ill of anyone. We never lie or deceive. We always remain calm. We always respect our opponents. We talk with reason, not with passion. That's how we campaigned against the US facilities in Iejima. For thirty-four years we fought like this and we will just keep on fighting until they are all gone.

Here we all know the military facilities are bad. We are united when it comes to this issue on the island. We have once or twice been visited by noisy but unintelligent thug types, perhaps paid and entertained with sake by the Americans. On one occasion, when they became sober we gently told them what this struggle was all about, reasoned with them to leave us alone because we were fighting for our own land, not theirs, and that none of us would like to see our land used for war preparations.

Throughout our struggle we have received letters and parcels of support from all parts of Japan, but we hardly got anyone coming over to help physically. It was because the US authorities at the time claimed it was only a few rebels and outsiders who were interfering in the issue and the bulk of the islanders were cooperative. We did not want to give an inch to that kind of propaganda and decided to take on the US forces.

What happened after Reversion? The occupied area was reduced by one-

IKE'S PIKE

President Dwight D. Eisenhower came to Okinawa in June 1960. Earlier that year, the security treaty was re-signed in Washington by Ike and Prime Minister Kishi Nobusuke. Ike had intended to visit Japan, and Okinawa was added to his schedule during a tense moment of the cold war in May when a trip to the USSR had to be called off after the infamous U-2 Incident, in which a US spy plane was downed over the USSR. Ike had to pike out from his Tokyo tour, too, because there were massive street demos against the deal he'd struck with Kishi. He touched down at Kadena Air Base and motorcaded along Military Highway 1 to Naha. The friendly US flag-wavers suddenly disappeared and were replaced by a mass of red banners advocating an alternative political system not favoured in the USA at the time.

The red flag-wavers made their point. Ike ordered his motor fleet straight to Naha airport, where he caught a chopper to Kadena, and then flew away to Korea, having spent only two and a half hours in Okinawa.

third, but now the Japanese government and the prefecture [at the time a conservative administration] are paying much more rent so really there has been no change here since 1972, the time of Reversion!

What are you doing now?

Opposition to the US facility has always been from the bottom up and the local leaders used to side with us. But the bases meant money from the government and they basically bought their silence. Soon they accepted the lease agreement and some of them even tried to secure longer terms. In the beginning there were 1000 of us but now only a dozen of us.

There are reasons for the decline. Many have given up opposition because some of the land underneath the base structures has been too spoilt to recultivate, and other land has been destroyed by continuous bombing exercises. They can't see it being productive again.

The other reason was the generational change. Our opposition was largely supported by those who experienced first-hand the bloodbath of the Battle of Okinawa. We were committed to oppose anything that could lead us to a war.

Now they are either dead or retired. We have a new generation who never questions that there won't be another war. Or worse, they think if there is one, we'll go up in one bang anyway so what's the difference?

All consumer prices are on the increase, while sugar prices and the price of their agricultural products are on the decrease, so people have more and more debt and they need the money from the bases. Hence the decline in the opposition movement.

Unfortunately the opposition won't be revived in this island, but throughout Okinawa as a whole, the movement is growing and gathering momentum. It will get stronger in ten years time.

As to what we do here, well we do go inside the bombing range when they don't practice and on Sundays about five,

PYLE'S FILE

Many thousands of US servicemen died in the long Battle of Okinawa including, towards the end, the man in charge, Lt-Gen. Simon Bolivar Buckner Jr, who was hit by a direct hit from an antitank gun. Another fatality, probably better known at the time, was war correspondent Ernie Pyle, who 'revolutionised' war reporting because he filed his reports from his infantry experiences with GIs and marines not with generals and majors. His reports from Europe, North Africa and the Pacific were published by hundreds of newspapers throughout the USA. He was popular because he 'humanised' the war. His dispatches won him a Pulitzer Prize. The soldiers he wrote about had names—even nicknames—and he himself was very 'human', a thin little guy the opposite of the gung-ho war hero.
However the humanisation process didn't extend to the Japanese. In one report he admitted that while they thought the Germans were 'still people', US troops saw Japanese as 'subhuman and repulsive' and had invented the word 'Japes' to suggest they were part ape. Ernie shared some of these feelings, describing some prisoners he saw as giving him 'the creeps'. He also couldn't get over the fact of how at first the invasion of Okinawa seemed to be a piece of cake. The first landings on the main island put 60 000 troops ashore with hardly any resistance—less than a hundred dead or missing. A fortnight later Ernie was killed on Iejima. There's a small plaque marking the spot where he is buried that says the GIs had 'lost a buddy'.

sometimes ten, of us, walk in and do a bit of digging and planting. We just walk through the gate. We're friendly to the soldiers on guard. We just chat them up, give them cups of tea and there's no hostility or antagonism at all.

Sometimes we get a bit of extra help if we've got some heavy equipment to move in. Other times, at weekends, we have picnics there—go in with families and kids.

Some of us have started preparations for the full 'take over'. My plot is facing the beach, so I have to start by growing the trees for a windbreak. We've dug some ponds. Water's scarce here. Then wherever there is soil still left, like my plot, we will start planting sugarcane and other crops.

To plant trees I've grown seedlings here and then transplanted them inside the fence. The US soldiers came to check us out when we were planting, got as close as fifty metres, and let us do what we were doing. We thought they would dig them up later, but they are still intact. It's just the start of a long battle.

This is our message from Iejima. Some people criticise us for our opposition to the bases. There are others who are only interested in the pursuit of self-interest. Peace cannot be constructed by these people.

ANOTHER SIGNIFICANT DATE

April 28 is another significant date in the Okinawan calendar. It was the day the 1952 Peace Treaty between the Japanese and US governments signed in San Francisco the previous year came into effect, as did the US–Japan Mutual Security Treaty (AMPO).

Article 3 of the Peace Treaty states:

'Japan will concur in any proposal of the United States to the United Nations to place under its trusteeship system, with the United States as the sole administering authority, Nansei Shoto south of 29° north latitude (including the Ryukyu Islands and the Daito Islands), Nanpo Shoto south of Sofu Gan (including the Bonin Islands, Rosario Island, and the Volcano Islands) and Parece Vela and Marcus Island. Pending the making of such a proposal and affirmative action thereon, the United States will have the right to exercise all and any powers of administration, legislation, and jurisdiction over the territory and inhabitants of these islands, including their territorial waters.'

And so the legal status of Okinawa was decided. Because the governing authority was defined as transitional until they became UN trust territories, the US was practically given the right to rule indefinitely; and it never proposed to turn Okinawa over to UN trusteeship.

Because their fate was decided without their opinion being sought and the treaties ratified in a parliament in which they had no representation, Okinawans remember April 28 as a day of shame.

While the US administration talked about autonomy and set up a government of the Ryukyu Islands just prior to the treaty taking effect, in reality it ruled by decree, as it had done in the first few months of the Occupation throughout Japan. Many civil positions including the top administrator were appointed by the US military.

Nearly two decades later, April 28 assumed significance for the Left factions in mainland Japan, and they nominated it as Okinawa Day, an occasion on which to mount opposition against the way Okinawa was to be reverted. The New Left factions chose the date to coordinate confrontations against the authorities and throughout the late sixties and early seventies it was marked by various violent demos and bombings.

REVERT TO GOD KNOWS WHERE

Under the US Occupation, Okinawans had no constitution, long-term legal or economic framework and no representation in Washington or Tokyo. They were war orphans.

As soon as it was realised the USA's intention was not to liberate them but to stay, occupy and fortify, a powerful movement sprang up in favour of 'going back to Japan'. Not because people wanted to be under the control of Tokyo but because they believed they should share in the material, social and political benefits of Japan's postwar democracy, especially the 'war-renouncing' Constitution, which included guarantees of human rights and equality which might end the years of discrimination they had experienced. While the USA did replace some war-damaged infrastructure and refurbish some institutions, it was mainly to suit their armed forces based in Okinawa. The islands missed out totally on the benefits of Japan's boom decade of the sixties. A quarter of a century after Reversion, people now look back with mixed feelings.

During the late forties, the loss of Okinawa was hardly even an issue for mainlanders. In 1946, for example, the Japan Communist Party defined Okinawans as an 'ethnic minority' who were 'liberated' from Japan's imperialism. The Socialists were not much different. In 1947, when the foreign minister expressed his wish that Okinawa revert to Japan, they criticised him for the 'violation' of the Potsdam declaration—which confiscated all Japan's former colonies.

As the Left gradually realised the US forces were not liberators and that Okinawa had become the 'keystone' of their anticommunist strategy, demands for Reversion were taken up in the fifties.

By the sixties however the issue had been more or less hijacked by the conservatives. LDP cabinets raised it with successive US administrations and it was on the agenda for the 1965 'summit' between President Johnson and Prime Minister Sato Eisaku. Because of its usefulness to the Vietnam intervention, Reversion was delayed for a further seven years and Richard Nixon set the final date. All the Japanese Left could do was study the details of the agreement to discover what was 'coming back' with Okinawa. The conditions were declared to be 'nonconditional', which really meant business as usual with no questions asked.

The organised parties of the Left had by this time less and less impact on grassroots politics; the 'initiative' was seized by New Left groups—students and other radicals with more extreme agendas including armed struggle and total revolution. In the long run their impact on real politics was just as futile but along with the Narita airport 'struggle', Okinawa become one of the most intense and fiercely violent issues around which such radicals could claim to be bringing on their political Armageddon.

The Red Army Faction was born around this time and advocated a military confrontation with the state over the pending Reversion of Okinawa and the renewal of the security treaty in 1970 as the core assault zones. Both were integral to the imperialist strategy that the USA and Japan were using to destroy liberation struggles in Asia and advance their own economic interests.

The Chukaku-ha, or Middle Core Faction, wanted Okinawa back without the military bases, to deprive the USA of its forward fortress in Asia. The Marxist-Leninist Faction claimed the mainland Japanese people and its government had no right to determine the future and that only Okinawans should decide their future. The Kakumaru-ha urged people to throw out the Reversion agreement because it was a 'bourgeois' solution.

Okinawa Day on April 28 became a rallying point in both 1969 and 1970, with tens of thousands protesting in Okinawa and throughout Japan. Many were not aligned to factions and the wild riot in Koza on December 20, 1970, was less political than spontaneous. But the radicals were definitely 'focussed' in their rage. On the night the goverment signed the Reversion treaty—June 17, 1971—as more than 100 000 marched throughout the nation in protest, for the first time in the country a steel pipe bomb was hurled against riot police, injuring thirty-seven. It was thrown by a member of the Red Army Faction—nine of whom had already successfully carried out Japan's first plane hijacking in March 1970.

All attempts to stop Reversion failed and the bill was ratified in the Diet on November 24, 1971, but nationwide rallies continued and the radicals became more desperate in their zeal.

In September 1971, four Chukaku 'affiliate' youth members from Okinawa rammed a car into the Imperial Palace, throwing Molotov cocktails. On November 14 a riot engulfed the Shibuya district of the capital and a policeman was burnt to death in a street fight with Chukaku members. The faction lost one of its members too—incinerated when Molotov cocktails she and her comrades were carrying went off in a packed Yamanote loop train. There were 300 arrests but for twenty-four hours pitched battles were the order of day and night through the business district of Hibiya.

Once it reverted, Okinawa more or less disappeared from the mainland political agenda—until recently. The New Left factions either destroyed themselves or each other and their strategy of armed struggle was ignored by the majority of people.

Many Okinawans see the post-Reversion period as one of lost opportunity. The Japanese government pumped money in but it was never enough to make a difference. Okinawans still resented being treated as second-class citizens and the intense discrimination they experienced during the colonial period of Meiji and Showa Japan was not dispelled by the fruits of democracy. The Okinawan standard of living fell even further behind the national standard.

Successive Tokyo administrations never questioned Okinawa's value to the USA for its 'forward deployment' of forces, or took notice of the wishes of the locals for the reduction of the bases. Cold war considerations came first. Okinawa's 'usefulness' outweighed any need to rectify discrimination and inequity. Okinawa continued to be the 'internal colony'.

Okinawans have learned that their agenda has not been compatible with that of Tokyo and they are as passionate in their critique of the central authority as they are of the military presence. Beneath the rage and resentment against the bases there's an undeniable desire for autonomy, a feeling shaped by the broken promises of Reversion. The rest of Japan is learning that such attitudes need not be unique. Many people around the 'edges' have similar grievances and are watching hopefully to see if and how Okinawans achieve greater independence.

THANKS

THANKS TO...

Everyone we interviewed and those we met on the road;

- Tazaki Satoshi (Power House), Naha and Chinai Yoshifumi (Tenku Kikaku), who helped us organise meetings and interviews and were a continual source of general inspiration, and on earlier visits, Inamine Toshio and Taira Yoshiyuki;
- RAI Rome and Roz Cheney, editor, ABC Radio Audio Arts, Sydney, without whom we would not have gone to Okinawa in 1996;
- Kawabata Hideki (military expert) for fact-checking; Saijo Tetsuo *(Insider)* for his continuing support;
- the Okinawan Prefectural Government at Naha for whatever information we asked for—including permission to reproduce the prefectural logo;
- various people who introduced us to Okinawan music, in particular: Hosono Haruomi, Kubota Makoto, Sakamoto Ryuichi and Sandii; also Kamiya Kazuyoshi (Disk Akabana) and Watanabe Kenichi;
- Roger Grierson (Polygram Music Australia) for music and general encouragement;
- Geoff Parish, Sharon Davis and Roger Deakin for their assistance;
- as usual, Imbi Hepner and David Mardiste in Tallinn, who helped us keep in touch with Estonia;
- our publisher, for much faith and trust;
- Blixa Bargeld, who, after reading *Higher than Heaven,* introduced us to Die Gestalten Verlag, which, by the way has published *Hör mit Schmerzen* (Listen with pain), a biography by film director Klaus Maeck of Blixa's band, Einstürzende Neubauten;
- the crew at Randle Street, and our immediate family members, friends, fellow travellers, cyber guest workers and mentors far too many to mention individually, but they must know who they are by now.

This book would never have been possible without help and encouragement from all these people; however, all editorial responsibility lies with the authors.

PICTURE CREDITS

Where not in the public domain, we have made a reasonable effort to contact all relevant copyright holders of illustrations.
Front-cover art: based on an old postcard titled 'Okinawa. Beautiful', believed to have been produced around 1941.
Video grabs, album covers, stills and film posters are credited.

RESOURCES

Japanese-language sources are listed with an English translation for readers' information.

BOOKS

Ahagon Shoko 1985, *Beigun to nomin* (US forces and the farmers), Iwanami, Tokyo
Arasaki Moriteru 1987, *Nihon ni natta Okinawa* (The Okinawa which has become Japan), Yubikaku, Tokyo
Archer, Jules 1973, *The Plot to Seize the White House,* Hawthorn Books, New York
Bartu, Friedemann 1993, *The Ugly Japanese,* Yenbooks, Tokyo
Bowring, Richard & Kornicki, Peter (eds) 1993, *The Cambridge Encyclopaedia of Japan,* Cambridge University Press, Cambridge
Chibana Shoichi 1992, *Burning the Rising Sun,* South Wind, Kyoto
—1996, *Moeru Okinawa, Yuragu AMPO* (Okinawa's outrage undermines AMPO), Shakai Hihyo Sha, Tokyo
Dennis, Felix & Simmons, Paul 1974, *The Beginner's Guide to Kung-fu,* Wildwood House, London
Dower, John 1986, *War without Mercy,* Pantheon, New York
—1993, *Japan in War and Peace,* New Press, New York
Feifer, George 1992, *Tennozan: The Battle of Okinawa and the Atomic Bomb,* Tickner & Fields, New York
Fitzgerald, James 1988, *Soviet-American Relations in the Nuclear Age,* Nelson, Melbourne
Gow, Ian 1986, *Okinawa 1945: Gateway to Japan,* Grub Street, London
Griffin, Richard 1964, *Fodor's Guide to Japan and East Asia,* Fodor, London
Hayes, Peter, Zarsky, Lyuba & Bello, Walden 1986, *American Lake: Nuclear Peril in the Pacific,* Penguin Australia, Ringwood
Higa Tomiko 1991, *The Girl with the White Flag,* Kodansha, Tokyo
Higa Kobun & Iwadare Hiroshi 1994, *Okinawa nyumon* (Introduction to Okinawa), Dojidaisha, Tokyo
Higaonna Morio 1993, *Traditional Karate-do: Okinawa Goju Ryu,* Sugawara Martial Arts, Tokyo
Ienaga Saburo 1978, *The Pacific War, 1931–45,* Random House, New York
Katz, Ephraim 1994, *The Film Encyclopedia,* Harper, New York
Kerr, George H. 1989, *Okinawa: The History of an Island People,* Tuttle, Tokyo
Lieven, Anatol 1994, *The Baltic Revolution,* Yale University Press, New Haven
Matlin, Leonard 1988, *TV & Video Guide,* Signet, New York
Matsumoto Kayoko 1984, *Goya ryori 60 sen* (Sixty recipes using bitter melon), Shinnihon Kyoiku Tosho, Shimonoseki
Miki Takeshi 1990, *Iriomote tanko gaishi* (Condensed history of mining in Iriomote), Hirugi, Naha
Nakata Toichi 1996, *'To and from Fiction: Imamura Shohei Interviewed',* Projections 6, Boorman, John & Donohue, Walter (eds), Faber & Faber, London
Oe Kenzaburo 1989, *Okinawa noto* (Okinawa notes), Iwanami, Tokyo
Okinawa Times (ed.) 1973, *Okinawa no shogen* (Testimonies from Okinawa), Okinawa Times, Naha
Ota Masahide 1984, *The Battle of Okinawa,* Kume, Tokyo
—1982, *Okinawa: Senso to heiwa* (Okinawa: war and peace), Shakai shinsho, Tokyo
Reynolds, Clark G. 1990, *War in the Pacific,* Military Press, New York
Ryukyu Shimpo (ed.) 1993, *Ehagaki ni miru Okinawa* (Okinawa captured on postcards), Ryukyu Shimpo, Naha
—1993, *Mukashi Okinawa* (Old Okinawa), Ryukyu Shimpo, Naha
Skates, John Ray 1994, *The Invasion of Japan,* University of South Carolina Press, Columbia
Spector, Ronald H. 1985, *Eagle against the Sun,* Free Press, New York
Salaman, Redcliffe N. 1949, *The History and Social Influence of the Potato,* Cambridge University Press, Cambridge
Steinberg, Rafael 1978, *Island Fighting,* Time-Life Books, Alexandria, Virginia
Takaki, Ronald 1995, *Hiroshima: Why America Dropped the Atomic Bomb,* Little, Brown, Boston
Tamamori Terunobu & James, John C. 1995, *A Minute Guide to Okinawa: Society and Economy,* Bank of the Ryukyus International Foundation, Naha

Takasawa Koji, Takagi Masayuki & Kurata Keisei 1995, *Shinsayoku nijunenshi* (Twenty-year history of the new left), Shinsensha, Tokyo

Takara Kurayoshi 1993, *Ryukyu Okoku* (The Ryukyu kingdom), Iwanami, Tokyo

—1994, *Okinawa rekishi monogatari* (Tales from Okinawa's history), Hirugisha, Naha

Takemoto Shozo 1985, *Daikan kokuki gekitsui jiken: Giwaku no koseki* (Shooting down of the KAL plane: Traits of suspicion), Ushio shuppan, Tokyo

Tenku Kikaku (ed.) 1992, *Uchina Pop: Okinawa Culture Book* (Okinawa pop: Okinawa culture book), Tokyo Shoseki, Tokyo

Tanimichi Kenta (ed.) 1996, *Fensu no muko no Amerika tanken* (Expedition to the USA across the fence), Sand K, Tokyo

Teruya Rinken 1995, *Nankuru gurashi* (A take-it-easy life), Chikuma Shobo, Tokyo

Toland, John 1970, *The Rising Sun,* Random House, New York

Tomiki Kenji 1988, *'Karate', Encyclopedia of Japan,* vol. 4, Kodansha, Tokyo

Watabe Tadayo (ed.) 1987, *Ine no Ajia shi* (The history of rice in Asia), 3 vols, Shogakukan, Tokyo

Yanagida Kunio 1993, *Kaijo no Michi* (The ocean road), Iwanami Bunko, Tokyo

MAGAZINES AND JOURNALS

AMPO: *Japan-Asia Quarterly Review* 1982, vol. 14, no. 4

—1996, vol. 27, no. 1

Campbell, Duncan 1985, 'What Really Happened to KE 007', *New Statesman,* Apr. 26

Duncan, David D. 1945, 'Okinawa: Threshold to Japan', *National Geographic,* vol. 87, no. 4, Oct.

Hayashi Rumi 1996, 'Okinawa ga kataru' (Okinawa talks), *Weekly Asahi Graph,* Mar. 29

Katayama Masahiko 1984, 'Daikan kokuki gekitsui jiken no kyojitsu' (Myths of the KAL downing), Sekai, Mar.

Masuo Yoshitaro 1985, 'Daikan kokuki jiken to jieitai' (Shooting down of KAL and the SDF), Sekai, May

Okinawa Rito Joho (Guidebook to the Okinawan islands), 1996, spring

Pearce, Fred 1996, 'Living Sea Walls Keep Floods at Bay', *New Scientist,* June 1

Pearson, David 1984, 'K.A.L. 007: What the U.S. Knew and When We Knew It', *Nation,* Aug. 18–25

Pearson, David & Keppel, John 1985, 'New Pieces in the Puzzle of Flight 007', *Nation,* Aug. 17–24

Schwartz, William L. 1945, 'Peacetime Rambles in the Ryukyus', *National Geographic,* vol. 87, no. 5, May

Ukai Teruyoshi 1991, 'Okinawa: Desecration of the Spirit', *AMPO,* vol. 22, no. 4

Walker, J. Samuel 1995, 'History, Collective Memory and the Decision to Use the Bomb', *Diplomatic History,* vol. 19, no. 2

Yoshioka Shinobu 1996, 'NHK kaitai shinsho' (White paper on dissolution of the NHK), *Shincho* 45, June

OTHER

Takamine Go 1996, *Mugen Ryukyu* (Love's love: An Okinawan dream), film script

Watanabe Akio 1966, Japanese Attitudes towards the Okinawa Problem, 1945–1965, PhD thesis, Australian National University, Canberra

GENERAL

Australian Broadcasting Corporation Radio and TV, *Asahi,* the *Australian, Australian Financial Review,* BBC World Service, *Eesti Ringvaade, Far Eastern Economic Review, Guardian Weekly, Insider, Japan Times, Mainichi, Nihon Keizei (Nikkei),Okinawa Times, Ryukyu Shimpo, Sapio, Shimauta Paradise, Sydney Morning Herald, Tokyo KaleidoScoop, Yomiuri*

INDEX

Aborigines 33, 46
AC-130 91
Adak Island 101
Adams, Will 118
Africa 160
African-Americans 18, 160
Ahagon Shoko 170, 198–206
airport, need for 126, 139
Ajima 114
Akahachi 68
akamai (red rice) 72
Akihito, Crown Prince 203
Akonaha 140
Aleutian Islands 101, 105
Alexander the Great 200
All Nippon Airways 16
Amami Oshima island 135, 179
Amawari 200
American Indians 202; *see also* Hopi
American Lake (Hayes) 200
American Ninja 43
AMPO 57, 145
AMPO treaty see Japan–US Mutual Security Treaty
ancestors 48, 58, 60
Anchorage 100
anti-Americanism 5, 11, 77, 91, 94–5, 202; US personnel on 183–4, 186, 187, 188–9, 190
anti-base movement: attitude of US government towards 19; compared to Reversion movement 46; ebb and flow 4, 5, 6, 76, 78, 170–1, 205; impact on US occupation forces 19, 106, 183, 184, 192–3, 204; landowners and 11, 28, 77, 81, 166, 199, 204, 205–6; mass support 11, 39, 65, 69, 98; Memi on 91; 1996 referendum 14; opposition to 119; origins 198–9, 202; rape cases and 79, 144; Shimoji on 144, 147; tactics 199, 204, 205–6; Tamaki on 139; see also protests
Aoki Konyo 118
Aquapolis 125
Arasaki Moriteru 75
Arasato Keiji 32
archaeology 67–8
Archer, Jules 188
architecture 63, 66, 110–1, 182, 191
Argentina 181
ASAP Sisters 107
'Asatoya Yunta' 52–3
ASEAN 86
Ashiya 196
A-Sign Days 64
A signs 64
assimilation 32–3, 74, 75, 82–3; *see also* cultural survival
AUSMIN 192
Australia 16, 30, 33, 46, 78, 97, 192
autonomy 141, 207, 209; aspects of 81, 89, 129; Ota on 5, 78, 82–3, 86–7; practicality of 121–2, 124–7, 142–3, 164; *see also* independence
Avildsen, John 43
AWACS 91, 95, 126
awamori 7, 53, 57, 123, 132, 152, 172–8
Axis alliance 203

Baba Shigeyuki 128, 129
Bagley, Richard 30
Bahasa Indonesia 51
Ballad of Narayama 64
Baltic states 5
'Banana Boat Song' 49, 181
banian trees 110
Bartu, Friedemann 133
baseball 181
Base Return Action Program 48
bases *see* Japanese Self-Defense Forces, Okinawan bases; US bases; *specific* bases
Basra 50
The Battle of Midway 43
Battle of Okinawa (film) 65
Battle of Okinawa (1945) 4, 27, 30, 77; casualties 75, 78, 83, 201, 203, 206; commemorated 17, 146; significance to marines 185–6, 192; Yamato and 82
The Battle of Okinawa (Ota) 79
beaches 63, 155, 156; private 15
Bello, Walden 200
Berlin Wall 5, 199
Bernard, Thomas 100–1
Bible 50, 203
Blood Line 47, 49
Board, William 175
Bodhidharma 42
Boeing 707 95, 99
Bolivia 181
bombing see target practice
Bon Voyage Co. 52
The Boom 53
'Born to Be Wild' 64
Brazil 180, 181
Broome (Australia) 180–1
B-36 200
B-29 200
Buckner, Simon 206
Buddhism 42, 140, 149
bukubuku cha 54
bullet train 147
bullfighting 57
bulu rice 179
Bungei Shunju 161
Burma 176
Burning the Rising Sun (Chibana) 27, 31
buses 41
Butler, Smedley 188
B-yen 68, 69
Byrne, David 44, 46

California, emigration to 180
The Cambridge Encyclopaedia of Japan 42
Camp Foster (Zukeran) 167, 182, 196
Camp Hansen 29
Camp Kinser 167
Camp Lejeune (N. Carolina) 20
Camp Lester (Kuwae) 117, 186
Camp Pendleton (California) 20
Camp Smedley D. Butler 182, 186, 196
Camp Zama (mainland Japan) 186
Camp Zukeran see Camp Foster
Canada 126; emigration to 180
Cape Hedo 38
Carradine, David 42, 43
cars 41, 92, 117
centralism see regionalism
Central Texas College 92
ceramics 193
Chakura 44
champon 51
champru 51, 52–3, 137, 181
Champrus (album) 53
Champruse (band) 46, 51, 53, 102, 107
Chibana ammunition depot 14–15
Chibana Shoichi 26–30, 31, 65, 92, 203; on Ota and lease renewals 29
Chibichiri cave mass suicide 27, 30, 31, 65
Chien-chen (Ganjin) 140
Chile 181
China 85, 106, 148, 161, 169; foodstuffs and 72, 118, 179; martial arts 36, 42; Ryukyus and 59, 70, 74, 140–1; trade with 84, 121, 125
China Sadao 53
chirudai 60–1, 62
chopsticks 132, 133
Christians 199
Chukaku-ha (Middle Core Faction) 203, 208, 209
cigarettes 69–70
Clark Air Base (Philippines) 94, 197
climate 13, 57, 110, 114, 122, 147
Clinton, Bill 15, 76, 112–13, 163, 170
coal mining 14, 155
coexistence 202
cold war 100–1, 148, 204; end of 76, 96, 195; impact of 4, 5, 57; US hegemony after 4, 6
colonialism: Japanese 85, 145, 154, 155, 161, 180, 193, 200; US 153, 155, 175, 188; *see also* imperialism
Columbus, Christopher 119
comfort women 11, 25
Commission on Human Rights 201
Communists see Japan Communist Party
Condition Green 52
C-130 series 94; AC-130 91; C-130 Hercules 94
C-135 series: EC-135 100; KC-135 91, 92, 99; RC-135 92, 100–1; WC-135 100
Confucius 42
Constitution 33, 81, 208
construction industry 48, 143, 145; tourism and 4–5, 86
convict labour 155
Cooder, Ry 44, 47, 107
Cook, James 97
coral 66, 86, 123, 124
Coral Bio-Tech Co. 123
Coral Calcium 123
corruption 126
Cosmopolitan City Plan 81, 87, 167
cost of living 23, 24, 167, 205
Coy, Sergeant 189–90
crime: US personnel and 21, 24, 25, 184, 185; see also rape cases; US military behaviour
The Crow 43
cultural survival 32–3, 35, 37–8, 45; *chirudai* and 61, 62; imported forms and 136–7; language and 115, 130, 132–3, 134, 135, 138, 159, 160; music and 45, 46, 47–8, 131, 132; *see also* assimilation
currency 68–9; *see also* exchange rates
Da Capo, Lieut 183–4
dance 60, 83, 137
Dari Sunda 107
Darwin 30, 192
DDT 71
Death-Defying Unit to Proclaim the Ownership of the Senkaku Shoto 85
Defense Facilities Administration Agency 171, 203
democracy 75, 149, 166, 208
Denver Post 100–1
dependency on Japan 121, 142, 143, 145; see also subsidies; US bases, impact of
Desert Storm *see* Gulf War
development *see* economic development
Diamantes 181
Diaoyu Tai (Uotsuri, Yukun) 85
Dido 107
disarmament 11, 49; see also militarism; peace studies
discrimination 16, 61, 81, 160, 165, 209; language 33, 83, 132–4
Disneyland 147
disposals 81–2
diving 21, 190
'Do Nothing' era 81
Dunkin' Donuts 131
Dutch village replica 147
Dutko, Tania 90, 91, 93–6

Eastern Europe 5, 6
EC-130 94
EC-135 100
economic development 84, 86, 87, 121–2, 124–5, 143, 167–8; tourism and 13, 16–17, 125, 147
Edo see Tokyo
Egypt 195
18th Air Wing (US) 90–1, 92
82nd Reconnaissance Squadron (US) 91–2
eisa 114, 131, 168
Eisenhower, Dwight 200, 204
electricity 67, 124
'Elephant Cage' 27, 28, 29, 101
ELINT 27, 28
emigration 97, 126, 169, 180–1; *see also* immigration; migration

Emperor system 30, 31, 65, 74–5, 83, 203
employment 157; on US bases 24, 95, 96, 98, 144, 187, 189; *see also* unemployment
Enter the Dragon 43
environment 84, 86, 89, 124; greens 48; pollution 6, 25, 26, 72, 73, 133; *see also* nuclear power; nuclear weapons
erosion 124, 128, 129
Eskelson, T. Edward 100–1
Estonia 88–9, 146
ethnology 60, 179
E-3 Sentry 91, 95
Euphrates river 50
Even Cowgirls Sing the Blues 43
exchange rates 19, 24, 193; see also currency
exports 177, 179; *see also* free trade; protectionism; trade

famine 118
Far East Network 52
farmers 72, 86, 87, 92–3, 147, 153, 170; expropriations of 80
fascists see ultranationalists
Feifer, George 78, 185
Feng Shui 110
F-15 Eagle 91, 92, 93
Field, Norma 27
Fifth Air Force (US) 92
filmmaking 55–6, 58, 64–5, 66, 138–9
films: martial arts 42–3; Okinawan 54, 58, 60–1, 62, 64–5, 66, 117
Fisher, Morgan 107
fishing 72, 128, 129, 152, 153
Fists of Fury 43
Florida Keys 128
Fodor's Guide to Japan and East Asia (Griffin) 57
food 128, 133; dishes 51, 123, 132, 137, 190; place of 39, 150–3; *see also* rice, sweet potato
foreign policy 84, 86–7
France 143
free trade 143; zones 122, 126, 147; *see also* protectionism
Fuji Sankei media group 161
Fukien, China 36, 86, 110, 118
Fukui region 89
Fukuoka Dome 147
fun park 147
Futenma Air Station 23; plans for 147; return of 11–12, 22, 87, 92, 112, 116, 163, 171, 199

Ganjin (Chien-chen) 140
Germany 92, 146, 180, 197, 202, 203, 206
Get Rhythm 53
Gima Shinjo 86
Ginowan city 12, 23, 41, 49, 196
The Girl with the White Flag (Higa) 30
Godzilla 65, 111
Godzilla v. the Bionic Monster 111
'Going Back to Okinawa' 53
Gold Coast (Queensland) 16
Golden Week 151
Gosamaru 200
goya 51, 123, 153, 190
goya champru 51, 137
Goya Day 137
graves 39, 60
Griffin, Stuart 57
Guelpa, Beatrice 91, 94–6
guest houses *(minshuku)* 150, 151, 152, 153, 157
Gulf War 21–2, 28, 92, 93, 95, 96, 99, 104
Gusukuyama 198, 199

habu snake 39, 155
Haemida beach 155
'Hai Sai Ojisan' 44, 45, 52, 158
Hakata 147
Haley, Alex 160
'Hana' (song) 44–5, 47, 107, 108, 158, 168
Hana (album) 107
Han dynasty 140
Hashimoto Ryutaro 23, 76, 112–13, 163
Hateruma island 67, 157
Havel, Václav 79
Hawaii 16, 92; emigration to 180; Marines in 20, 197; similarity with Okinawa 97
Hawaiian Champru 52
Hayes, Peter 200
HC-130 94
Hemingway, Ernest 65
Hendrickson, John 30
Henoko 161
Hentona 38, 39
Henza island 116
HH-60 Black Hawk 91
Hibiya district 209
Hickam Air Force Base (Hawaii) 92
Hideyoshi see Toyotomi Hideyoshi
Higa Distillery 172
Higa Masahiro 98
Higa Masakuni 173–4, 176–8
Higa Tomiko 30, 146
Highway 58 38, 191
hijacking, JAL 209
Hika Shuncho 32
himpun 110
hinomaru 65; burnt by Chibana Shoichi 30, 65, 203
Hirohito, Emperor 12, 141
Hiroshima 13, 161
Hirotsu Kazuo 32
Hitler, Adolf 200
HMS *Prince of Wales* 82
HMS *Repulse* 82
Hokkaido 29, 101
Hokkaido Development Agency 145
home pages 43
homogeneity 4, 70, 103, 115–16, 142, 143, 159, 201
Hong Kong 42, 84, 85, 121, 125, 138, 163
Honshu 89
Hopi 46, 168; see also American Indians
Hoshisuna beach 63
Hosono Haruomi 52, 53, 61, 65
hospitality 39, 40, 105, 151, 154;

US personnel on 183–4, 186, 187, 188–9
host-nation sensitivities *see* crime; rape cases; US military behaviour 19, 21
housing 110, 167, 190
Huis Ten Bosch 147

ICBMs 101
Iejima Auxiliary Facility 198
Iejima island 85, 170, 196, 198–9; land loss to US bases 24, 199, 202
Iigunkuba (Senkaku Shoto) 85
Ikawu 114
Imamura Shohei 64–5
immigration 88, 119, 181; see also emigration; migration
imperialism 208 see also colonialism
Imperial Palace 203, 209
Inamine Keiichi 120–2, 124–7
Inchon 122
independence 86–7, 88; economic 147, 167; political 59, 60, 78, 143, 166; see also autonomy
independents 149
India 47, 202
Indica rice 72, 174, 176, 179
Indies 74
indigenous peoples 33, 46, 48, 49, 168, 202
Indonesia 51, 84, 125, 179
inns *(ryokan)* 150
intelligence-gathering 27, 28, 29, 91–2, 95, 100–1, 126, 192, 196–7
internationalisation 138
International Society for Mangrove Ecosystems 128, 129
interoperability 92
In the Realm of the Dying Emperor (Field) 27
Iran 126
Iraq 50
Iriomote island 63, 88, 155–7; coal mining 14, 155; mangroves and 128; pollution 73; roads 41; Taiwan and 84
Ishigaki island 55, 65, 66, 67; airport 17, 86; revolt against Ryukyu Kingdom 68; roads 41; Senkakus and 85; shrines 63; Taketomi and 71, 151, 152, 175
island revival movement 88
Israel 93
Italy 203
Itokazu Keiko 10–15, 17, 155; on US bases 11–12; on women 10–11
Itoman 35, 72, 117, 172, 203
Iwakuni (Japan) 12

Japan: atom bombing of 78, 201; Axis alliance and 203; colonialism in Asia 85, 145, 154, 155, 161, 180, 193; fallacy of homogeneity 4, 70, 103, 115–16, 142, 143, 159, 201; Meiji era 6, 45, 72; militarism 11, 25, 30, 74–5, 85, 97, 106, 146, 161, 164, 200–4; national goals 6, 89; resistance to Communism from 196; Showa era 33, 75; takeover of Okinawa 36, 45, 46, 59, 68, 74, 82; Tokugawa shogunate 74, 118; US Occupation of 42, 105, 207; weakening of centralism 5–6, 14, 61–2, 89, 149
Japan Airlines 16
Japan Communist Party 69, 148, 149, 208
Japanese government: Defense Facilities Administration Agency 171, 203; funding of US bases 92, 113, 142, 143, 196, 197, 205; Ministry of Agriculture 129, 179; Ministry of Defense 112, 144; Official Development Assistance program 124, 145; rape case and 5; unwillingness to act 15, 129
Japanese Imperial Army 176; behaviour 25, 146, 161; *see also* Japanese Self-Defense Forces
Japanese Self-Defense Forces 29, 93, 101, 104–5, 134, 146; Okinawan bases 126, 159, 196; *see also* Japanese Imperial Army
'Japanisation' *see* assimilation
Japan Social Democratic Party see Social Democratic Party of Japan
'Japan's other Voices' 4, 76
Japan Tobacco Monopoly 70
Japan–US Mutual Security Treaty (AMPO) 77, 146, 148, 185, 203, 207, 208; consequences for Okinawa 27, 28, 29, 80; protests against 47, 204
Japan–US security alliance 4, 76–7, 93, 100–1, 143; China and 85, 148; north Korea and 21, 96, 106, 148; SACO and 12, 20, 163
Japan Youth Federation 85
Japonica rice 72, 174–5, 179
Javanica rice 72, 179
Jesus 168
'Jidai no nagare' 58–9
jimami tofu 123
JJJ-FM 44
jodam omote 57
'Johnny B. Goode' 64
John Birch Society 100
Johnson, Lyndon 80, 208
Joint Reception Center 21
Jones, Byron D. 158–62, 164–8
Jones, Jim 31
judo (ju-jitsu) *see* martial arts
jungle 157
Junkermann, Jan 65

Kabira village 55
kachashi 60, 137
Kadekaru Rinsho 54, 58–9, 66
Kadena Air Base 90–3, 95, 96, 101, 196; Futenma and 12; Koza and 57, 98, 117; plans for 14–15, 84, 116, 126–7, 138–9, 167; return of 87
Kadena city 98; land loss to US bases 24;
Kadena city *(continued)*: post-base plans 14–15
Kagoshima 178
Kai's Bar 54
Kakumaru-ha 209
Kanemaru Shin 197

Kansai 181
karaoke 47, 53, 175
karate see martial arts
Karate Kid films 43
Kawamura Yosuke 53
KC-130 94
KC-135 91, 92, 99
kemari 57
Kennedy, John F. 47
Kerr, George 141, 164
'Keystone of the Pacific' 177
KE 007 100–1
kimigayo 30
Kina Keiko 102–3, 105
Kina Shoei 44, 45, 53
Kina Shokichi 44–50, 51, 52, 53; Chibana Shoichi and 28; Jones and 158, 168; Newman and 102–3, 105, 107–8; Tamaki and 131, 136; on US bases 48–9
Kina Tomoko 47, 107
Kin bay 89
Kin city 26–7, 170–1, 175
King Shii-saa 111
Kin Mon Club 77
Kishi Nobusuke 204
Kiyan Mary 64
Koda Yoshihiro 128, 129
Kohama Haeko 151–4
Kohama island 72, 157
Kokusaidori street 44, 109
Komei 149
Konoe Fumimaro, Prince 200
Korea 6, 100, 140, 145, 155, 193; comfort women 11; Japan–US security alliance and north 21, 96, 106, 148; trade with 84, 100, 125
Korean Airlines 100–1
Koreans 64, 155, 193
Korean War 28, 104, 200
Koza city 51, 53, 57, 112, 113, 139; origins 131, 136; riot 117, 209
Kubasaki High School 161
Kubota Makoto 52, 53, 107
Kudaka island 72
Kume village 169
kung fu *see* martial arts
'Kung Fu' (TV) 42
Kurnia, Detty 107
kusu 173, 175
Kyoto 54, 55, 179
Kyushu island 87, 135, 141, 147, 175, 179

land: lost to US bases 24, 65, 80, 92, 199, 202; post-base plans for 116, 123, 126–7, 138–9, 144, 147, 166–7; prices 23, 24; use 24, 92–3, 179
landowners: accepting rent 12–13, 93, 143–4, 170; anti-base 11, 28, 77, 81, 166, 199, 204, 205–6
language 161, 168, 181; cultural survival and 115, 130, 132–3, 134, 135, 138, 159, 160; discrimination 33, 83, 132–4; romanisation 7; US personnel on barrier of 187, 190
lao-rong 175
Lao Tzu 42
Latvia 88, 146
'Lay Down Your Weapons and Take Up Musical Instruments' 107
leases, expiration of 28, 29, 81
Lee, Brandon 43
Lee, Bruce 42, 43
legends 49–50, 68
Liberal Democratic Party 126, 142, 148, 149, 208
Lili'uokalani, Queen 97
lion-dogs *(shii-saa)* 110–11, 193
Lithuania 88
Lockheed Corp. 94, 125
L-188 Electra 126
longevity 13, 48, 123, 125, 175
Lord, Winston 196
Luxembourg 146
Luzon 118
mabui 56, 61
'Mabui Dance' 61
MacArthur, Douglas 105, 153, 200
McDonald, Lawrence 100
McDonnell Douglas Corp. 93
Maki 14
Makiminato 167
malaria 71
Malay Peninsula 82
Malaysia 84, 125
Manchuria 85, 145, 199, 202
mangroves 63, 124, 128–9
Manila 115
manufacturing 122–3, 147, 157
Mariana Islands 180
marine biology 122, 124, 128–9
Marine Expo (1975) 16, 111, 125, 203
martial arts 35–8, 42–3, 82
Mary and Medusa 64
Marxist-Leninist Faction 208–9
mass suicides 75; Chibichiri cave, 27, 30, 31, 65; Itoman 203; Jonestown, Guyana 31; Saipan 180
Mecha-Godzilla 111
Medal of Honor 188
media 161, 171, 206; rape case and 5
Medicine Compilation 61
Meiji era 6, 45, 72
Mekas, Jonas 54
Memi, Ed 90–6, 98, 163
Meri, Lennart 88
Michiko, Princess 203
Middle Core Faction (Chukaku-ha) 203, 208, 209
Middle East 104, 106
Mikado 53
migration 68, 72; *see also* emigration; immigration
MiG-23 101
militarism: Ahagon on 200–4; Butler on 188; Chibana Shoichi on 30, 31; Higa Masakuni on 177; Itokazu on women and 11; Japanese 11, 25, 30, 74–5, 85, 97 106, 146, 161, 164, 200–4; Kina Shokichi on 48–9; Newman on 106; opposition to 5, 39; Ota on 83; US 25, 97, 164, 188, 200–4; *see also* disarmament; peace studies
Military Highway 1 80, 191, 204
mimiga sashimi 123
Minatogawa 67

Ming dynasty 140
Miniatures 107
mining 14, 155
Ministry of Agriculture 129, 179
Ministry of Defense 112, 144
minshuku (guest houses) 150, 151, 152, 153, 157
minyo 47, 53, 66, 169, 175
Misawa base 29
missiles 101
Mitsui 155
Miyagi 43
Miyako island 72, 88, 133
Moeru Okinawa, Yuragu AMPO (Chibana) 27
Mongolia 176, 178
monorail 41
monuments 63, 75
Morita Noriyuki (Pat) 43
Motobu 16, 125, 198
mountains 157
Mt Fuji 196
Mugen Ryukyu 65
Murasaki 52
Musashi 82
museums 67, 73, 199, 201
music 58–9, 64, 65, 88–9, 169; *champru* 51, 52–3, 131, 181; cultural survival and 45, 46, 47–8, 131, 132; Jones on 160, 161, 162, 168; Kina Shokichi on 45–8, 49–50; Latin American influences 181; Newman on 102, 107–8; Tamaki on 130, 131, 132, 136, 137; Teruya Rinken on 113–15; Webster on 189
Mussolini, Benito 200
MX missile 101
Myers, Colonel 184–6, 193

Nagasaki 13, 51, 118, 147, 164–5
Nago 191
Naha 23, 42, 44, 47, 53, 55, 66, 109, 118, 171; airport 126; anti-Americanism in 94; development of 125; free-trade zone 122, 147; Tsuboya district 193
Naha port 83, 125
nakami 123
Nakano Akiyoshi 65
Nakasone Yasuhiro 4, 70, 76
Nansei Shoto 141
Narita airport 208
nasi campur 51
National Geographic 181
National Security Agency (US) 100–1
NATO 101
Nemuro 101
Nenes 49, 52, 53, 114, 131, 136
Netherlands 126, 147
Nevers, Lance Corporal 190, 192–3
New Left 203, 207, 208, 209
Newman, Paul 102–8
New Year 151
New Zealand 202
nicknames: for Okinawa 57; see also Okinawa, use of term; Ryukyu, use of term
1955 system 148
'Ninja' 43
nirai kanai 49, 58
Nirai Kanai (album) 49
Nishie Masayuki 159
Nixon, Richard 163, 208
Nobel Prize 80, 161
Nomo Hideo 181
nonmaterialist culture 48
Noriega, Manuel 94
Norris, Chuck 43
Northern Territory (Australia) 30, 92
Northern Training Area 12
North Korea see Korea; Korean War
nonviolence 36, 37, 49, 68, 82, 184, 199
Nuchi du Takara *awamori* 177
nuclear power 6, 14, 73, 89
nuclear weapons, 48, 98, 103–5, 163; atom bombing of Japan 78, 201; future war with 201, 205; Korea and 21, 96, 200; Oe on 161; in Tahiti 143
Nye Report 81

Obon festival 114
The Ocean Road 60
Oda Nobunaga 200
Oe Kenzaburo 161
Official Development Assistance program 124, 145
Ogarkov, Nikolai 100, 101
Ogata Ken 64
Okamoto Kihachi 65
Okinawa city 98, 131, 159, 161; see also Koza
Okinawa Club 180
Okinawa Day 207, 209
Okinawa Development Agency 85, 145, 162
Okinawa Electrical Power Co. 124
Okinawa (Hika et al.) 32
Okinawa island 38, 55, 67, 133, 135, 140, 179; Battle of Okinawa and 27; land loss to US bases 24
Okinawa–Korea Association 35
Okinawa Marine 183, 184
Okinawan Boys 64, 68, 69, 117
Okinawan Chirudai 60–1, 62, 65
Okinawan islands see Hateruma island; Henza island; Iejima island; Iriomote island; Ishigaki island; Kohama island; Kudaka island; Miyako island; Okinawa island; Ryukyu Shoto; Sakishima islands; Taketomi island; Yaeyama islands; Yonaguni island
Okinawa Noto (Oe) 161
Okinawan Women Act against Military Violence 10
Okinawan Women's Peace Caravan 10, 15
Okinawan Youth League 32
'Okinawa: Orphan of the Pacific' 57
Okinawa–Peru Association 35
Okinawa Shoto 140
Okinawa Sugar Company 87
Okinawa: The History of an Island People (Kerr) 141, 164
Okinawa Times 104, 171
Okinawa University 75
Okinawa: use of term 140–1, 163; see also nicknames
Okuma 15, 17

The Old Man and the Sea 65
Olympic Games: 1996 Arts Festival 44, 47, 107; revamped 49; Tokyo 42
Omura bay 147
Onna 139
Operation Just Cause 94
Operation Restore Hope 195
opinion polls 77, 86
Oregon 168
origins of human settlement 67–8
Osaka 41, 86, 89, 103, 181
Osaki Chizuru 156–7
Osborne, Susan 107
Otaka Sizuru 107
Ota Masahide 5, 76, 77–84, 86–7, 164; lease renewals and 29, 81; negotiating attempts 15, 80–1, 164, 167; opposition to assimilation by 74, 75, 82–3; support for 11, 149, 170; tourism and 13, 14, 17

Pacific Air Force (US) 92
Pacific–Asia Resource Centre 145
Pakistan 129
Panama 94
Paradise View 54, 58, 61, 65
Paraiso 52
parks 128, 155, 171
passports 16, 69
peace studies 13, 15; see also disarmament; militarism
Peace Treaty (1952) 69, 196, 200, 207
Pearl Harbor 97, 201
Peppermint Tea House 47
perestroika 199
Perry, Matthew C. 153, 155, 175
Pershing missile 101
Persian Gulf 195
Peru 181
Philippines 19, 94, 97, 105, 115, 118, 179; emigration to 180; trade with 84, 122
Phuket 16
pineapples 157
Pine Gap (Australia) 192
The Plot to Seize the White House (Archer) 188
plutonium 73
political parties: independents 149; Japan Communist Party 69, 149; Komei 149; Liberal Democratic Party 126, 142, 148, 149; Shinshinto 149; Social Democratic Party of Japan 148, 149, 208; Social Mass Party 149
pollution *see* environment
population 41, 84, 88, 96
postage stamps 70
postcolonial theory 32
Potsdam declaration 208
pottery 193
poverty 6, 77, 84, 88, 118, 119, 165, 209; emigration and 180, 181
prawns 153
prefectural government 199; Base Return Action Program 48; opposition to private beaches 15; post-base plans 6, 12, 84; prefectural assembly 10, 86; reaction to SACO interim report 20
Prefectural Road 104 170
preservation orders 17, 73
Profound Desire of the Gods 64–5
prostitution 19, 64, 155
protectionism 143, 163; see also free trade
protests: against AMPO 47, 204; against Emperor system 30, 65, 203; against nukes 143; against *Samayoeru Ryukyu-jin* 32; Kin city 26, 27, 170–1; Koza riot 117, 209; rape case 5, 78, 120, 164, 170; Reversion 80, 207, 208–9; *see also* anti-base movement
P-3 Orion 91, 126
P-2 Neptune 126
Pulitzer Prize 206
pumpkin 153
Pusan 122
Pyle, Ernie 206

radio 44, 52, 76, 84
rafute 123
railways 41
rainforest 155, 191
rape case (1955) 80
rape case (1995) 4, 11, 12, 78; Dutko on 95; Japanese government and 5; Jones on 164, 165; Myers on 185; Ota on 79; Wagner on 19; *see also* crime; US military behaviour
Rape of Nanking 161
RC-135 92, 100–1
Reagan, Ronald 76, 101
Red Army, Soviet 146
Red Army Faction 208, 209
red rice *(akamai)* 72
Red Sea 195
referenda 14
regionalism 70–1; growth of 5–6, 14, 61–2, 89, 149; Ota on 82–3, 86–7; *see also* autonomy
Remove Troops from Okinawa Network 104
Rengo Okinawa 14
returnees see immigration
revenue: from tourism 16, 96; from rent for US bases 24, 87, 144
Reversion 45, 46, 69, 80, 165–6, 208–9; hopes for 4, 75, 81, 163; impact of 47, 149, 184, 204–5; opinion polls on 77, 86; protests 80, 207, 208–9; treaty 209
rice 119, 153, 173, 174, 175, 176; origins of 60, 72, 179; *see also* food
Riga 146
Rinken Band 112, 114–15, 130, 131, 132, 134, 136
Ritsu Buddhism 140
roads 38, 41, 71, 80, 170, 191
romanisation: of Asian languages 7, 140–1
'Roo Choo Gumbo' 52
Roots (Haley) 160
ryokan (inns) 150
Ryukyu Kingdom 4, 5, 61, 86; and China 59, 70, 74; dissolution 6, 45, 68, 164; unification 35, 70,

71, 88; Yaeyama revolt against 68
Ryukyu Shoto 141
Ryukyu: use of term 32, 35, 50, 140–1
Ryuseki Corp. 120

sabani 50, 63, 72
'Sabani' (song) 50
SACO see Special Action Committee on Okinawa
Sakamoto Ryuichi 52
sake 173, 175, 176
Sakhalin Island 100
Sakishima islands 135, 141
Saipan 39, 180
Saitama 196
Sai Yoichi 64
Sandii and the Sunsetz 52, 107
San Francisco 207
Samayoeru Ryukyu-jin (Hirotsu) 32, 33
samba 169
sanshin 7, 45, 53, 66, 83, 114, 115, 160, 161, 169
Sanshin Trio 53
Sasebo Naval Station 196
Sato Eisako 80, 163, 208
Satsuma region 36, 68, 71, 74, 82, 118, 193
Saudi Arabia 93
Scotch whisky 176, 178
Scotland 178
Sea of Japan 29
seawater therapy 125
secession see independence
Second World War *see* World War II
security alliance *see* Japan–US security alliance
Senaba 159
Senaga-jima 159
Senaga Kamejiro 69
Senaha Shigetoshi 36–8
Senkaku Shoto (Iigunkuba) 85
Seoul 100
Seventh Fleet 196
shamisen 169
Shelton, Jerry 32
Shemya Island 101
Shesirs 111
Shibuya district 111, 209
shii-saa (lion-dogs) 110–11, 193
Shii-saas (band) 111
shimadaiko 115, 169
shima okoshi movement 88
Shimazu clan 36, 68, 71, 118, 174, 179
Shimeisai festival 38, 39, 60
Shimoji Mikio 142–4, 147
Shimota Shoji 32
Shimuku cave 31
Shinano 82
Shinjo Taku 64, 68, 117
Shinshinto 149
Shiroma, Alberto 181
Shochiku Kageki Dan troupe 130–1, 134
shochu 174, 175, 177
Sho dynasty 35, 70
Sho En 70
Sho Ha Shi 70
Sho Sen 70
Sho Shin 68, 70
Showa era 33, 75
Shuri 35, 42, 70
Shuri dialect 133, 134
Singapore 84, 88, 121, 125, 164
Sino-Japanese War 74–5, 85
Sino–Ryukyu Association 35
slavery 49
Small Business Association of Okinawa 70
soba 39, 132, 133
Sobe Communications Site 27, 28, 93; possible return of 29
Social Democratic Party of Japan 148, 149, 208
Social Mass Party 149
Soka Gakkai Buddhism 149
soki 123
solar power 124
Somalia 195
Sony 130
South-east Asia 72, 74, 84, 128, 167, 179
South Korea *see* Korea; Korean War
South Pacific 143
Soviet Union 5, 6, 47, 88, 89, 96, 100, 101, 146, 200, 202, 204
Spanish colonialism 118
Special Action Committee on Okinawa (SACO) 6, 11–12; interim report 20; Japan–US security alliance and 12; Memi on 94; Wagner on 19
spying *see* intelligence-gathering
SS-X-25 missile 101
Statue of Peace 31
Status of Forces Agreement (SOFA) 170; legal protection for US personnel of 5, 21, 25, 117
stereotyping 32, 33, 206
strategic importance 4, 76, 148, 195, 197, 200, 209; Chibana Shoichi on 28; Memi on 92, 94, 96, 98; Newman on 104, 105, 106; Wagner on 19
Strategic Reconnaissance and Bombing Group (US) 197
Subic (Philippines) 122
subsidies 143, 144, 145, 162, 209; *see also* dependency; US bases, funding
Sudan 195
SU-15 100, 101
sugarcane 86, 87, 157, 160, 161
suicide see mass suicides
Sui Shu 140
'Sukiyaki' 107
Sumerian civilisation 50
Sunda 67
Sunset Gang 52
Supreme Commander for the Allied Powers 105
Supreme Court 81
surveillance see intelligence-gathering
'Suzie Q' 64
Suzuki, Sandii 52, 107
sweet potato 57, 116, 118–19; *see also* food
Sweet Potato Association 119
Sydney 192
Syracuse University 77

Tachikawa base 196
Tahiti 143
Taisho era 174
Taisho island 85
Taiwan 85, 89, 94, 140, 179; comfort women 11; emigration to 154, 180; Japanese occupations of 85, 145, 154, 155, 200; martial arts 35; trade with 84, 121, 125, 142
Takamine Go (Tsuyoshi) 54–6, 58–62, 65, 66, 117; on US bases 62
Takasato Suzuyo 57
takeover of Okinawa: by Japan 36, 45, 46, 59, 68, 74, 82; by Satsuma 37, 71, 74, 82
Takeshima islands (Tok-do islands) 140
Taketomi 66–7, 128; distinctness 68, 71; Ishigaki and 71, 151, 152, 175; music 52–3; pollution 72; tourism and 17, 73, 151–4, 157
Tallinn (Estonia) 146
Tamaki Mitsuru 130–4, 136–9
Tanaka Kakuei 126
Tanetori festival 152
Taoism 110
target practice 26, 170, 191; Iejima 198, 200, 201, 203
Taruganini, James 137
Tawu (Yami) people 140
taxes 71–2, 144, 165
Tekketsu Kinno Tai 77
television 42–3
tennoism see Emperor system
Tennozan: The Battle of Okinawa and the Atomic Bomb (Feifer) 78, 185
Teruya Rinken 53, 112, 113–16
Teruya Rinsuke 113, 116, 136, 169
Thailand 16, 30, 84, 125, 174, 175, 176; rice 173, 174, 175
theatre 113, 130–1, 134, 136, 137–8
31st Marine Expeditionary Unit (US) 195
32nd Forces (Japan) 146
353rd Special Operations Group (US) 91
tobacco 69–70
Todai Wajo Toseiden 140
tofu 123, 152, 190
Togawa Jun 65
Toho film company 65, 111
Tojo Hideki 200
Tok-do islands (Takeshima islands) 140
Tokyo (Edo) 41, 75, 89, 103; as Edo 153, 174
'Tokyo's Burning' 6
Tokugawa shogunate 74, 118
Tomari 42
Torii Station 186
tourism 5, 84–5, 124, 147; construction industry and 4–5, 86; economic development and 13, 16–17, 125, 147; guide training 13, 14, 17; impact of 16–17, 88, 106; Iriomote 155–7; statistics 16, 73, 97; Taketomi 17, 73, 151–4
Townsville (Australia) 192
Toyama Kyuzo 180
Toyotomi Hideyoshi 68, 193, 200
trade 70, 71, 74, 88, 118; *see also* exports; free trade; protectionism
trade unions *see* unions
traditionalists 134, 136
traffic: accidents 41, 117; pattern 184
trams 41
transport 38, 41, 66–7, 121–2, 145, 152
Tropical Dandy 52
Truman, Harry 78
t-shirts 109
Tsuboya district 193
Tsuburaya Eiji 65
typhoons 57, 110, 145, 147

Uchima Kanamaru 70
Uchina 57, 140
Uchinan-chu 140, 141
Uchina Pop 57
udon 132
Uesedo Yoshinori 67–73; on US bases 71
The Ugly Japanese 133
ultranationalists 31, 85
uminchu 72, 161
underemployment 162, 164
unemployment 84, 124, 139, 144; *see also* employment
unions 14, 170, 171
United Nations 49, 88, 166, 207; Commission on Human Rights 201; 1995 women's conference 10, 11
United States; hegemony 4, 6, 105, 166, 185, 188, 202; influences 41, 47, 191; militarism 25, 97, 164, 188, 200–4; trade 92
United States government; High Commission for Okinawa 196, 207; House International Relations Committee 196
University of East Anglia 129
University of Maryland 92
University of the Ryukyus 76, 124, 165
Untama Giru 54, 65
Uotsuri (Diaoyu Tai, Yukun) 85
Ur 50
Urauchi river 63, 155
Uruma 50
US Air Force 95, 196; 18th Air Wing 90–1, 92; 82nd Reconnaissance Squadron 91–2; facilities 186; Fifth Air Force 92; Pacific Air Force 92; 353rd Special Operations Group 91
US Army 186, 196
US bases: Ahagon on 200–6; Camp Foster (Zukeran) 167, 182, 186, 196; Camp Hansen 29; Camp Kinser 167; Camp Lester (Kuwae) 117, 186; Camp Smedley D. Butler 182, 186, 196; Camp Zama (mainland Japan) 186; Chibana ammunition depot 14–15; closure 29–30, 186, 196; Dutko on 93–6; employment of Okinawans 24, 95, 96, 98, 144, 187, 189; funding 92, 113, 142, 143, 196, 197, 205; Futenma Air

Station 11–12, 22, 87, 92, 112, 116, 163, 171, 199; Iejima Auxiliary Facility 198; impact of 10–11, 24, 186, 193; Inamine on 126–7; Iwakuni (Yamaguchi prefecture) 12; Jones on 162, 164, 165–8; Kadena Air Base see main entry; Kina Shokichi on 48–9; land loss from 24, 65, 80, 92; legality of 81; Memi on 91–6, 98; Myers on 186; Misawa (Honshu) 29; Naha port 83, 87; Nevers on 192–3; Newman on 106; Northern Training Area 12; Ota on 79, 80–1, 83; Philippines, loss of 19–20; revenue from, compared to tourism 16, 87, 96; Sasebo Naval Station (mainland Japan) 196; Sobe Communications Site 27, 28, 29, 93; Senaha Shigetoshi on 38; statistics 4, 80, 83, 91, 92, 94, 95, 196, 197; Tachikawa base (mainland Japan) 196; Takamine on 62; Teruya Rinken on 116; Torii Station 186; transfer of functions 12, 20, 29–30, 78, 92, 112–13, 186, 192; Uesedo on 71; women and 12; Yokosuka Naval Station (mainland Japan) 187, 196; Yokota Air Base (mainland Japan) 92; *see also* revenue, from rent for US bases; *specific overseas* bases

US Coast Guard 94

US High Commission for Okinawa 196, 207

US–Japan Mutual Security Treaty *see* Japan–US Mutual Security Treaty

US Marine Corps 162; Butler on 188; Expeditionary Command 197; Newman and 102, 103–5; role and structure 20, 22, 185, 192, 195; statistics 20–1, 196; 31st Marine Expeditionary Unit 195; women in 183

US military: behaviour 19, 21, 79, 91, 93; compared to Imperial Japanese Army 25, 71; legal protections for 5, 21, 25, 117; personal relations with Okinawans 93–5, 98, 183–4, 186, 187, 188–9, 190; police 117; troop strength 20–1, 92, 94, 195, 196, 197; *see also* crime; rape cases; United States, militarism

US Navy 20, 91, 97, 187, 193, 196

US Occupation (1945–72) 196, 207, 208; encouragement of Okinawan culture 33, 75; restrictions under 16, 42, 64, 68–9, 83, 184, 208; of Yaeyama islands 71

US Pacific Command 97

USS *McClusky* 21

USS *Missouri* 153

USSR *see* Soviet Union

Usudeku 116

U-2 Incident 204

Van Damme, Jean-Claude 43

Vietnam 84, 125, 129, 197

Vietnam War 28, 99, 104, 208

vinaya Buddhism 140

Võidupüha 146

Võnnu (Ceisis) 146

Wagner, Stuart 18–22

Wakkanai 101

Waseda University 77, 159

Watabe Tadayo 179

WC-135 100

weaving 67

Webster, Todd 187–9

wind power 124

women 10–11, 39–40, 116, 123, 170, 175, 183; US bases and 12, 39

Wonder, Stevie 107

World War I, 180

World War II 38, 39, 82, 83, 97, 114, 164; atom bombings in 78, 201; Battle of Saipan 180; Japanese surrender 153; in Yaeyama islands 71; *see also* Battle of Okinawa

Wright, James 101

wu shu see martial arts

Yaeyama islands 66, 68, 70, 71, 88, 155, 179

Yamato 82

Yami (Tawu) people 140

Yanagida Kunio 60, 179

Yanbaru forest 48

Yasukuni shrine 75

Yellow Magic Orchestra 52

Yogi Park 171

Yokosuka Naval Station 187, 196

Yomitan village 27, 65, 185, 193

Yonabaru 12

Yonaguni island 17, 65, 84

Yukun (Diaoyu Tai, Uotsuri) 85

Yuntanza Okinawa 65

Zarsky, Lyuba 200

Zen Buddhism 42

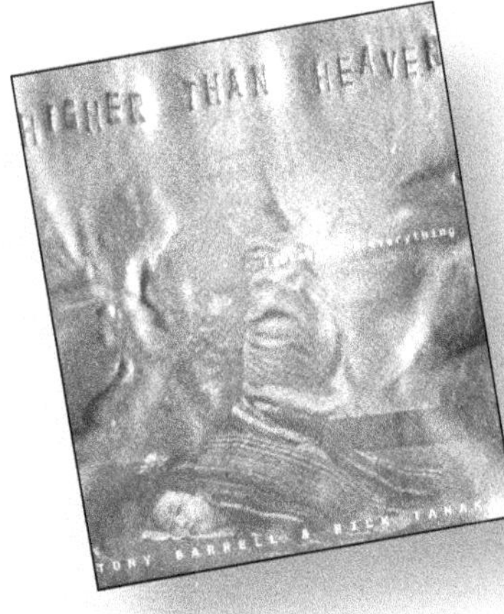

If you've enjoyed *Okinawa Dreams OK*, you'll be interested in the authors' previous book:

Higher than Heaven: Japan, War and Everything

By Tony Barrell and Rick Tanaka
published by Private Guy International
(ISBN 0 646 23187 1)

A comprehensive and fast-moving post–cold war story of a century of manipulation by and of Japan. Here's what's been said around the world:

'Succinct laid-back style ... compulsive reading.'
Elizabeth Kata
Author, Tokyo fire-bombing survivor, Sydney

'A great travel book in its way. I like the visual jokes. The disappearing emperor is my favourite!'
David Mardiste
Eesti Ringvaade, Tallinn, Estonia

'A very important book about the Emperor system.'
Kogawa Tetsuo
Media critic, sociologist, Tokyo

'Pictures of Hirohito planting rice fading into the column on his war responsibility is most apt and amusing.'
Kurihara Satoshi
Hot Wind, Seoul

'Unlike anything else I've read on the Japanese Occupation!'
Sharon Lim
Elle, Singapore

'Well researched.'
Nick Bornoff
Japan Insight, London

'Very readable and looks great.'
Blixa Bargeld
Artist, Berlin

'War-related history freed from the grip of military historians.'
Takano Hajime
Insider, Tokyo

'History with Attitude.'
Linda Jaivin
Rolling Stone, Sydney

'Neither revisionist nor Japan-basher, free from national stereotypes, it is a must-be-translated book.'
Ogura Toshimaru
Honyaku no sekai, Tokyo

'Impassioned and sustained.'
Brad Glosserman
Japan Times, Tokyo

'Lively and unconventional.'
David Cozy
Asahi Evening News, Tokyo

'A couple of tabloid comedians.'
Jeffrey Grey
Australian Defence Force Academy, Canberra

'Thorough research, painstaking editing and witty presentation.'
Richard McGregor
The Australian, Sydney

Higher than Heaven is available in bookshops throughout the world or directly from:
Private Guy International, 16 Fourteenth Street, Hepburn, VIC 3416, Australia
e-mail: privateguy@zoho.com

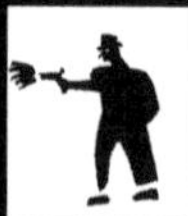

www.ingramcontent.com/pod-product-compliance
Ingram Content Group UK Ltd.
Pitfield, Milton Keynes, MK11 3LW, UK
UKHW051206260726
13967UKWH00011B/3129